D0375185

CCNA Security Portable Command Guide

Bob Vachon

Cisco Press

800 East 96th Street

Indianapolis, Indiana 46240 USA

CCNA Security Portable Command Guide

Bob Vachon

Copyright © 2016 Cisco Systems, Inc.

Published by:

Cisco Press

800 East 96th Street

Indianapolis, IN 46240 USA

Printed in the United States of America

4 17

Library of Congress Control Number: 2016931906

ISBN-13: 978-1-58720-575-0

ISBN-10: 1-58720-575-0

Warning and Disclaimer

This book is designed to provide information about CCNA Security (210-260 IINS) exam and the commands needed at this level of network administration. Every effort has been made to make this book as complete and as accurate as possible, but no warranty or fitness is implied.

The information is provided on an "as is" basis. The authors, Cisco Press, and Cisco Systems, Inc. shall have neither liability nor responsibility to any person or entity with respect to any loss or damages arising from the information contained in this book or from the use of the discs or programs that may accompany it.

The opinions expressed in this book belong to the author and are not necessarily those of Cisco Systems, Inc.

Trademark Acknowledgments

All terms mentioned in this book that are known to be trademarks or service marks have been appropriately capitalized. Cisco Press or Cisco Systems, Inc., cannot attest to the accuracy of this information. Use of a term in this book should not be regarded as affecting the validity of any trademark or service mark.

Special Sales

For information about buying this title in bulk quantities, or for special sales opportunities (which may include electronic versions; custom cover designs; and content particular to your business, training goals, marketing focus, or branding interests), please contact our corporate sales department at corpsales@pearsoned.com or (800) 382-3419.

For government sales inquiries, please contact governmentsales@pearsoned.com.

For questions about sales outside the U.S., please contact intlcs@pearson.com.

Feedback Information

At Cisco Press, our goal is to create in-depth technical books of the highest quality and value. Each book is crafted with care and precision, undergoing rigorous development that involves the unique expertise of members from the professional technical community.

Readers' feedback is a natural continuation of this process. If you have any comments regarding how we could improve the quality of this book, or otherwise alter it to better suit your needs, you can contact us through email at feedback@ciscopress.com. Please make sure to include the book title and ISBN in your message.

We greatly appreciate your assistance.

Publisher: Paul Boger

Associate Publisher: Dave Dusthimer

Business Operation Manager, Cisco Press: Jan Cornelssen

Executive Editor: Mary Beth Ray

Managing Editor: Sandra Schroeder

Development Editor: Chris Cleveland

Project Editor: Mandie Frank

Copy Editor: Geneil Breeze

Technical Editor: Dave Garneau

Editorial Assistant: Vanessa Evans

Designer: Mark Shirar

Composition: codeMantra

Indexer: Tim Wright

Proofreader: Paula Lowell

CISCO

Americas Headquarters
Cisco Systems, Inc.
San Jose, CA

Asia Pacific Headquarters
Cisco Systems (USA) Pte. Ltd.
Singapore

Europe Headquarters
Cisco Systems International BV
Amsterdam, The Netherlands

Cisco has more than 200 offices worldwide. Addresses, phone numbers, and fax numbers are listed on the Cisco Website at **www.cisco.com/go/offices**.

CCDE, CCENT, Cisco Eos, Cisco HealthPresence, the Cisco logo, Cisco Lumin, Cisco Nexus, Cisco StadiumVision, Cisco TelePresence, Cisco WebEx, DCE, and Welcome to the Human Network are trademarks; Changing the Way We Work, Live, Play, and Learn and Cisco Store are service marks; and Access Registrar, Aironet, AsyncOS, Bringing the Meeting To You, Catalyst, CCDA, CCDP, CCIE, CCIP, CCNA, CCNP, CCSP, CCVP, Cisco, the Cisco Certified Internetwork Expert logo, Cisco IOS, Cisco Press, Cisco Systems, Cisco Systems Capital, the Cisco Systems logo, Cisco Unity, Collaboration Without Limitation, EtherFast, EtherSwitch, Event Center, Fast Step, Follow Me Browsing, FormShare, GigaDrive, HomeLink, Internet Quotient, IOS, iPhone, iQuick Study, IronPort, the IronPort logo, LightStream, Linksys, MediaTone, MeetingPlace, MeetingPlace Chime Sound, MGX, Networkers, Networking Academy, Network Registrar, PCNow, PIX, PowerPanels, ProConnect, ScriptShare, SenderBase, SMARTnet, Spectrum Expert, StackWise, The Fastest Way to Increase Your Internet Quotient, TransPath, WebEx, and the WebEx logo are registered trademarks of Cisco Systems, Inc. and/or its affiliates in the United States and certain other countries.

All other trademarks mentioned in this document or website are the property of their respective owners. The use of the word partner does not imply a partnership relationship between Cisco and any other company. (0812R)

About the Author

Bob Vachon is a professor in the Computer Systems Technology program at Cambrian College in Sudbury, Ontario, Canada, where he teaches networking infrastructure courses. He has worked and taught in the computer networking and information technology field since 1984. He has collaborated on various CCNA, CCNA Security, and CCNP projects for the Cisco Networking Academy as team lead, lead author, and subject matter expert. He enjoys playing the guitar and being outdoors.

About the Technical Reviewers

Dave Garneau is a customer support engineer on the High Touch Technical Support (HTTS) Security team at Cisco Systems. He has also worked at Rackspace Hosting on its Network Security team. Before that, he was the principal consultant and senior technical instructor at The Radix Group, Ltd. In that role, Dave trained more than 3,000 students in nine countries on Cisco technologies, mostly focusing on the Cisco security products line, and worked closely with Cisco in establishing the new Cisco Certified Network Professional Security (CCNP Security) curriculum. Dave has a bachelor of science degree in mathematics from Metropolitan State University of Denver. Dave lives in McKinney, Texas, with his wife, Vicki, and their twin girls, Elise and Lauren.

Dedications

This book is dedicated to my students. Thanks for reminding me why I do this stuff.

I also dedicate this book to my beautiful wife, Judy, and daughters, Lee-Anne, Joëlle, and Brigitte. Without their support and encouragement, I would not have been involved in this project.

Acknowledgments

I would like to start off with a big thanks to my friend Scott Empson for involving me with this project. Your *Portable Command Guide* series was a great idea and kudos to you for making it happen.

Thanks to the team at Cisco Press. Thanks to Mary Beth for believing in me and to Chris for making sure I got things done right and on time.

Special thanks to my Cisco Networking Academy family. A big thanks to Jeremy and everyone else for involving me in these very cool projects. You guys keep me young.

Finally, a great big thanks to the folks at Cambrian College for letting me have fun and do what I love to do ... teach!

Contents at a Glance

Reader Services

Register your copy at www.ciscopress.com/title/9781587205750 for convenient access to downloads, updates, and corrections as they become available. To start the registration process, go to www.ciscopress.com/register and log in or create an account*. Enter the product ISBN 9781587205750 and click Submit. Once the process is complete, you will find any available bonus content under Registered Products.

*Be sure to check the box that you would like to hear from us to receive exclusive discounts on future editions of this product.

Table of Contents

Command Syntax Conventions

The conventions used to present command syntax in this book are the same conventions used in the IOS Command Reference. The Command Reference describes these conventions as follows:

- **Boldface** indicates commands and keywords that are entered literally as shown. In actual configuration examples and output (not general command syntax), boldface indicates commands that are manually input by the user (such as a **show** command).

- *Italics* indicate arguments for which you supply actual values.

- Vertical bars (|) separate alternative, mutually exclusive elements.

- Square brackets [ ] indicate optional elements.

- Braces { } indicate a required choice.

- Braces within brackets [{ }] indicate a required choice within an optional element.

Introduction

Welcome to CCNA Security! Scott Empson had an idea to provide a summary of his engineering journal in a portable quick reference guide. The result is the *Portable Command Guide* series. These small books have proven to be valuable for anyone studying for Cisco certifications or as a handy quick reference resource for anyone tasked with managing Cisco infrastructure devices.

The *CCNA Security Portable Command Guide* covers the security commands and GUI steps needed to pass the 210-260 Implementing Cisco Network Security certification exam. The guide begins by summarizing the required fundamental security concepts. It then provides the CLI commands required to secure an ISR. Examples are included to help demonstrate the security-related configuration.

The last part of the book focuses on securing a network using an Adaptive Security Appliance (ASA). It provides the CLI commands and the ASA Security Device Manager (ASDM) GUI screenshots required to secure an ASA 5505. Again, examples are included to help demonstrate the security-related configuration.

I hope that you learn as much from reading this guide as I did when I wrote it.

Networking Devices Used in the Preparation of This Book

To verify the commands in this book, I had to try them out on a few different devices. The following is a list of the equipment I used in the writing of this book:

- Cisco 1941 ISR running Cisco IOS release 15.4(3)M2

- Cisco 2960 switches running Cisco IOS release 15.0(2)SE7

- Cisco ASA 5505 running Cisco ASA IOS software version 9.2(3) with a Base License and the ASA Security Device Manager (ASDM) GUI version 7.4 (1)

Who Should Read This Book

This book is for people preparing for the CCNA Security (210-260 IINS) exam, whether through self-study, on-the-job training and practice, study within the Cisco Academy Program, or study through the use of a Cisco Training Partner. There are also some handy hints and tips along the way to make life a bit easier for you in this endeavor. The book is small enough that you can easily carry it around with you. Big, heavy textbooks might look impressive on the bookshelf in your office, but can you really carry them all around with you when working in some server room or equipment closet?

Organization of This Book

The parts of this book cover the following topics:

- **Part I, "Networking Security Fundamentals"**—Introduces network security-related concepts and summarizes how security policies are implemented using a lifecycle approach. It also summarizes how to build a security strategy for borderless networks.

- **Part II, "Protecting the Network Infrastructure"**—Describes how to secure the management and data planes using the IOS CLI configuration commands.

- **Part III, "Threat Control and Containment"**—Describes how to secure an ISR against network threats by configuring ACLs, a zoned-based firewall, and IOS IPS.

- **Part IV, "Secure Connectivity"**—Describes how to secure data as it traverses insecure networks using cryptology and virtual private networks (VPNs). Specifically, site-to-site IPsec VPNs are enabled using the IOS CLI configuration commands.

- **Part V, "Securing the Network Using the ASA"**—Describes how to secure a network using ASA data as it traverses insecure networks using cryptology and virtual private networks (VPNs). Specifically, remote access SSL VPNs are enabled using the IOS CLI configuration commands and ASDM.

CHAPTER 1

Networking Security Concepts

The chapter covers the following topics:

Basic Security Concepts

- Security Terminology
- Confidentiality, Integrity, and Availability
- Data Classification Criteria
- Data Classification Levels
- Classification Roles

Threat Classification

- Trends in Information Security Threats
- Preventive, Detective, and Corrective Controls
- Risk Avoidance, Transfer, and Retention

Drivers for Network Security

- Evolution of Threats
- Data Loss and Exfiltration
- Tracking Threats

Malicious Code: Viruses, Worms, and Trojan Horses

- Anatomy of a Worm
- Mitigating Malware and Worms

Threats in Borderless Networks

- Hacker Titles
- Thinking Like a Hacker
- Reconnaissance Attacks
- Access Attacks
- Password Cracking
- Denial-of-Service Attacks
- Distributed DoS Attacks
- Tools Used by Attackers

Principles of Secure Network Design

- Defense in Depth

Basic Security Concepts

Security Terminology

Six terms associated with security management include:

Asset	Anything of value to an organization that must be protected
Vulnerability	A weakness in a system or its design that could be exploited by a threat
Exploit	The mechanism used to leverage a vulnerability to compromise an asset
Threat	A potential danger to an asset such as information or network functionality
Risk	The likelihood that a particular threat will exploit a particular vulnerability of an asset that results in an undesirable consequence
Countermeasure	A protection that mitigates a potential threat or risk

Confidentiality, Integrity, and Availability (CIA)

To provide adequate protection of network assets, three things must be guaranteed:

Confidentiality	Only authorized users can view sensitive information.
Integrity	Only authorized users can change sensitive information. It can also guarantee the authenticity of data.
Availability (system and data)	Authorized users must have uninterrupted access to important resources and data.

Data Classification Criteria

Factors when classifying data include the following:

Value	The number one criteria and is based on the cost to acquire, develop, and replace.
Age	The importance of data usually decreases with time.
Useful life	The amount of time in which data is considered valuable and must be kept classified.
Personal association	Data that involves personal information of users and employees.

Data Classification Levels

Data classification terms commonly used by government and military include the following:

Unclassified	Data that has little or no confidentiality, integrity, or availability requirements, and therefore little effort is made to secure it.
Sensitive but unclassified (SBU)	Data that could prove embarrassing if it is revealed, but no great security breach would occur.
Confidential	Data must be kept secure.
Secret	Data for which significant effort is made to keep it secure. Few individuals have access to this data.
Top secret	Data for which great effort and sometimes considerable cost is made to guarantee its secrecy. Few individuals on a need-to-know condition have access to top-secret data.

Data classification terms commonly used by the public sector include the following:

Public	Data that is available publicly, such as on websites, publications, and brochures
Sensitive	Data that is similar to SBU data and that might cause some embarrassment if revealed
Private	Data that is important to an organization and an effort is made to maintain the secrecy and accuracy of this data
Confidential	Data that companies make the greatest effort to keep secure, such as trade secrets, employee data, and customer information

Classification Roles

Roles related to data include the following:

Owner	Person responsible for the information
Custodian	Person in charge of performing day-to-day data maintenance, including securing and backing up the data
User	Person using the data in accordance to established procedures

Threat Classification

Three categories of threat classification exist:

Administrative	Policy and procedure based, including change/configuration control, security training, audits, and tests
Technical	Controls that involve hardware and software
Physical	Controls for protecting the physical infrastructure

Trends in Information Security Threats

Motivation	The attack motivation is no longer for fame and notoriety. Motivation now includes insidious reasons such as for political and financial reasons aimed at economic espionage and money-making activities.
Targeted	Attacks are now targeted with mutating and stealth features.
Application layer	Threats are consistently focusing on the application layer such as known web browser vulnerabilities and looking for new web programming errors.
Social engineering	Users are the weakest link, and social engineering sites are a huge source of information. Increasingly, attackers are not only trying to steal an identity, but also trying to assume the identity of the user.
Borderless	Attackers are also targeting mobile platforms because data is in more places. You must now protect the device, protect the network, and protect the cloud.

Preventive, Detective, and Corrective Controls

Incident and exposure management entails the following five categories:

Preventive	Preventing the threat from coming in contact with a vulnerability, such as using a firewall, physical locks, and a security policy
Detective	Identifying that the threat has entered the network or system using system logs, intrusion prevention systems (IPSs), and surveillance cameras
Corrective	Determining the underlying cause of a security breach and then mitigating the effects of the threat being manifested, such as updating virus or IPS signatures
Recovery	Putting a system back into production after an incident
Deterrent	Discouraging security violations

Risk Avoidance, Transfer, and Retention

Countermeasures to managing risk can be categorized as follows:

Risk avoidance	Avoiding activity that could carry risk.
Risk reduction	Involves reducing the severity of the loss or the likelihood of the loss from occurring.
Risk sharing or transfer	Involves sharing the burden of loss or the benefit of gain with another party.
Risk retention or acceptance	Involves accepting the loss, or benefit of gain, from a risk when it occurs.

Drivers for Network Security

Key factors to consider when designing a secure network include the following:

- Business needs
- Risk analysis
- Security policy
- Industry best practices
- Security operations

Evolution of Threats

Threats have evolved in the following manner over the years:

First generation (early 1990s)	Threats took days to propagate and targeted individual computers and networks using macro viruses, email viruses, spam, denial-of-service (DoS) attacks, and limited hacking.
Second generation (early 2000s)	Threats were propagated in hours and targeted multiple networks using network DoS, blended threats (worm + virus + Trojan horses), turbo worms, and widespread hacking.
Third generation (late 2000s)	Threats took minutes to propagate and targeted regional networks using infrastructure hacking, Adobe Flash compromises, distributed DoS (DDoS), and worms and viruses with damaging payloads.
Next generation	Threats now propagate in seconds and target global networks, websites, critical infrastructure services, and consumer electronics and include virtualization exploits, memory scraping, hardware hacking, and IPv6-based attacks.

Data Loss and Exfiltration

This refers to the means by which data leaves the organization without authorization, including the following:

Email attachments	Email attachments containing sensitive information can be intercepted or might accidentally be sent to the wrong person.
Unencrypted devices	Smartphones, personal devices, and laptops do not usually encrypt their content. If compromised, an attacker can steal data.
Cloud storage services	Users may use cloud storage services to transfer large files, which can result in sensitive data being posted on the cloud storage server.
Removable storage devices	Sensitive data could be intentionally transferred to a removable storage drive. Data on a USB stick could also be accidentally lost.

Tracking Threats

Various organizations classify and keep track of threats, including the following:

- **CAPEC (Common Attack Pattern Enumeration and Classification):** http://capec.mitre.org

- **MAEC (Malware Attribute Enumeration and Characterization):** http://maec.mitre.org/

- **OWASP (Open Web Application Security Project):** https://www.owasp.org

- **WASC TC (Web Application Security Consortium Threat Classification):** http://www.webappsec.org/

- **ISC (Internet Storm Center):** http://isc.sans.org/

Malware

The following highlights common types of malicious code (malware) that can be used by hackers:

Viruses	Infectious malicious software that attaches to another program to execute a specific unwanted function on a computer. Most viruses require end-user activation and can lay dormant for an extended period and then activate at a specific time or date. Viruses can also be programmed to mutate to avoid detection.
Worms	Infectious malware, worms are self-contained programs that exploit known vulnerabilities with the goal of slowing a network. Worms do not require end-user activation. An infected host replicates the worm and automatically attempts to infect other hosts by independently exploiting vulnerabilities in networks.
Spyware	Spyware is typically used for financial gain and collects personal user information, monitoring web-browsing activity for marketing purposes, and routing of HTTP requests to advertising sites. Spyware does not usually self-replicate but can be unknowingly installed on computers.
Adware	Refers to any software that displays advertisements, whether or not the user has consented, sometimes in the form of pop-up advertisements.
Scareware	Refers to a class of software used for scamming unsuspecting users. They can contain malicious payloads or be of little or no benefit. A common tactic involves convincing users that their systems are infected by viruses and then providing a link to purchase fake antivirus software.

Trojan horses	These are applications written to look like something else such as a free screensaver, free virus checker, and so on. When a Trojan horse is downloaded and opened, it attacks the end-user computer from within. Trojan horses may be created to initiate specific types of attacks, including the following: ■ Remote access ■ Data sending (key logging) ■ Destructive ■ Security software disabler ■ Denial of service

Anatomy of a Worm

Upon successful exploitation, the worm copies itself from the attacking host to the newly exploited system and the cycle begins again.

Most worms have the following three components:

Enabling vulnerability	A worm installs itself using an exploit mechanism (email attachment, executable file, Trojan horse) on a vulnerable system.
Propagation mechanism	After gaining access to a device, the worm replicates itself and locates new targets. It spreads without human intervention and scans for other hosts to infect.
Payload	Any malicious code that results in some action. Most often, this is used to create a back door to the infected host.

Mitigating Malware and Worms

The primary means of mitigating malware is antivirus software. Antivirus software helps prevent hosts from getting infected and spreading malicious code. It requires much more time (and money) to clean up infected computers than it does to purchase antivirus software and maintain antivirus definition updates.

Worms are more network based than viruses and are more likely to have infected several systems within an organization. The security staff response to a worm infection usually involves the following four phases:

Containment	The goal is to limit the spread of infection and requires segmentation of the infected devices to prevent infected hosts from targeting other uninfected systems. Containment requires using incoming and outgoing access control lists (ACLs) on routers and firewalls at control points within the network.
Inoculation	The goal is to deprive the worm of any available targets. Therefore, all uninfected systems are patched with the appropriate vendor patch. The inoculation phase often runs parallel to or subsequent to the containment phase.

Quarantine	The goal is to track down and identify the infected machines. Once identified, they are disconnected, blocked, or removed from the network and isolated for the treatment phase.
Treatment	Infected systems are disinfected of the worm. This can involve terminating the worm process, removing modified files or system settings that the worm introduced, and patching the vulnerability the worm used to exploit the system. In severe cases, the system may need to be re-imaged.

Threats in Borderless Networks

Possible adversaries to defend against attacks include the following:

- Nations or states
- Terrorists
- Criminals
- Government agencies
- Corporate competitors
- Disgruntled employees
- Hackers

Hacker Titles

Various hacker titles include the following:

Hackers	Individuals who break into computer networks to learn more about them. Most mean no harm and do not expect financial gain.
White hat and blue hat	Names given to identify types of good hackers. White hats are ethical hackers such as individuals performing security audits for organizations. Blue hats are bug testers to ensure secure applications.
Crackers	Hackers with a criminal intent to harm information systems or for financial gain. They are sometimes called "black hat hackers."
Black hat and gray hat	Names given to identify types of crackers. Black hat is synonymous with crackers, and gray hats are ethically questionable crackers.
Phreakers	Hackers of telecommunication systems. They compromise telephone systems to reroute and disconnect telephone lines, sell wiretaps, and steal long-distance services.
Script kiddies	Hackers with very little skill. They do not write their own code but instead run scripts written by more skilled attackers.
Hacktivists	Individuals with political agendas who attack government sites.

Thinking Like a Hacker

The following seven steps may be taken to compromise targets and applications:

Step 1	Perform footprint analysis.	Hackers generally try to build a complete profile of a target of easily available tools and techniques. They can discover organizational domain names, network blocks, IP addresses of systems, ports, services that are used, and more.
Step 2	Enumerate applications and operating systems.	Special readily available tools are used to discover additional target information. Ping sweeps use Internet Control Message Protocol (ICMP) to discover devices on a network. Port scans discover TCP/UDP port status. Other tools include Netcat, Microsoft EPDump and Remote Procedure Call (RPC) Dump, GetMAC, and software development kits (SDKs).
Step 3	Manipulate users to gain access.	Social engineering techniques may be used to manipulate target employees to acquire passwords. They may call or email them and try to convince them to reveal passwords without raising any concern or suspicion.
Step 4	Escalate privileges.	To escalate their privileges, a hacker may attempt to use Trojan horse programs and get target users to unknowingly copy malicious code to their corporate system.
Step 5	Gather additional passwords and secrets.	With escalated privileges, hackers may use tools such as the pwdump and LSADump applications to gather passwords from machines running Windows.
Step 6	Install back doors.	Hackers may attempt to enter through the "front door," or they may use "back doors" into the system. The backdoor method means bypassing normal authentication while attempting to remain undetected. A common backdoor point is a listening port that provides remote access to the system.
Step 7	Leverage the compromised system.	After hackers gain administrative access, they attempt to hack other systems.

Reconnaissance Attacks

This is where the initial footprint analysis and discovery of applications and operating systems are done. Reconnaissance is analogous to a thief surveying a neighborhood for vulnerable homes to break into.

Reconnaissance attacks typically involve the unauthorized discovery and mapping of systems, services, or vulnerabilities using the following:

Internet information queries	Uses readily available Internet tools such as WHOIS, which is widely used for querying databases that store the registered users or assignees of an Internet resource.
Ping sweeps	Method is used to discover a range of live IP addresses.
Port scanners	An application program designed to probe a target host for open ports and identify vulnerable services to exploit.
Packet sniffers	An application program that can intercept, log, and analyze traffic flowing over a network (also referred to as a packet analyzer, network analyzer, or protocol analyzer).

Access Attacks

The goal of access attacks is to discover usernames and passwords to access various resources. The following are common methods to conduct an access attack:

Blended threats	Blended threats are attack mechanisms that combine the characteristics of viruses, worms, Trojan horses, spyware, and others. If the threat is successfully initiated, the access attack attempts to gather user information.
Phishing	Phishing attacks masquerade as a trustworthy entity to get unsuspecting users to provide sensitive information (and are usually used for identity theft). The attacks are usually carried out using email, instant messaging, or phone contact. *Spear phishing* is when a phishing attack is directed at a specific user. *Whaling* is when the attack is targeted at a group of high profile individuals such as top-level executives, politicians, famous people, and more. The term is a play on "landing a big fish."
Pharming	Pharming is an attack aimed at redirecting the traffic of a website to another website. Such attacks are usually conducted by exploiting a vulnerable Domain Name System (DNS) server.
Man-in-the-middle attacks	In a man-in-the-middle attack, a hacker positions himself between a user and the destination. The actual implementation can be carried out in a variety of ways, including using network packet sniffers or altering routing and transport protocols. This type of attack is used for session hijacking, theft of information, sniffing and analyzing network traffic, corrupting data flows, propagating bogus network information, and for DoS attacks.
IP and MAC address spoofing	In IP address spoofing attacks, a hacker forges IP packets with trusted IP source addresses. MAC address spoofing similarly forges trusted host MAC addresses on a LAN. The attacks are commonly used to create a man-in-the-middle situation.

Trust exploitation	Trust exploitation refers to when a hacker has compromised a target and that host is trusted by another host (new target).
Social engineering	This is using social skills, relationships, or understanding of cultural norms to manipulate people inside a network and have them willingly (but usually unknowingly) participate and provide access to the network.

Password Cracking

Attackers can capture passwords using Trojan horse programs, key loggers, or packet sniffers. In addition, they can attempt to crack passwords using the following methods:

Password guessing	The attacker manually enters possible passwords based on informed guesses. The attack can also use software tools to automate the process.
Dictionary lists	Programs use dictionary and word lists; phrases; or other combinations of letters, numbers, and symbols that are often used as passwords. Programs enter word after word at high speed until they find a match.
Brute force	This approach relies on power and repetition, comparing every possible combination and permutation of characters until it finds a match. It eventually cracks any password, but it may be very time-consuming.
Hybrid cracking	Some password crackers mix a combination of techniques and are highly effective against poorly constructed passwords.

Denial-of-Service Attacks

The goal of a DoS attack is to deny network services to valid users. A DoS situation can be caused in a variety of ways. For instance, an attacker conducts a DoS attack by using a host to send an extremely large number of requests to a server or edge device. The intent is to overwhelm the target and make it unavailable for legitimate access and use. This is the most publicized form of attack and among the most difficult to eliminate.

A DoS situation could also be caused unintentionally, such as when an administrator misconfigures network access denying access to authorized users.

Types of DoS attacks include the following:

Buffer overflow	A DoS attack in which the attacker provides input that is larger than the destination device expected. It may overwrite adjacent memory, corrupt the system, and cause it to crash.
Ping of death	Legacy attack in which the attacker would craft a packet specifying a packet size greater than 65,536 bytes. Servers receiving these packets would crash causing a DoS situation. Modern servers are no longer susceptible to this attack. However, similar attacks using malformed SNMP, syslog, DNS, or other UDP-based protocol messages are now being used.

ICMP flood	A DoS attack that sends a large number of ICMP requests or ICMP responses (e.g., a Smurf attack) to a destination device in an attempt to overwhelm it, slow it down, or even crash it.
UDP flood	A DoS attack that sends a large number of UDP packets to a destination device in an attempt to overwhelm it, slow it down, or even crash it.
TCP SYN flood	A DoS attack that exploits the TCP three-way handshake operation. The attacker sends multiple TCP SYN packets with random source addresses to the target host. The victim replies with a SYN ACK, adds an entry in its state table, and waits for the last part of the handshake, which is never completed. The large number of requests consumes the resources of the target.
Reflection	A DoS attack that sends a flood of protocol request packets with a spoofed source IP address to numerous target hosts. These target hosts become reflectors because they all reply to the spoofed IP address of the victim.
Amplification	A DoS attack that amplifies a reflection attack by using a small request packet to solicit a large response from the victim. For instance, a small DNS query that results in a large reply by the DNS server.
Other attacks	Other attacks to compromise availability include cutting electrical power, or sabotaging the computer environment.

Distributed Denial-of-Service Attacks

An attacker can enlist a network of controlled hosts to create a distributed DoS (DDoS) attack. DDoS attacks are more effective than DoS attacks.

DDoS attacks require the following:

Bots	This is self-propagating malware designed to infect a host and make it surrender control to an attacker's command and control server. Bots can also log keystrokes, gather usernames and passwords, capture packets, and more.
Botnets	Describes a collection of compromised zombie systems that are running bots.
Zombie	Describes a host compromised with a bot. The zombie is logged in to the command and control server and quietly waits for commands.
Command and control server	Describes the attacker's host, which remotely controls the botnets. The attacker uses the master control mechanism on a command and control server to send instructions to zombies.

Tools Used by Attackers

Several tools are used by attackers. Some of these tools are legitimate tools used by network administrators and security penetration testing firms. Other tools are explicitly written for nefarious reasons.

Tools used by attackers can be located from the following:

sectools.org	Website maintained by the Nmap Project that lists the top security tools in order of popularity from the network security community. Tools include password auditors, sniffers, vulnerability scanners, packet crafters, exploitation tools, and more.
Kali Linux	Linux distribution that provides access to more than 300 security tools. It can also be easily booted from removable media or installed in a virtual machine.
Metasploit	Security engineer tool used to develop and test exploit code.

Principles of Secure Network Design

Guidelines to secure a network infrastructure include the following:

Defense in depth	Architecture uses a layered approach to create security domains and separate them by different types of security controls.
Compartmentalization	Architecture segments the network where different assets with different values are in different security domains, be it physical or logical. Granular trust relationships between compartments would mitigate attacks that try to gain a foothold in lower-security domains to exploit high-value assets in higher-security domains.
Least privilege	Principle applies a need-to-know approach to trust relationships between security domains. This results in restrictive policies, where access to and from a security domain is allowed only for the required users, applications, or network traffic. Everything else is denied by default.
Weakest link	Architecture uses a layered approach to security, with weaker or less-protected assets residing in separated security domains. Humans are often considered to be the weakest link in information security architectures.
Separation and rotation of duties	Concept of developing systems where more than one individual is required to complete a certain task to mitigate fraud and error. This applies to information security controls, and it applies to both technical controls and human procedures to manage those controls.

Mediated access	Principle is based on centralizing security controls to protect groups of assets or security domains such as using firewalls, proxies, and other security controls to act on behalf of the assets they are designed to protect, and mediate the trust relationships between security domains.
Accountability and traceability	Architecture should provide mechanisms to track the activity of users, attackers, and even security administrators. It should include provisions for accountability and nonrepudiation. This principle translates into specific functions, such as security audits, event management and monitoring, forensics, and others.

Defense in Depth

Defense in depth provides a layered security approach by using multiple security mechanisms. The security mechanisms should complement each other but not depend on each other. The use of this approach can eliminate single points of failure and augment weak links in the system to provide stronger protection with multiple layers.

Recommendations for a defense-in-depth strategy include the following:

Defend in multiple places	Threat vectors can occur from various locations. Therefore, an organization must deploy protection mechanisms at multiple locations to resist all classes of attacks. Includes defending the networks and infrastructure, enclave boundaries, and the computing environment.
Build layered defenses	All products have inherent weaknesses. Therefore, an effective countermeasure is to deploy multiple defense mechanisms between the adversary and the target.
Use robust components	Specify the security robustness based on the value of the asset to be protected. For instance, deploy stronger mechanisms at the network boundaries than at the user desktop.
Employ robust key management	Deploy robust encryption key management and public key infrastructures that are highly resistant to attack.
Deploy intrusion detection/prevention systems (IDSs/IPSs)	Deploy infrastructures to detect and prevent intrusions and to analyze and correlate the results and react accordingly.

CHAPTER 2

Implementing Security Policies

The chapter covers the following topics:

Managing Risk

- Quantitative Risk Analysis Formula
- Quantitative Risk Analysis Example
- Regulatory Compliance

Security Policy

- Standards, Guidelines, and Procedures
- Security Policy Audience Responsibilities
- Security Awareness

Secure Network Lifecycle Management

- Models and Frameworks
- Assessing and Monitoring the Network Security Posture
- Testing the Security Architecture

Incident Response

- Incident Response Phases
- Computer Crime Investigation
- Collection of Evidence and Forensics
- Law Enforcement and Liability
- Ethics

Disaster-Recovery and Business-Continuity Planning

Managing Risk

Risk needs to be framed, assessed, monitored, and responded to. Risk, compliance, and security policies are major components of security architectures. The primary purpose of risk analysis is to quantify the impact of an individual potential threat.

There are two types of risk analysis:

Quantitative risk analysis	Uses a mathematical model using an estimated value for an asset multiplied by the likelihood of a threat being realized. Quantitative risk analysis provides an actual monetary figure of expected losses, which is then used to estimate an annual cost. The resulting numbers can also be used to justify proposed countermeasures.
Qualitative risk analysis	Uses a scenario model. Can be performed in a shorter period of time and with less data. Qualitative risk assessments are descriptive versus measurable. Qualitative risk assessments may precede a quantitative analysis.

Quantitative Risk Analysis Formula

Risk management is based on its building blocks of assets and vulnerabilities, threats, and countermeasures. Quantitative analysis relies on specific formulas to determine the value of the risk decision variables. Figure 2-1 displays the quantitative risk analysis formula.

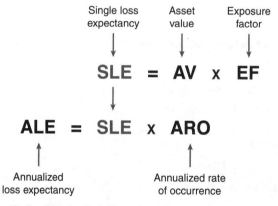

Figure 2-1   Quantitative Risk Analysis Formula

Quantitative risk analysis terms include the following:

Asset value (AV)	This estimated value includes the purchase price, the cost of deployment, and the cost of maintenance. Assets of low value would have a limited effect on CIA. Assets of moderate value would have a serious effect on CIA. Assets of high value would have a severe effect on CIA.
Exposure factor (EF)	This estimates the degree of destruction that may occur. It is represented as a percentage that a realized threat could have on an asset.

Single loss expectancy (SLE)	This calculation represents the expected loss from a single occurrence of the threat. The SLE is defined as the AV × EF.
Annualized rate of occurrence (ARO)	This is the estimated frequency that a threat is expected to occur. It is the number of times that one may reasonably expect the risk to occur during one year. This estimate is very difficult and is usually based on past experience.
Annualized loss expectancy (ALE)	This is the expected financial loss that an individual threat may cause. The ALE is a monetary value derived from the formula SLE × ARO. This number is used to justify the least-cost security measures.

Quantitative Risk Analysis Example

An administrator of a data center must provide a projection for a flood disaster. Assume that the overall value of a data center is $10,000,000 (AV). It is estimated that 60% (EF) of the data center would be destroyed in the event of a flood (risk):

- SLE = AV × EF
- SLE = $10,000,000 × 60% = $6,000,000

The SLE assigns a monetary value for a single occurrence. It represents the organization's potential loss amount if a specific threat exploits a vulnerability.

The ALE is the total amount of money that the organization will lose in 1 year if nothing is done to mitigate the risk. It is often used to justify the lowest-cost security measure. If the likelihood of a flood occurring is estimated at once in 100 years (1/100), the ARO equals 1%:

- ALE = SLE × ARO
- ALE = $6,000,000 × 1% = $60,000

The ALE provides a value that the organization can work with to budget the cost to establish controls or safeguards to prevent this type of damage.

Regulatory Compliance

The current regulatory landscape is broader and more international. Compliance regulations define not only the scope and parameters for the risk and security architectures of an organization, but also the liability for those who do not comply.

The following are compliance regulations, their geographic scope, and which organizations a regulation applies to:

Regulation	Geographic Boundary	Description
DMCA	U.S.	The Digital Millennium Copyright Act (DMCA) protects against copyright infringement. It heightens the penalties for copyright infringement on the Internet.
FISMA	U.S.	The Federal Information Security Management Act (FISMA) of 2002 requires that the U.S. government federal agencies, service organizations, and affiliated parties be subject to yearly cybersecurity audits.
GLB	U.S.	The Gramm-Leach-Bliley (GLB) Act (also known as the Financial Services Modernization Act of 1999) applies mostly to banks, investment companies, and insurance agencies and governs the collection, disclosure, and protection of consumer information.
HIPAA	U.S.	The Health Insurance Portability and Accountability Act (HIPAA) of 2000 includes a set of national standards for healthcare transactions that provide assurances that the electronic transfer of confidential patient information will be as safe as, or safer than, paper-based patient records.
SOX	U.S.	The Sarbanes-Oxley (SOX) Act of 2002 governs the accounting and reporting practices of publicly traded companies in the United States. It was created in response to accounting scandals, including those affecting Enron, Tyco International, Peregrine Systems, and WorldCom.
PCI DSS	U.S.	The Payment Card Industry Data Security Standard (PCI DSS) governs organizations processing branded credit card data.
PIPEDA	Canada	The Personal Information Protection and Electronic Documents Act governs how private-sector organizations collect, use, and disclose personal information in the course of commercial business.
NERC	North America	The North American Electric Reliability Corporation (NERC), a nonprofit corporation that seeks to ensure the reliability of the North American bulk electric power system, applies to users, owners, and operators in that system.
EU Data Protection Directive	European Union	This act contains eight "data protection principles" that specify how personal data is securely collected, maintained, and disposed of. It applies to all organizations operating in the 27 member countries.

Regulation	Geographic Boundary	Description
Safe Harbour Act	European Union	It prohibits European firms from transferring personal data to overseas jurisdictions with weaker privacy laws.
Basel II	Global	An international standard with which banking regulators must comply. It requires them to put aside enough capital to guard against risk. It applies to all internationally active banks with assets of more than $250 billion.

Security Policy

A security policy is a set of objectives for the company, rules of behavior for users and administrators, and requirements for system and management that collectively ensure the security of network and computer systems in an organization.

It is a "living document," meaning that the document is never finished and is continuously updated as technology and employee requirements change. One document will not likely meet the needs of the entire audience of a large organization.

The audience of the security policy should be employees, contractors, suppliers, or customers who have access to your network.

Figure 2-2 displays a common corporate policy structure for most organizations:

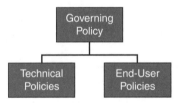

Figure 2-2   Comprehensive Security Policy Components

Governing policy	It details the company's overall security policy philosophy. It defines information security concepts at a high level, describes why they are important, and details the organization's stand. It supports the technical and end-user policies.
Technical policies	Security staff creates technical policies to implement the security requirements outlined in the governing policy. These policies describe what the security staff does but do not dictate how the security staff performs its functions.
End-user policies	Documents contain security policies important to end users.

Technical policies can be categorized as follows:

General policies	Define the use of equipment, computing services, and security guidelines. May include an acceptable use policy (AUP), account access policy, password policy, acquisition policy, audit policy, information sensitivity policy, risk assessment policy, and global web server policy.
Remote-access policies	Defines the standards for connecting to the organization network from an external host or network. Typically include a virtual private network (VPN) security policy.
Network policies	Define standards to secure all wired and wireless networks' data ports. May also include general network access polices and policies to access routers, switches, servers, and extranets.
Email policies	Define standards to protect the email infrastructure of the organization. May also include an automatic forwarding of email policy and junk email (i.e., spam) policy.
Other policies	Other categories may include telephony policies, application use policies, and wireless policies.

Standards, Guidelines, and Procedures

Security policies establish a framework within which to work, but they are usually too general to be of much use to individuals responsible for implementing these policies.

Therefore, more detailed documents exist, including the following:

Standards	Allow IT staff to be consistent by specifying the use of technologies. They are usually mandatory and help provide consistency, uniformity, and efficiency.
Guidelines	These are best practices that provide a list of suggestions on how things can be done better. They are similar to standards, but are more flexible and are not usually mandatory.
Procedures	Documents include the details of implementation, usually with step-by-step instructions and graphics.

Figure 2-3 provides a hierarchical view of the information security policy framework.

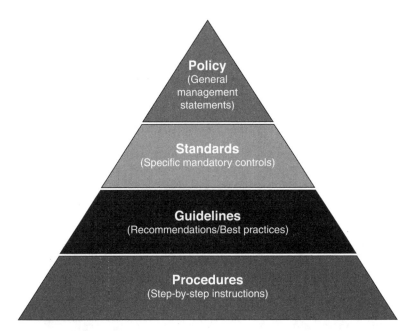

Figure 2-3   Information Security Policy Framework

Security Policy Audience Responsibilities

Key individuals in an organization responsible for the security policy are as follows:

Senior management (CEO)	Is ultimately responsible
Senior security IT management (CSO, CIO, CISO)	Are responsible for the security policy
Senior security IT staff	Have input on the security policy and possibly draft sections of the security policy
Security IT staff	Are responsible for implementing the security policy
End users	Are responsible for complying with the security policy

Security Awareness

An effective computer security awareness and training program requires proper planning, implementation, maintenance, and periodic evaluation. In general, a computer security awareness and training program should encompass the following seven steps:

1. Identify program scope, goals, and objectives.

2. Identify training staff.

3. Identify target audiences.

   4. Motivate management and employees.

   5. Administer the program.

   6. Maintain the program.

   7. Evaluate the program.

Secure Network Lifecycle Management

The lifecycle approach may also help you understand the framing of information security.

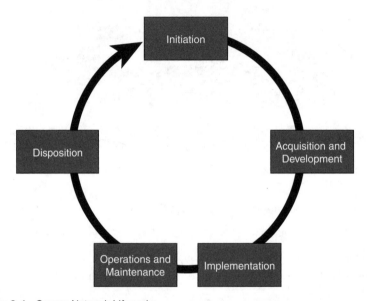

Figure 2-4   Secure Network Lifecycle

Figure 2-4 illustrates the five phases of the lifecycle approach. The five-phase approach gives context to the process of designing, creating, and maintaining security architectures. It is based on Publication 800-64 revision 2 of the National Institute of Standards and Technology (NIST).

When applied to information security, these phases are used as follows:

Initiation	Includes security categorization and preliminary risk assessment steps.
Acquisition and development	Includes steps such as risk assessment, security functional requirements analysis, security assurance requirements analysis, cost considerations and reporting, security planning, security control development, developmental security test and evaluation, and other planning components.
Implementation	These security tasks include inspection and acceptance, system integration, security certification, and security accreditation steps.

Operations and maintenance	Includes configuration management and control and continuous monitoring steps.
Disposition	Includes information preservation, media sanitization, and hardware- and software-disposal steps.

Models and Frameworks

The following frameworks and models are alternatives to the lifecycle approach and provide similar security architecture guidance:

Control Objectives for Information and Related Technology (COBIT)	Includes best practices from a consensus of experts that focus on IT controls and IT metrics, which is useful for IT governance and audits. These good practices help optimize IT-enabled investments, ensure service delivery, and provide a measure against which to judge when things do go wrong.
ISO 27000 Standards	Includes a comprehensive set of controls comprising best practices in information security. It is also a certified and globally recognized information security standard that focuses on risk identification, assessment, and management.
Information Technology Infrastructure Library (ITIL)	Includes a set of eight practice guidebooks covering most aspects of IT service management.
National Institute of Standards and Technology (NIST)	The NIST 800 series provides detailed documents on how to secure a networked infrastructure. It is also available for free and is used for FISMA.

Assessing and Monitoring the Network Security Posture

The security posture should be assessed at multiple points of the lifecycle. By assessing all aspects of the networked business environment, it is possible to determine the ability of the organization to detect, defend against, and respond to network attacks.

Key assessment activities include the following:

Security posture assessment	Consists of a thorough assessment of the network devices, servers, desktops, and databases. Analyzes the effectiveness of the network security against recognized industry best practices to identify the relative strengths and weaknesses of the environment and document specific vulnerabilities that could threaten the business.
Internal assessment	Consists of a controlled network attack on internal systems, applications, and network devices and is used to identify steps that are needed to prevent intentional attacks or unintentional mistakes from trusted insiders to effectively secure valuable information assets.

External assessment	The goal is to quantify the security risk associated with Internet-connected systems.
Wireless assessment	Tests the wireless network within the organization and identifies risks and exposures associated with a wireless deployment.
Security posture assessment analysis and documentation	Quantifies the security posture of the organization network by using metrics and graphs. The report should explain methods that would likely be used to compromise network devices and systems. It should also prioritize the vulnerabilities and recommend actions to correct the security risks and detail remediation steps to prevent future exploitation.

Testing the Security Architecture

The security infrastructure should be tested within the context of risk management. Some testing techniques are predominantly manual, and other tests are highly automated. Staff that conducts the security testing should have significant security and networking knowledge.

Many types of testing techniques are available, including the following:

- Network and vulnerability scanning
- Password cracking
- Log review
- Integrity checkers, virus checking
- War dialing and war driving
- Penetration testing

Incident Response

Risk cannot be completely eliminated, which makes incident response critical.

Incident Response Phases

The incident response process has several phases:

Preparation	Involves getting ready before an incident happens. Prepare the facilities and team contact information. Define the tools required and know how to use them. Define prevention procedures.
Detection and analysis	Define the threat vector, analyze and implement tools for log and error correlation.

Containment, eradication, and recovery	After an incident has been detected, it must be contained before it can spread. All containment strategies should also include steps to eradicate the threat and vulnerabilities, or at least mitigate them, and steps to recover operating systems, hardware components, and productive time.
Post-incident activity	A crucial step, document what happened and how it was mitigated. This should provide insight for future incidents.

Computer Crime Investigation

To successfully prosecute computer crimes, investigators must prove three things:

Motive	Did the perpetrators have a reason to commit the crime?
Opportunity	Were they available to commit the crime?
Means	Were they capable of committing the crime?

Collection of Evidence and Forensics

In response to security breaches, the infected system must be immediately isolated. Dump the memory to disk and create multiple master copies of the hard drive.

These master copies are usually locked in a safe for investigators who will use working copies for both the prosecution and the defense.

Law Enforcement and Liability

Most countries have three basic categories of laws:

Criminal	Concerned with crimes, and its penalties usually involve the risk of fines or imprisonment or both.
Civil	Civil law focuses on correcting wrongs that are not crimes, such as a company infringing on a patent.
Administrative	Involves government agencies enforcing regulations, such as paying employees their due vacation pay.

Organizations are required to practice due diligence and due care. While laws may make it difficult to prosecute intrusions, this does not diminish liability issues on the part of the organization. Companies can be found liable for not properly protecting their systems from being compromised (data breach, data leakage).

Ethics

Ethics is a standard higher than the law. It is a set of moral principles that govern civil behavior. Individuals who violate the code of ethics can face consequences such as loss of certification, loss of employment, and even prosecution by criminal or civil courts.

Disaster-Recovery and Business-Continuity Planning

Disaster recovery is the process of regaining access to the data, hardware, and software necessary to resume critical business operations after a natural or human-induced disaster or the unexpected or sudden loss of key personnel.

A disaster-recovery plan is part of business-continuity planning and requires extensive planning. The goal is to define objectives for the recovery of host computing systems that run the applications that support the business processes. Terms associated with business continuity include the following:

Maximum tolerable downtime (MTD)	Total amount of time the system owner or authorizing official is willing to accept for an outage or disruption
Recovery time objective (RTO)	The maximum amount of time that a system resource can remain unavailable before there is an unacceptable impact on other system resources, supported mission, or business processes
Recovery point objective (RPO)	The point in time, prior to a disruption or system outage, to which mission or business process data can be recovered after an outage

CHAPTER 3

Building a Security Strategy

The chapter covers the following topics:

Cisco Borderless Network Architecture

- Borderless Security Products

Cisco SecureX Architecture and Context-Aware Security

- Cisco TrustSec
- TrustSec Confidentiality
- Cisco AnyConnect
- Cisco Talos

Threat Control and Containment

Cloud Security and Data-Loss Prevention

Secure Connectivity Through VPNs

Security Management

Cisco Borderless Network Architecture

Traditional approaches to network security used well-defined borders to protect inside networks from outside threats and malware. Employees used corporate computers secured with antivirus and personal firewalls. Perimeter-based networks were protected using network-scanning devices (firewalls, web proxies, and email gateways).

Today, network borders are dissolving as users want to access to resources from any location, on any type of endpoint device, using various connectivity methods. Cisco has addressed this with the Borderless Network Architecture, which integrates the following components:

Borderless end zone	The zone offers deployment flexibility and strong security services in multiple dimensions as users connect to the network. End-user access is based on the security posture of the connecting endpoint using the Cisco AnyConnect SSL VPN Client. Infrastructure protection is provided using firewalls, intrusion prevention systems (IPSs), web security, and email security.
Borderless Internet	Implemented by performing Layer 2 through Layer 7 scanning engines managed by enterprises and cloud providers. Scanning engines assume the role of firewalls, intrusion detection/prevention systems (IDSs/IPSs), network proxies, and web gateways.

| Borderless data center | Layers virtualized components on top of existing infrastructure components to provide security solutions for the cloud. |
| Policy management layer | The security policy is managed in central locations and then enforced throughout the network based on context-specific variables. It provides the following:

■ Access policy (who, what, when, where, and how)

■ Dynamic containment policy

■ Policy for on and off premise |

Borderless Security Products

The architectural approach to security found in the Borderless Network Architecture results in distinct categories of Cisco products, technologies, and solutions:

■ SecureX and context-aware security

■ Threat control and containment

■ Cloud security and data-loss prevention

■ Secure connectivity through VPNs

■ Security management

Cisco SecureX Architecture and Context-Aware Security

To respond to the evolving security needs of today's borderless network environments, Cisco developed the SecureX architecture. It is a new context-aware security architecture that enforces security policies across the entire distributed network, not just at a single point in the data stream.

The architecture starts with a solid network technology foundation that ensures the network infrastructure is not compromised in any way. It has security enforcement elements in the form of appliances, modules, or cloud services built on top. This architecture can deal with the full spectrum of devices, ranging from the traditional corporate PC or Mac, all the way to next-generation mobile devices such as iPads and Androids. With Cisco AnyConnect, security is enforced in the network by tethering these myriad devices into the security infrastructure at the most optimal point and attaching seamlessly.

The components of the SecureX strategy include the following:

■ Context awareness

■ Cisco TrustSec

■ Cisco AnyConnect

■ Cisco Talos

Figure 3-1 illustrates the components of the SecureX strategy.

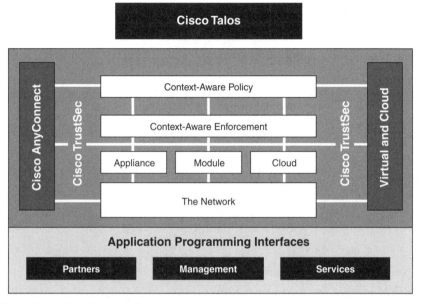

Figure 3-1   Cisco SecureX Components

Components of the Cisco SecureX strategy include the following:

Context-aware policies	Allows enforcement elements such as infrastructure devices to use user information (for example, user identity, security posture of the connecting device, and the point of access to the network) to define the access policy.
Cisco TrustSec	TrustSec is an intelligent and scalable access control solution that mitigates security access risks across the entire network to provide access to anyone, anywhere, anytime.
Cisco AnyConnect Client	AnyConnect Client provides for secure connectivity across a broad set of PC- and smartphone-based mobile devices. The enforcement devices provide posture assessment, access control services, and policy enforcement.
Cisco Talos	Cisco Talos Security Intelligence and Research Group (Talos) correlates data of almost a million live data feeds from deployed Cisco email, web, firewall, and IPS solutions to detect, analyze, and protect against both known and emerging threats. Information is shared with Cisco customers and devices on demand.

Cisco TrustSec

TrustSec is an umbrella term that encompasses the Cisco next-generation Network Access Control (NAC) framework, including the following:

- Policy-based access control
- Identity-aware networking based on roles
- Data confidentiality
- Data integrity

It does so by incorporating the following technologies:

- IEEE 802.1x (Dot1x)
- Cisco NAC Appliance
- Profiling technologies
- Guest services
- Security group tags (SGTs) and security group ACLs (SGACLs)
- MACSec (802.1AE)
- Access Control Server (ACS)
- Identity Services Engine (ISE)

When user TrustSec identities are not based on IP addresses or usernames, they are role based. When users authenticate, their privileges are based on their SGT and SGACL.

Cisco ISE combines the functionality of other Cisco products—such as the Cisco Secure Access Control Server (ACS) for authentication, authorization, and accounting (AAA) services, and Network Admission Control (NAC)—into this next-generation policy server.

TrustSec Confidentiality

TrustSec implementation follows this process:

1. A user connects to a switch using 802.1X. The switch relays the authentication credentials to an ISE. The ISE authenticates the user and assigns the user an SGT.

2. Traffic from the authenticated user is tagged with its specific SGT. Network devices along the data path read this tag and enforce its associated policy by restricting access to predetermined network destinations and resources. The devices do so by using SGACLs.

3. TrustSec can also provide data confidentiality by using MACSec. For example, if a policy requires that data should be secured, Cisco TrustSec understands this policy and dynamically encrypts the user data.

Cisco AnyConnect

Cisco AnyConnect protects mobile employees on PC-based or smartphone platforms using an SSL or IP Security (IPsec) virtual private network (VPN) to deliver a more seamless, always-on, and always-protected experience to end users, while enabling IT administrators to enforce policies and block malware with cloud-based or hybrid web security.

Cisco AnyConnect provides the following:

- Device support regardless of device type (for example, PC, laptop, smartphone, tablet, or PDA)

- Multifunctional security by combining multiple security controls in one client application

- Consistent experience by providing an always-on intelligent connection for seamless experience and performance

Cisco Talos

Cisco Talos combines the Cisco Security Intelligence Operations (SIO) and Sourcefire VRT to provide collective security intelligence. Talos baselines the current global state of threats and provides the network with valuable information to detect, prevent, and react to threats. It operates as an early-warning system by correlating threat information from the SensorBase, analyzed by the Threat Operations Center. This information is then provided to enforcement devices such as the Cisco Adaptive Security Appliance (ASA), Integrated Services Router (ISR), and IPS device for real-time threat prevention.

Threat Control and Containment

The Cisco threat control and containment solution regulates network access, isolates infected systems, prevents intrusions, and protects critical business assets. This solution counteracts malicious traffic before it affects a business.

Threat prevention products include the following:

Cisco ASAs	The Adaptive Security Appliance devices provide proven firewall services and integration of VPN and IPS technologies.
Cisco ISRs	Integrated Services Routers provide network security controls using zone-based policy firewall (ZPF), IOS IPS, and VPN technologies.
Cisco IPS	Intrusion prevention is provided using dedicated appliances or is integrated into ASA and ISR devices. These IPS sensors support a variety of IPS technologies, including signature-based, anomaly-based, policy-based, and reputation-based techniques.

Cloud Security and Data-Loss Prevention

Adding to the complexity of securing a network is the fact that many modern network designs now incorporate cloud computing. Threats in cloud computing include the following:

- Abuse of cloud computing
- Account or service hijacking
- Data loss in the cloud
- Unsecure interfaces and application programming interfaces (APIs)
- Malicious insiders

Administrators, because they are ultimately responsible for data residing on networks over which they have no control, must also consider the consequences if the cloud environment is not properly secured.

Two following traditional key services must now be secured in the cloud:

Securing web access	Cisco Cloud Web Security (CWS), formerly known as Cisco ScanSafe, is a cloud-based solution that provides comprehensive web security as a service (SaaS). Cisco CWS provides enhanced security for all endpoints while they access Internet websites using publicly available wireless networks including hotspots and mobile cellular networks. With Cisco CWS, administrators can set and enforce specific web use policies to control access to websites and specific content in web pages and applications as well as SaaS applications.
	Cisco Web Security Appliance (WSA) is a type of firewall and threat monitoring appliance that provides secure web access, content security, and threat mitigation for web services. It also provides advanced malware protection, application visibility and control, insightful reporting, and secure mobility.
Securing email access	Cisco Email Security Appliance (ESA) is a type of firewall and threat monitoring appliance for email traffic. It provides the capability to quickly block new email-based blended attacks, to control or encrypt sensitive outbound email, control spam, and more.

Secure Connectivity Through VPNs

There are two VPN-based solutions to implement secure connectivity:

Secure communications for remote access	Provides secure customizable access to corporate networks and applications by establishing an SSL or IPsec VPN tunnel between the remote host and central site
Secure communications for site-to-site connections	Provides secure site-to-site IPsec VPN access between two or more sites

Security Management

Cisco network management systems help automate, simplify, and integrate a network to reduce operational costs; improve productivity; and achieve critical functions such as availability, responsiveness, resilience, and security.

The hierarchy of tools available for security management is as follows:

Device managers	Web interface tool that simplifies the configuration and monitoring of a single device.
Cisco ASA Security Device Manager (ASDM)	A GUI-based device management tool for ASAs.
Cisco Security Manager	An enterprise-level application solution to configure and manage thousands of firewalls, routers, switches, IPS sensors, and other security solutions. Scalability is provided using intelligent policy-based management techniques that simplify administration.

CHAPTER 4

Network Foundation Protection

The chapter covers the following topics:

Threats Against the Network Infrastructure

Cisco Network Foundation Protection Framework

Control Plane Security

- Control Plane Policing

Management Plane Security

- Role-Based Access Control
- Secure Management and Reporting

Data Plane Security

- ACLs
- Antispoofing
- Layer 2 Data Plane Protection

Threats Against the Network Infrastructure

Common vulnerabilities and threats against a network infrastructure include the following:

Vulnerabilities	<ul><li>Design errors</li><li>Protocol weaknesses</li><li>Software vulnerabilities</li><li>Device misconfiguration</li></ul>
Threats	<ul><li>Trust exploitation</li><li>Login, authentication, and password attacks</li><li>Routing protocol exploits</li><li>Spoofing</li><li>Denial of service (DoS)</li><li>Confidentiality and integrity attacks</li></ul>

The impact of those threats and vulnerabilities includes the following:

Impact	<ul><li>Exposed management credentials</li><li>High CPU usage</li><li>Loss of protocol keepalives and updates</li><li>Route flaps and major network transitions</li><li>Slow or unresponsive management sessions</li><li>Indiscriminant packet drops</li></ul>

Cisco Network Foundation Protection Framework

The Cisco Network Foundation Protection (NFP) framework provides an umbrella strategy for infrastructure protection forming the foundation for continuous service delivery.

NFP logically divides a router and Catalyst switches into three functional areas:

Control plane	Provides the ability to route data correctly. Traffic consists of device-generated packets required for the operation of the network itself, such as Address Resolution Protocol (ARP) message exchanges, Open Shortest Path First (OSPF) protocol, or Enhance Interior Gateway Protocol (EIGRP) routing advertisements.
Management plane	Provides the ability to manage network elements. Traffic is generated either by network devices or network management stations using tools such as Telnet, Secure Shell (SSH), Trivial File Transfer Protocol (TFTP), File Transfer Protocol (FTP), Network Time Protocol (NTP), or Simple Network Management Protocol (SNMP).
Data plane (forwarding plane)	Provides the ability to forward data. Typically consists of user-generated packets being forwarded to another end station. It does not include traffic sent to the IOS device. Most traffic travels through the router via the data plane.

Figure 4-1 provides a conceptual view of the NFP framework.

Each of these planes must be protected to provide network availability and ensure continuous service delivery. The Cisco NFP framework provides the tools and techniques to secure each of these planes.

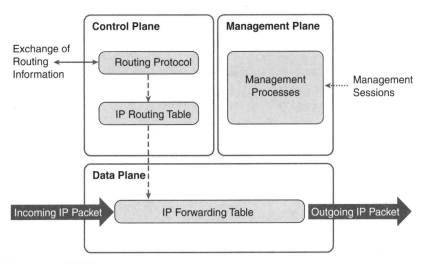

Figure 4-1   NFP Planes

Control Plane Security

Control plane security can be implemented using the following features:

Cisco AutoSecure	Cisco AutoSecure provides a one-step device lockdown feature to protect the control plane and the management and data planes. It is a script initiated from the command-line interface (CLI) to configure the security posture of routers and disables nonessential system processes and services. It first makes recommendations to address security vulnerabilities and then modifies the router configuration.
Routing protocol authentication	Neighbor authentication prevents a router from accepting fraudulent routing updates. Most routing protocols support neighbor authentication.
CoPP	Control Plane Policing (CoPP) is used on higher-end Cisco devices with route processors. It is a Cisco IOS feature designed to enable users to manage the flow of traffic managed by the route processor of their network devices.

Control Plane Policing

CoPP is designed to prevent unnecessary traffic from overwhelming the route processor. The CoPP feature treats the control plane as a separate entity with its own ingress (input) and egress (output) ports. Because the CoPP feature treats the control plane as a separate entity, a set of rules can be established and associated with the ingress and egress ports of the control plane.

CoPP consists of the following features:

CoPP	Control Plane Policing lets users configure a QoS filter that manages the traffic flow of control plane packets. This protects the control plane against reconnaissance and DoS attacks.
CPPr	Control Plane Protection is an extension of CoPP but allows a finer policing granularity. For example, CPPr can filter and rate-limit the packets that are going to the control plane of the router and discard malicious and error packets (or both).
Control Plane Logging	The Control Plane Logging feature enables logging of the packets that CoPP or CPPr drop or permit. It provides the logging mechanism that is needed to deploy, monitor, and troubleshoot CoPP features efficiently.

Management Plane Security

Management plane security can be implemented using the following features:

Login and password policy	Restrict device accessibility. Implement AAA to identify administrators as they log in to network devices (authentication). Control what each administrator is allowed to do (authorization). Provide audit trails that record what each administrator has done (Accounting).
Role-based access control	Ensure access is only granted to authenticated users, groups, and services. Role-based access control (RBAC) and authentication, authorization, and accounting (AAA) services provide mechanisms to effectively authenticate access.
Authorize actions	Restrict the actions and views permitted by any particular user, group, or service.
Secure management access and reporting	Log and account for all access. Record who accessed the device, what occurred, and when it occurred.
Ensure the confidentiality of data	Protect locally stored sensitive data from being viewed or copied. Use management protocols with strong authentication to mitigate confidentiality attacks aimed at exposing passwords and device configurations.
Present legal notification	Display legal notice developed with legal counsel.
Secure access using ACLs	Define ACLs for management purposes and limit which IP addresses are allowed to connect to the network device. It can also be configured to limit which other network device to connect to by applying an ACL to an outbound `access-class` line configuration command.
Use only secure management protocols	Define a network policy to use only secure network management protocols such as SSH instead of Telnet, HTTPS instead of HTTP, and SNMPv3 (authPriv mode) instead of earlier versions of SNMP.

Role-Based Access Control

RBAC restricts user access based on the role of the user. Roles are created for job or task functions and assigned access permissions to specific assets. Users are then assigned to roles and acquire the permissions defined for the role.

On some devices, such as Cisco Nexus data center switches, RBACs are automatically implemented. However, on Cisco IOS devices, the role-based CLI access feature is used to implement RBAC for management access. The feature creates different "views" that define which commands are accepted and what configuration information is visible. For scalability, users, permissions, and roles are usually created and maintained in a central repository server. This makes the access control policy available to multiple devices using it.

The central repository server can be an AAA server such as the Cisco Secure Access Control System (ACS) to provide AAA services to a network for management purposes.

Secure Management and Reporting

The management network is an attractive target to hackers. For this reason, the management module has been built with several technologies designed to mitigate such risks.

The information flow between management hosts and the managed devices can be out-of-band (OOB; information flows within a network on which no production traffic resides) or in-band (information flows across the enterprise production network, the Internet, or both).

Data Plane Security

Data plane security can be implemented using the following features:

Access control lists	Access control lists (ACLs) perform packet filtering to control which packets move through the network and where.
Antispoofing	ACLs can be used as an antispoofing mechanism that discards traffic that has an invalid source address.
Layer 2 security features	Cisco Catalyst switches have integrated features to help secure the Layer 2 infrastructure.
Firewalls	Cisco firewalls can recognize and allow legitimate data traffic while rejecting illegitimate data traffic.
Intrusion prevention systems	Cisco IPSs perform deep analysis of application layer data streams to recognize malicious content in the data streams and take action to prevent attack success.
Virtual private networks	Cisco VPNs can be enabled to protect data crossing untrusted networks, providing privacy, origin authentication, and data integrity.
Content security	Cisco content security appliances can analyze web and email traffic to enforce content policies and to mitigate attacks embedded in web and email data streams.

ACLs

ACLs are used to secure the data plane in a variety of ways, including the following:

Block unwanted traffic or users	ACLs can filter incoming or outgoing packets on an interface, controlling access based on source addresses, destination addresses, or user authentication.
Reduce the chance of DoS attacks	ACLs can be used to specify whether traffic from hosts, networks, or users can access the network. The TCP intercept feature can also be configured to prevent servers from being flooded with requests for a connection.
Mitigate spoofing attacks	ACLs enable security practitioners to implement recommended practices to mitigate spoofing attacks.
Provide bandwidth control	ACLs on a slow link can prevent excess traffic.
Classify traffic to protect other planes	ACLs can be applied on vty lines (management plane).
	ACLs can control routing updates being sent, received, or redistributed (control plane).

Antispoofing

Implementing the IETF best current practice 38 (BCP38) and RFC 2827 ingress traffic filtering renders the use of invalid source IP addresses ineffective, forcing attacks to be initiated from valid, reachable IP addresses that could be traced to the originator of an attack.

Features such as Unicast Reverse Path Forwarding (uRPF) can be used to complement the antispoofing strategy.

Layer 2 Data Plane Protection

The following are Layer 2 security tools integrated into the Cisco Catalyst switches:

Port security	Prevents MAC address spoofing and MAC address flooding attacks
DHCP snooping	Prevents client attacks on the Dynamic Host Configuration Protocol (DHCP) server and switch
Dynamic ARP inspection (DAI)	Adds security to ARP by using the DHCP snooping table to minimize the impact of ARP poisoning and spoofing attacks
IP source guard	Prevents IP spoofing addresses by using the DHCP snooping table

CHAPTER 5

Securing the Management Plane

The chapter covers the following topics:

Planning a Secure Management and Reporting Strategy

Securing the Management Plane

- Securing Passwords
- Securing the Console Line and Disabling the Auxiliary Line
- Securing VTY Access with SSH
- Securing VTY Access with SSH Example
- Securing Configuration and IOS Files
- Restoring Bootset Files

Implementing Role-Based Access Control on Cisco Routers

- Configuring Privilege Levels
- Configuring Privilege Levels Example
- Configuring RBAC via the CLI
- Configuring RBAC CLI Example
- Configuring Superviews
- Configuring a Superview Example

Network Monitoring

- Configuring a Network Time Protocol Master Clock
- Configuring an NTP Client
- Configuring an NTP Master and Client Example
- Configuring Syslog
- Configuring Syslog Example
- Configuring SNMPv3
- Configuring SNMPv3 Example

Planning a Secure Management and Reporting Strategy

Small networks are relatively easy to manage and monitor. However, device management and monitoring can be challenging on a large network, especially considering the number of infrastructure devices generating syslog data.

You must decide whether the network management data flows over an in-band (over the production network) or out-of-band (over a separate network) network.

Consider the following in-band management guidelines:

- Typically appropriate for smaller networks.
- Network information flows over a production network.
- Apply only to devices that need to be managed or monitored.
- Use secure protocols such as IPsec, Secure Shell (SSH), or Secure Sockets Layer (SSL) when possible.
- Decide whether the management channel needs to be open at all times.

Consider the following out-of-band (OOB) management guidelines:

- Typically implemented in larger networks.
- Network information does not flow over the production network.
- Provides the highest level of security.
- Eliminates the risk of passing unsecure management protocols over the production network.

NOTE: Regardless of which network management method you choose, you must secure the management plane.

NOTE: You can implement both in-band and OOB simultaneously.

Securing the Management Plane

Securing the management plane includes the following:

- Enforcing a secure password policy
- Securing console, vty, and auxiliary lines
- Securing and archiving configurations
- Enabling logging to record changes in real time, on demand, and scheduled reports .
- Using Network Time Protocol (NTP) to keep clocks synchronized because it can identify the order in which a specified attack occurred

- Choosing appropriate logging levels for each device while ensuring that the right data is being captured

- Implementing a change management policy

NOTE: The focus of this chapter is on securing the management plane.

Securing Passwords

Keep the following in mind when enforcing a password policy:

- Change passwords often.

- Include alphanumeric characters, uppercase and lowercase characters, symbols, and spaces.

- Password-leading spaces are ignored; all spaces after the first character are not ignored.

- Do not use dictionary words.

- Encrypt all passwords.

- Passwords should have a minimum of 10 characters.

`Router(config)# service password-encryption`	Encrypt all plaintext passwords to level 7.
`Router(config)# security passwords min-length length`	Enforce a minimum password length for all new passwords. Existing passwords are not affected.
	Length can be from 1 to 16. Ten characters or more are recommended.
`Router(config)# enable algorithm-type {md5	sha256	scrypt} secret password`	Encrypt the privileged EXEC mode (enable) password using either type 8 (sha256) or type 9 (scrypt) passwords. Type 8 and type 9 were introduced in Cisco IOS 15.3(3)M. Type 8 and type 9 use SHA encryption. However type 9 is slightly stronger. **NOTE:** The `enable secret` *password* command is still available but is now considered weak.

Securing the Console Line and Disabling the Auxiliary Line

`Router(config)# username name algorithm-type {md5	sha256	scrypt} secret password`	Create a local user database entry and encrypt the password using either type 8 (sha256) or type 9 (scrypt) passwords.
	This method is stronger than using the `username` *name* `secret` command. **TIP:** Always create the local user database accounts before enabling authentication.

Router(config)# `line console 0`	Enter line console config mode.
Router(config-line)# `login local`	Authenticate using the local database.
	This method is stronger than using the `password` and `login` combination because it requires a username.
Router(config-line)# `exec-timeout` *minutes* *seconds*	Sets the inactivity timer interval. The user will be logged out of the privilege EXEC mode if it is inactive for the defined period of time. Default is 10 minutes.
Router(config-line)# `line aux 0`	Enter line auxiliary mode.
Router(config-line)# `no exec`	Disable the auxiliary port.

Securing VTY Access with SSH

Router(config)# `hostname` *name*	A hostname other than Router must be configured.
Router(config)# `username` *name* `algorithm-type` {`md5` | `sha256` | `scrypt`} `secret` *password*	Create a local user database entry and encrypt the password.
Router(config)# `ip domain name` *name*	Configure a domain name. Required to implement SSH.
	The IOS also accepts the hyphenated command `ip domain-name`.
Router(config)# `crypto key generate rsa general-keys modulus` *modulus*	Generate the general usage RSA keys that SSH requires. Required to implement SSH.
Router(config)# `ip ssh version` [1|2]	Specify the version of SSH to enable. Choosing 1 only runs SSHv1. Choosing 2 only runs SSHv2.
	By default, SSH runs in compatibility mode, which means that both versions 1 and 2 are supported. To return to compatibility mode, enter the command `no ip ssh version`. **NOTE:** SSHv1 has known security issues. Therefore, it is recommended to use SSHv2 whenever possible.
Router(config)# `ip ssh time-out` *seconds*	(Optional) The number of seconds to wait for the SSH client to respond during the negotiation phase. Default is 120 seconds.
Router(config)# `ip ssh authentication-retries` *integer*	(Optional) Limit the number of login attempts. Default is 3.
Router(config)# `login block-for` *seconds* `attempts` *tries* `within` *seconds*	Configure enhanced vty login.

`Router(config)# line vty 0 4`	Enter line vty mode.
`Router(config-line)# login local`	Authenticate using the local database. **NOTE:** This command is available only if AAA is not enabled.
`Router(config-line)# transport input ssh`	Only allow incoming SSH sessions.
`Router(config-line)# access-class ACL-number`	Apply an access control list (ACL) to specify who can access the vty line.

Securing VTY Access with SSH Example

`Router(config)# hostname R1`	Change the hostname from Router.
`R1(config)# username Bob algorithm-type scrypt secret cisco123`	Create a local user database entry and encrypt the password.
`R1(config)# ip domain-name ccnasecurity.com`	Configure the required domain name.
`R1(config)# crypto key generate rsa general-keys modulus 1024`	Generate the general usage RSA keys that SSH requires. Required to implement SSH.
`R1(config)# ip ssh version 2`	Only allow SSH Version 2.
`R1(config)# ip ssh time-out 60`	Configure an SSH timeout period of 60 seconds.
`R1(config)# ip ssh authentication-retries 2`	Limit the number of login attempts.
`R1(config)# login block-for 60 attempts 3 within 30`	After three failed login attempts within a 30-second time span, do not display the login prompt for 60 seconds.
`R1(config)# line vty 0 4`	Enter line vty mode.
`R1(config-line)# login local`	Authenticate using the local database.
`R1(config-line)# transport input ssh`	Only allow incoming SSH sessions.
`R1(config-line)# access-class ADMIN-IN in`	Only permit users defined in the ACL ADMIN-IN to access the vty lines.

To SSH from a host, an SSH client such as PuTTY, OpenSSH, or TeraTerm is required.

To SSH from another router using the command-line interface (CLI), use the following command:

`R3# ssh-l Bob 10.1.1.1` `Password:`	The administrator on R3 is connecting to R1.

NOTE: Use the `show ssh` command to display the SSH connection's status. Use the `show ip ssh` command to display the SSH version and SSH configuration data.

Securing Configuration and IOS Files

Securing the router configuration and IOS image files is critical. The Cisco IOS Resilient Configuration feature secures working copies of these files by creating bootset files that cannot be erased from a router.

The following example secures the IOS image and configuration file on a 1941 Integrated Services Router (ISR) G2 running IOS 15.4(3).

R1(config)# `secure boot-image` R1(config)# *Oct 25 18:06:28.563: %IOS_ RESILIENCE-5-IMAGE_RESIL_ACTIVE: Successfully secured running image	Secure the IOS image by hiding it in flash. It can be seen only when in ROMMON mode.
R1(config)# `secure boot-config` R1(config)# *Oct 25 18:06:43.499: %IOS_ RESILIENCE-5-CONFIG_RESIL_ACTIVE: Successfully secured config archive [flash0:.runcfg-20151025-180642.ar]	Take a snapshot of the router running configuration and securely archive it in flash. It can be seen only when in ROMMON mode.
R1# `show secure bootset` IOS resilience router id FTX1636848Z IOS image resilience version 15.4 activated at 18:06:28 UTC Sun Oct 25 2015 Secure archive flash0:c1900- universalk9-mz.SPA.154-3.M2.bin type is image (elf) []file size is 75551300 bytes, run size is 75730352 bytes Runnable image, entry point 0x81000000, run from ram IOS configuration resilience version 15.4 activated at 18:06:43 UTC Sun Oct 25 2015 Secure archive flash0:. runcfg-20151025-180642.ar type is config configuration archive size 1343 bytes R1#	Display the status of Cisco IOS image and configuration resilience. This step is important to verify that the Cisco IOS image and configuration files have been properly backed up and secured. Of importance to note are the location and filenames of both files (for example, **flash0:c1900-universalk9-mz. SPA.154-3.M2.bin** and **flash0:. runcfg-20151025-180642.ar**).

Restoring Bootset Files

To restore a primary bootset from a secure archive after the router has been tampered with (by an NVRAM erase or a disk format), you must complete four steps.

The following example walks through the process of restoring bootset files to an ISR with a corrupt IOS that boots to ROMMON mode.

`Router# reload` `Proceed with reload? [confirm]`	Reload the router. Press **Enter** to continue.
`rommon 1 > dir flash:`	Enter ROMMON mode and display the bootset files.
`rommon 2 > boot c1900-univer-` `salk9-mz.SPA.154-3.M2.bin`	Boot the router using the listed image.

`Router(config)# secure`
`boot-config restore flash0:.`
`runcfg-20151025-180642.ar`
	Restore the secure configuration to the archive found in flash.

Implementing Role-Based Access Control on Cisco Routers

To control the level of access to network infrastructure devices, configure privilege levels or role-based access control (RBAC). RBACs are preferred.

Configuring Privilege Levels

`Router(config)# privilege mode` `{level level command	reset` `command}`	Assign commands to a custom privilege level between level 2 and 14.
	There are 16 privilege levels. Level 0 is entry level, level 1 is for user EXEC access, and level 15 is privileged EXEC mode. Levels 2–14 are customizable.
`Router(config)# enable` `algorithm-type {md5	sha256` `| scrypt} secret password`	Assign a password to the custom privilege level.
`Router>enable level`	Enter a custom privilege level.

NOTE: Use the `show privilege` command to display the current privilege level.

Configuring Privilege Levels Example

`R1(config)# privilege exec` `level 5 ping`	Add the `ping` command to level 5.
`R1(config)# privilege exec` `level 5 reload`	Add the `reload` command to level 5.

`R1(config)# enable`
`algorithm-type scrypt`
`secret level 5 cisco12345`
	Configure an enable password to enter level 5.

`R1>enable 5` `Password:`	The user logs in with privilege level 5. Along with the regular user EXEC commands, the level 5 user also has the `ping` and `reload` available.

`R1# show privilege`
`Current privilege level`
`is 5`
	Verify the privilege level.

Configuring RBAC

RBACs are used to configure views that contain administrator-selected commands for that view. AAA must be enabled. You must be logged in as a root user using the `enable view root` command and the enable secret password. The root account can create up to 15 views that identify permissible commands that can be executed as shown in Figure 5-1.

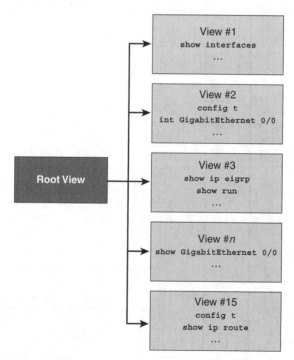

Figure 5-1   Root Account Creates User Views

`Router(config)# aaa new-model`	Enable AAA. AAA must be configured before you can enable a view.
`Router# enable view` `Password:`	Enter root view. Required to configure and alter views. Use the enable password when prompted. **NOTE:** The **enable secret** command must be previously configured.
`Router(config)# parser view` `view-name`	Create a view in global configuration mode. There is a maximum limit of 15 views in total excluding the root.
`Router(config-view)# secret` `password`	Assign a password to the view. This is a required step. **NOTE:** The scrypt and sha256 algorithm-type are not supported.

`Router(config-view)#`
 `commands parser-mode {include`
 `| include-exclusive |`
 `exclude} [all] [interface`
 `interface-name
	command]`	Assign commands to the current view. Views contain commands.

`Router# enable view view-name`	Enter and verify a view.

NOTE: Use the `show parser view` command to verify the current view. Root can also use the command `show parser view` to display all configured views.

Configuring RBAC via the CLI Example

`R1(config)# aaa new-model`	Enable AAA.
`R1# enable view` `Password:`	Enter root view.
`R1(config)# parser view` `SHOWVIEW`	Create a view called **SHOWVIEW.**
`R1(config-view)# secret` `cisco123`	Assign a password to the view.
`R1(config-view)# commands` `exec include show`	This view can use all **show** commands from privileged EXEC mode.
`R1(config-view)# commands` `exec include ping`	This view can use the **ping** command.
`R1# enable view SHOWVIEW` `Password:`	Log in to the SHOWVIEW view to verify it.

Configuring Superviews

A view can be shared or grouped into **superviews** as shown in Figure 5-2. However, commands cannot be configured for a superview. Commands can only be added to a view. Users who are logged in to a superview can access all the commands configured for any of the CLI views that are part of the superview.

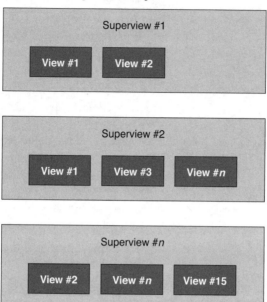

Figure 5-2   Root Account Creates User Views

Router(config)# **parser view** *view-name* **superview**	Create a superview in global configuration mode.
	A superview can only contain other views. A superview cannot contain commands.
Router(config-view)# **secret** *password*	Assign a password to the view. This is a required step.
Router(config-view)# **view** *view-name*	Assign an existing view to the superview. Multiple views can be assigned to a superview.
Router# **enable view** *view-name*	Enter and verify a view.

Configuring a Superview Example

R1(config)# **parser view JR-ADMIN superview**	Create a superview called **JR-ADMIN.**
R1(config-view)# **secret cisco12345**	Assign a password to the view.
R1(config-view)# **view SHOWVIEW**	Assign the SHOWVIEW view to the superview.
R1(config-view)# **view VERIFYVIEW**	Assign the VERIFYVIEW view to the superview.

`R1# show parser view all`
 	
`Views/SuperViews Present in System:`
 	
`SHOWVIEW`
 	
`VERIFYVIEW`
 	
`JR-ADMIN *`
`-------(*) represent super-`
`view-------`
 	
`R1#`
	Show all views.

`R1# enable view JR-ADMIN`
 	
`Password:`
	Enable a view. The JR-ADMIN superview has access to the commands listed in the other views.

`R1# show parser view`
 	
`Current view is 'JR-ADMIN'`
	Verify which view you are in.

`R1# show parser view all`
           `^`
`% Invalid input detected at '^'`
`marker.`
	The JR-ADMIN superview does not have permission to use the command as the `show parser view all` command is available only to the root view.

Network Monitoring

Network monitoring includes using syslog and Simple Network Management Protocol (SNMP) features. Regardless, all devices can be synchronized using NTP.

> **NOTE:** Network devices can produce huge amounts of logs. SIEM is a technology that can make the task of collecting, correlating, and acting on the information provided by the logs much easier. SIEM technology provides real-time analysis of security alerts generated by network devices.

Configuring a Network Time Protocol Master Clock

Time synchronization between devices is critical. Devices should be synchronized with a public time server on the Internet or with an internal time source.

You can configure a router to be an NTP master clock source when other sources are not available.

`Router(config)# ntp master stratum`	Configure the router to be the NTP master.
	The stratum number is optional and is the number of hops away from an authoritative time source, such as an atomic clock.
`Router(config)# ntp authenticate`	Enable NTP authentication.
`Router(config)# ntp authentication key key-number md5 key-value`	Define the NTP key and password and encrypt it using MD5.

Router(config)# **ntp trusted-key** *key-number*	Identify the trusted key on the master.
	To synchronize, an NTP client must provide the correct trusted key and password.

Configuring an NTP Client

Client(config)# **ntp server** *ntp-server-address*	Enable Router to be the master clock to which peers will synchronize.
Client(config)# **ntp authentication-key** *keynumber* **md5** *key-value*	Define the NTP key and password and encrypt it using MD5.
Client(config)# **ntp trusted-key** *key-number*	Identify the trusted key on the master.

NOTE: Other NTP-related commands are also available.

Configuring an NTP Master and Client Example

The following example configures R1 to be the master NTP clock:

R1# **clock set 9:00:00 july 1 2016**	Set the local device clock.
R1(config)# **ntp master 1**	Enable R1 to be the master clock to which clients will synchronize.
R1(config)# **ntp authentication-key 1 md5 cisco123**	Specify the NTP password and encrypt it using MD5. In this example, a peer router must authenticate with the password cisco123.
R1(config)# **ntp trusted-key 1**	Identify the trusted key on the master. A peer must also provide the correct trusted key in its NTP packets.
R1(config)# **ntp authenticate**	Enable NTP authentication.

The following example configures R3 to be the NTP client:

R3(config)# **ntp server 10.1.1.1**	Enable R1 to be the master clock with which peers will synchronize.
R3(config)# **ntp authentication-key 1 md5 cisco123**	Specify the NTP password and encrypt it using MD5. In this example, a peer router must authenticate with the password cisco123.
R3(config)# **ntp trusted-key 1**	Identify the trusted key on the master. A peer must also provide the correct trusted key in its NTP packets.

NOTE: It may take up to 2 minutes for the device clock to synchronize with the NTP master.

You can verify the clock settings using the `show clock, show ntp associations`, and `show ntp status` commands.

Configuring Syslog

Log messages can be sent to one of the following locations:

Console	Useful when modifying or testing the router while connected to the console, but messages are not stored.
VTY lines	Useful when accessing a device remotely, but messages are not stored.
Buffer	Messages are stored in the router memory but lost when it is rebooted or the buffer is full. Use the `show logging` command to view logging messages.
Syslog	Very useful message logging facility, which sends log messages to servers. The server provides a central long-term log storage capability for all networking devices.
SNMP server	Specific router events can be trapped and forwarded to an external SNMP server.

NOTE: To reduce the CPU load, disable logging to the console using the `no logging console` and instead send logging information to the local log buffer.

NOTE: When telnetting to a router, use the `terminal monitor` command to view log messages.

Router log messages typically contain time stamps, log messages, severity levels, and message text. Cisco router log messages fall into one of eight levels.

0	LOG_EMERG	Emergencies, such as when the router is unusable
1	LOG_ALERT	A condition that should be corrected immediately, such as a corrupted system database
2	LOG_CRIT	Critical conditions, such as hard device errors
3	LOG_ERR	Errors such as invalid memory size
4	LOG_WARNING	Warning messages, such as the crypto operation failed
5	LOG_NOTICE	Conditions that are normal but important
6	LOG_INFO	Informational messages, such as when a packet is denied
7	LOG_DEBUG	Messages that contain information normally of use only when debugging a program

Syslog requires a syslog server and a syslog client:

`Router(config)# service timestamps [debug|log] [uptime|datetime [msec]] [localtime] [show-timezone] [year]`	Enable time stamps on debug and logging messages.
`Router(config)# logging host [ip-address	hostname]`	Identify the syslog server address or hostname.
`Router(config)# logging trap level`	Limit messages logged to the syslog servers based on severity. Default is 0–6.
`Router(config)# logging source-interface interface-type interface-number`	Specify that syslog packets contain the IP address of a specific interface, regardless of which interface the packet uses to exit the router.
`Router(config)# logging on`	On by default, it sends messages to the buffer, vty lines, and syslog server.

Use the `show logging` command to display the state of system logging (syslog) and the contents of the standard system logging buffer.

Configuring Syslog Example

The following example configures R1 to send level 5 messages to a syslog server located at 192.168.1.100:

`R1(config)# service timestamps log datetime msec`	Enable time stamps on logging messages.
`R1(config)# service timestamps debug datetime msec`	Enable time stamps on debug messages.
`R1(config)# logging host 192.168.1.100`	Identify the syslog server IP address.
`R1(config)# logging trap 5`	Limit log messages to severity level 0–5.
`R1(config)# logging source-interface loopback 0`	Specify the Lo0 interface as the source interface from this router.
`R1(config)# logging origin-id string Router-R1`	Specifies that syslog packets contain the text label Router-R1.

Configuring SNMPv3

SNMP enables network administrators to manage network performance, find and solve network problems, and plan for network growth. SNMP is used to capture (trap) log information, but can also be configured to get information as needed and to send configuration changes to a device.

Three versions of SNMP are available: SNMPv1 (legacy), SNMPv2, and SNMPv3. SNMPv3 should be enabled as it is the most secure version because it offers message integrity and authentication, encryption, and access control. Use SNMPv2 only if SNMPv3 is not supported.

NOTE: To send SNMP messages to an SNMP server, SNMPv1 and SNMPv2 use read-only community strings to authenticate with a server. To authenticate configuration changes from an SNMP server, SNMP uses read-write community strings.

TIP: Change the default names of the read-only and read-write community strings.

Router(config)# `ip access-list` `standard` `acl-name` Router(config-std-nacl)# `permit` `source_net`]	Configure an ACL to permit the protected management network.
Router(config)# `snmp-server view` `view-name oid-tree` {`included` | `excluded`}	Configure an SNMP view. Include only the MIB OIDs necessary for monitoring and managing the network.
Router(config)# `snmp-server group` `group-name` `v3` `priv` `read` `view-name` `access` [`acl-number` | `acl-name`]	Configure an SNMP group.
Router(config)# `snmp-server user` `username group-name` `v3` `auth` {`md5` | `sha`} `auth-password` `priv` {`des` | `3des` | `aes` {`128` | `192` | `256`}} `privpassword`	Configure a user as a member of the SNMP group.

Use the `show run` \| `include snmp` command to display the SNMP configuration. Use the `show snmp user` command to view the user information.

Configuring SNMPv3 Example

Create an SNMP group and user permitting SNMPv3 read access to router R1 from the 192.168.1.0/24 network:

R1(config)# `ip access-list` `standard` `PERMIT-ADMIN` R1(config-std-nacl)# `permit` `192.168.1.0` `0.0.0.255`	Create an ACL permitting the users on the 192.168.1.0/24 network.
R1(config)# `snmp-server view` `SNMP-RO` `iso` `included`	Configure an SNMP view.
R1(config)# `snmp-server group` `ADMIN` `v3` `priv` `read` `SNMP-RO` `access` `PERMIT-ADMIN`	Configure an SNMP group, enable version 3, require authentication and encryption, associate a view to the group and give it only read access, and specify the ACL.
R1(config)# `snmp-server user` `BOB` `ADMIN` `v3` `auth` `sha` `cisco12345` `priv` `aes` `128` `cisco54321`	Configure a user as a member of the SNMP group. Enable version 3, set the authentication type to sha, and require encryption using 128-bit AES with the password cicso54321.

CHAPTER 6

Securing Management Access with AAA

This chapter covers the following topics:

Authenticating Administrative Access

- Local Authentication
- Server-Based Authentication
- Authentication, Authorization, and Accounting Framework

Local AAA Authentication

- Configuring Local AAA Authentication Example

Server-Based AAA Authentication

- TACACS+ Versus RADIUS
- Configuring Server-Based AAA Authentication
- Configuring Server-Based AAA Authentication Example

AAA Authorization

- Configuring AAA Authorization Example

AAA Accounting

- Configuring AAA Accounting Example

802.1X Port-Based Authentication

- Port-Based Authentication
- Configuring 802.1X Port-Based Authentication
- Configuring 802.1X Port-Based Authentication Example

Authenticating Administrative Access

Securing administrative access to your infrastructure devices is paramount. This chapter describes various methods to authenticate administrative users.

Local Authentication

Administrative access to console, vty, and AUX lines can be authenticated locally using the following:

| Line passwords | Easy to implement using the `password` and `login` commands, but this is the least-secure method and very vulnerable to brute-force attacks. There is also loss of accountability because the password can be shared. |

Local authentication	Implemented to improve security because the user must now provide a username and password, which are compared to entries in the local device database.
Local AAA	Also called self-contained AAA, this method is similar to local authentication but can provide backup methods of authentication.

NOTE: Authenticating locally is not very scalable.

Server-Based Authentication

A more scalable method is to use a server-based solution using one of the following methods:

Cisco Secure Access Control System	The Cisco ACS software runs either on a dedicated appliance such as the Secure Network Server 3415 Appliance for Secure Access Control System 5.8 or older Secure Access Control 1121 appliances.
ACS for VMWARE	A method growing in popularity where the Cisco ACS server is installed as a virtual machine on VMware ESX or ESXi 5.0, 5.1, 5.5, or 6.0.
Cisco Identity Services Engine (ISE)	A dedicated appliance that consolidates features of Cisco ACS and Network Admission Control (NAC) to provide AAA, profiling, posture, and guest management. It is a component of the Cisco TrustSec solution.

NOTE: Cisco Secure Access Control Server (ACS) for Windows Server is a legacy solution that may still be in use in some installations.

Authentication, Authorization, and Accounting Framework

Authentication, authorization, and accounting (AAA) is a standards-based framework that you can implement to control who is permitted to access a network (authenticate), what they can do while they are there (authorize), and audit what actions they performed while accessing the network (accounting).

Local AAA Authentication

The following are the general steps to configure a Cisco router to support local AAA authentication:

1. Add usernames and passwords to the local router database.

2. Enable AAA globally on the router using the `aaa new-model` command.

3. Configure authentication policies using the `aaa authentication` command and specified method lists.

4. (Optional) Configure authorization policies using the `aaa authorization` command and specified method lists.

5. (Optional) Configure accounting policies using the `aaa accounting` command and specified method lists.

6. Confirm and troubleshoot the AAA configuration.

NOTE: Other variations of the `aaa authentication` command include `aaa authentication ppp`, `aaa authentication enable`, and `aaa authentication dot1x`.

NOTE: Other configurable parameters include `aaa authentication banner`, `aaa authentication username-prompt`, `aaa authentication password-prompt`, and `aaa authentication fail-message`.

`Router(config)# username name algorithm-type {md5	sha256	scrypt} secret password`	Add a username and password to the local security database.
`Router(config)# aaa new-model`	Enable AAA.
`Router(config)# aaa authentication login {default	list-name} {method1 [method2...]}`	Defines the login authentication method to use when accessing console, vty, and AUX lines. A `default` list applies to all lines; a `list-name` can be defined and applied to specific lines. If a `list-name` is defined, the `login authentication list-name` command must be applied to the line. You can specify up to four methods. The additional methods of authentication are used only if the previous method returns an error, not if it fails. Method choices include `local`, `local-case`, and `enable`. **NOTE:** Passwords are always case sensitive. The `local-case` method makes the password and username case sensitive.

Optional `aaa authentication` commands include the following:

`Router(config)# aaa authentication username-prompt text-string`	Replace the default Username: prompt. If this text string contains spaces, it must be enclosed in double quotes.

`Router(config)# aaa authentication password-prompt` *text-string*	Replace the default Password: prompt. If this text string contains spaces, it must be enclosed in double quotes.
`Router(config)# aaa local authentication attempts max-fail` *number*	Secure AAA user accounts by locking out accounts that have exceeded the maximum number of failed attempts specified. Account stays locked until it is cleared by an administrator with the `clear aaa local user lockout {username` *username* ` | all}` command.

Use the **show aaa local user lockout** privileged EXEC command to display a list of all locked-out users. Use the **show aaa sessions** privileged EXEC command to display the attributes collected for one AAA session.

Configuring Local AAA Authentication Example

`R1(config)# username JR-ADMIN algorithm-type scrypt secret Str0ng3rPa55w0rd`	Create an entry in the local database. **NOTE:** Always configure at least one local database entry before enabling AAA.
`R1(config)# aaa new-model`	Enable AAA.
`R1(config)# aaa authentication login default local-case`	All lines automatically enforce the default login policy and require case-sensitive username and password access.
`R1(config)# aaa authentication login VTY-IN local-case enable`	Command specifies a list called VTY-IN using the `local-case` method, which makes the username and password case sensitive. If no local database has been configured, use the enable password.
`R1(config)# aaa authentication username-prompt "Enter your Username: "`	Replace the default Username: prompt.
`R1(config)# aaa authentication password-prompt "Enter your Password: "`	Replace the default Password: prompt.
`R1(config)# aaa local authentication attempts max-fail 8`	Lock out the account after eight failed attempts.
`R1(config)# line console 0`	Enter line console mode.
`R1(config-line)# login authentication VTY-IN`	Applies the VTY-IN list-name to the interface. **TIP:** Use `login authentication default` to disable the `list-name` method.

Server-Based AAA Authentication

Maintaining a local authentication database for each Cisco device in a large network is not feasible. Large networks require an AAA server-based solution. Routers communicate with AAA servers, which can be installed on a Windows server or on dedicated appliances, or the Cisco Identity Services Engine (ISE).

When users connect to a router, they are prompted for a username and password. The router passes the credentials to the AAA server, which in turn authenticates the user.

TACACS+ Versus RADIUS

Routers communicate with AAA servers using either TACACS+ or RADIUS protocols to implement AAA functions:

	TACACS+	**RADIUS**
Functionality	Uses the AAA architecture separating authentication, authorization, and accounting	Combines the functions of authentication and authorization together; provides detailed accounting when configured
Standard	Cisco proprietary	Open standard and widely supported by most vendors
Transport protocol	TCP port 49	UDP ports 1645 or 1812 for authentication and UDP ports 1646 or 1813 for accounting
Confidentiality	Encrypts all packets exchanged between the client (router) and AAA server	Encrypts only the password in the Access-Request packet from the client (router) to the AAA server
Customization	Provides authorization of router commands on a per-user/group basis per-user/group basis	Can pass a privilege level down to the router, which can then be used locally for command authorization
Accounting	Captures limited information	Captures more detailed information
Deployment	Common in Cisco deployments and where multiprotocol support is required	Popular in VoIP installations and to support 802.1x

NOTE: Depending on the solution chosen, the configuration commands differ slightly.

The following are the general steps to configure a Cisco router to support server-based authentication:

1. Configure the AAA servers and groups.

2. Enable AAA globally on the router.

3. Configure authentication policies using the `aaa authentication` command and specified method lists.

4. (Optional) Configure authorization policies using the `aaa authorization` command and specified method lists.

5. (Optional) Configure accounting policies using the `aaa accounting` command and specified method lists.

6. Confirm and troubleshoot the AAA configuration.

Configuring Server-Based AAA Authentication

To configure the TACACS+ server specifics:

`Router(config)# tacacs server server-name`	Enter TACACS+ server configuration mode.
`Router(config-server-tacacs)# address ipv4 ip-address`	Identify the IP address of the server.
`Router(config-server-tacacs)# single-connection`	Enhance TCP performance by having the TCP connection maintained for the life of the session. **TIP:** The command makes the TCP session more efficient.
`Router(config-server-tacacs)# key secret-key`	Configure the shared secret key to encrypt the data transfer between the TACACS+ server and AAA-enabled router.

To configure a RADIUS server specifics:

`Router(config)# radius server server-name`	Enter RADIUS server configuration mode.
`Router(config-radius-server)# address ipv4 ip-address [auth-port port-# | acct-port port-#]`	Identify the IP address of the server. Specify a RADIUS host. Port numbers and key are optional. **NOTE:** If **auth-port** and **acct-port** are not specified, the default value of auth-port is 1645 and the default value of acct-port is 1646. Other common port values are 1812 for authentication and 1813 for accounting.
`Router(config-radius-server)# key secret-key`	Configure the shared secret key to encrypt the data transfer between the RADIUS server and AAA-enabled router.

Finally, configure the login authentication method list to use the identified servers:

`Router(config)# aaa authentica-`
`tion login {default | list-name}`
`{method1 [method2 ...]}`
	Defines the default login authentication method to use when accessing lines.
	
	Server-based method choices include the following:
	
	■ `group radius`
	
	■ `group tacacs+`
	
	■ `group group-name`
	
	NOTE: It is recommended to add the local router database as a fallback method, in case communication to the AAA servers fails.

Configuring Server-Based AAA Authentication Example

The first step of configuring AAA servers is to configure AAA server objects:

`R1(config)# username JR-ADMIN`
`algorithm-type scrypt secret`
`Str0ng3rPa55w0rd`
	Create an entry in the local database.

`R1(config)# aaa new-model`	Enable AAA.
`R1(config)# radius server SERVER-R`	Enter RADIUS server configuration mode.

`R1(config-radius-server)# address`
`ipv4 192.168.1.100 auth-port 1812`
`acct-port 1813`
	Specify a RADIUS server located at IP address 192.168.1.100 and use UDP port numbers 1812 and 1813.

`R1(config-radius-server)# key` `RADIUS-Pa55w0rd`	Configure the shared secret key of **RADIUS-Pa55w0rd** to encrypt the password between the RADIUS server and R1.
`R1(config)# tacacs server SERVER-T`	Enter TACACS+ server configuration mode.
`R1(config-server-tacacs)# address` `ipv4 192.168.1.101`	Specify a TACACS+ server located at 192.168.1.101.
`R1(config-server-tacacs)#` `single-connection`	Enhance TCP performance by having the TCP connection maintained for the life of the session.
`R1(config-server-tacacs)# key` `TACACS-Pa55w0rd`	Configure the shared secret key of **TACACS-Pa55w0rd** to encrypt the data transfer between the TACACS+ server and R1.

`R1(config)# aaa authentication`
`login default group tacacs+ group`
`radius local-case`
	Configure logins to consult the TACACS+ server for authentication.
	If it is not reachable, the consult the RADIUS server.
	Finally, if the RADIUS server is not reachable, the local database is consulted.

NOTE: The preceding configuration is for example only. In production networks, a TACACS+ server is typically never backed up by a RADIUS server for AAA authentication. The reason is because TACACS+ is used for device admin access, which RADIUS typically does not support, and RADIUS is generally used for authenticating network access, which TACACS+ does not support.

AAA Authorization

Authorization policies set parameters that restrict administrative EXEC access to the routers or user access to the network.

NOTE: Authorization and accounting rules follow a similar approach using method lists to define the location of the authorization permissions and the accounting logs.

`Router(config)# aaa authorization` `{exec	network	commands level}` `{default	list-name} {method1` `[method2 ...]}`	Defines the authorization policy to use when accessing lines: ■ **exec** is used to authorize whether the user is allowed to run an EXEC shell. ■ **network** is used to authorize network-related service requests, such as PPP. ■ **command** is used to implement authorization for all commands for a specific privilege level.

Configuring AAA Authorization Example

`R1(config)# aaa authorization exec` `default group tacacs+`	EXEC command authorization will be provided by the TACACS+ server.

AAA Accounting

A AAA server serves as a central repository for accounting information, essentially tracking events that occur on the network. This stored information can prove helpful for management, security audits, capacity planning, and network-usage billing.

Method lists for accounting define the way accounting will be performed and the sequence in which these methods are performed. AAA supports six different types of accounting: network, connection, exec, system, command, and resource:

`Router(config)# aaa accounting`
`{system | network | exec`
`| commands level} {default`
`| list-name} {start-stop |`
`wait-start | stop-only | none}`
`[method1 [method2]]`
	Define the accounting method to use for a specific service. It keeps track of requested services for billing or security purposes.
	
	■ **system** tracks system-level events such as reloads.
	
	■ **network** tracks network-related service requests such as PPP.
	
	■ **exec** tracks EXEC shell sessions.
	
	■ **commands** tracks all commands at the specified privilege level.

Configuring AAA Accounting Example

`R1(config)# aaa accounting exec` `default start-stop group tacacs+`	The router sends a start accounting notice at the beginning of the requested event and a stop accounting notice at the end of the event.

802.1X Port-Based Authentication

The IEEE 802.1X is a specification that provides port-based access control to restrict unauthorized hosts from connecting to a LAN. Each host must be authenticated to receive network access.

IEEE 802.1X commonly uses the Extensible Authentication Protocol over the LAN (EAPOL) protocol to secure the initial communication between a wired host and switch. Depending on the 802.1X configuration, a host may only be able to use EAPOL, DHCP, and ARP until it is authenticated. Once authenticated, normal network traffic from the host is permitted through the port.

Figure 6-1 illustrates the components of 802.1X.

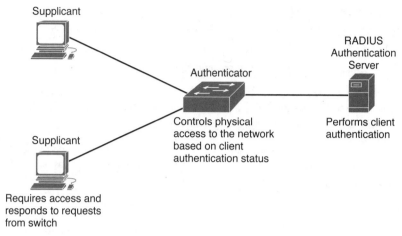

Figure 6-1   802.1X Components

Supplicant	A host running 802.1X-compliant client software that requests access to the LAN and responds to requests from the switch. It communicates with the Authenticator using a Layer 2 EAPOL protocol.
Authenticator	The switch that controls physical access to the network. The switch communicates with the supplicant using EAPOL and relays the EAP frames using RADIUS to an Authentication Server.
RADIUS Authentication Server	The AAA RADIUS server that verifies the identity of the supplicant (i.e., the host) and notifies the authenticator (i.e., the switch) whether the client is authorized to access the LAN and switch services.

Configuring 802.1X Port-Based Authentication

The following are the general steps to configure an 802.1X authentication on a Cisco switch port:

1. Enable AAA globally on the switch.

2. Configure the 802.1X port-based authentication policies using the `aaa authentication dot1x` global configuration command.

3. Globally enable 802.1X port-based authentication using the `dot1x system-auth-control` global configuration command.

4. Enable 802.1X port-based authentication on the port using the `authentication port-control auto` interface configuration command.

5. Set the port to be a Port Access Entity (PAE) authenticator using the `dot1x pae authenticator` interface configuration command.

Switch(config)# **aaa new-model**	Enable AAA.
Switch(config)# **radius server** *server-name*	Enter RADIUS server configuration mode.
Switch(config-radius-server)# **address ipv4 ip-address** [**auth-port** *port-#* | **acct-port** *port-#*]	Identify the IP address of the server. Specify a RADIUS host. Port numbers and key are optional. **NOTE:** If **auth-port** and **acct-port** are not specified, the default value of **auth-port** is 1645 and the default value of **acct-port** is 1646. Other common port values are 1812 for authentication and 1813 for accounting.
Switch(config-radius-server)# **key** *secret-key*	Configure the shared secret key to encrypt the data transfer between the RADIUS server and AAA-enabled router.
Switch(config)# **aaa authentication dot1x** {**default** | *list-name*} **group radius**	Create an 802.1X port-based authentication method list.
Switch(config)# **dot1x system-auth-control**	Globally enable 802.1X port-based authentication.
Switch(config-if)# **switchport mode access**	Configure the port as an access port.
Switch(config-if)# **authentication port-control auto**	Enable 802.1X port-based authentication on the port. The port begins in unauthorized state, enabling only EAPOL frames to be sent and received through the port. When the link state of the port transitions to up (authenticator initiation) or when an EAPOL-start frame is received (supplicant initiation) the switch requests the identity of the client and begins relaying authentication messages to the authentication server.
Switch(config-if)# **dot1x pae authenticator**	Set the port to be a Port Access Entity (PAE) authenticator. PAE makes the interface act only as an authenticator and to not respond to any messages meant for a supplicant.

Configuring 802.1X Port-Based Authentication Example

`S1(config)#aaa new-model`	Enable AAA.
`S1(config)#radius server CCNAS`	Enter TACACS+ server configuration mode.
`S1(config-radius-server)#address ipv4 10.1.1.50 auth-port 1812 acct-port 1813`	Identify the IP address of the server.
`S1(config-radius-server)#key RADIUS-Pa55w0rd`	Configure the shared secret key.
`S1(config)#aaa authentication dot1x default group radius`	Create an 802.1X port-based authentication method list.
`S1(config)#dot1x system-auth-control`	Globally enable 802.1X port-based authentication.
`S1(config-if)#switchport mode access`	Configure the port as an access port.
`S1(config-if)#authentication port-control auto`	Enable 802.1X port-based authentication on the port.
`S1(config-if)#dot1x pae authenticator`	Set the port to be a Port Access Entity (PAE) authenticator.

CHAPTER 7

Securing the Data Plane on Catalyst Switches

This chapter covers the following topics:

Common Threats to the Switching Infrastructure

- Layer 2 Attacks
- Layer 2 Security Guidelines

MAC Address Attacks

- Configuring Port Security
- Fine-Tuning Port Security
- Configuring Optional Port Security Settings
- Configuring Port Security Example

VLAN Hopping Attacks

- Mitigating VLAN Attacks
- Mitigating VLAN Attacks Example

DHCP Attacks

- Mitigating DHCP Attacks
- Mitigating DHCP Attacks Example

ARP Attacks

- Mitigating ARP Attacks
- Mitigating ARP Attacks Example

Address Spoofing Attacks

- Mitigating Address Spoofing Attacks
- Mitigating Address Spoofing Attacks Example

Spanning Tree Protocol Attacks

- STP Stability Mechanisms
- Configuring STP Stability Mechanisms
- Configuring STP Stability Mechanisms Example

LAN Storm Attacks

- Configuring Storm Control
- Configuring Storm Control Example

Advanced Layer 2 Security Features

- ACLs and Private VLANs
- Secure the Switch Management Plane

Common Threats to the Switching Infrastructure

Layer 2 and Layer 3 switches are targets of attack and must be secured. If a Layer 2 switch is compromised, Layers 3–7 are also affected.

Layer 2 Attacks

Layer 2 Attack	Attack Description	Catalyst Switch Mitigation Solution
MAC address attacks	Attacker generates thousands of bogus MAC addresses per second, which a switch adds to its MAC address table. This quickly fills up the table and makes the switch forward all frames out of all ports except the port on which it came in. An attacker could then capture the frames.	- Configure port security.
VLAN attacks	There are two types of attacks: - Trunk with a switch - Double tagging also known as VLAN hopping	- Disable trunking and DTP on access ports. - Explicitly configure trunk ports and change native VLAN. - Secure unused ports.
DHCP attacks	There are two types of attacks: - DHCP spoofing attack - DHCP starvation attack	- Configure DHCP snooping and rate limit untrusted access ports.

Layer 2 Attack	Attack Description	Catalyst Switch Mitigation Solution
ARP attacks	Attacker conducts an ARP poisoning attack by generating a gratuitous ARP containing a spoofed source MAC address (e.g., the default gateway). The switch updates its CAM table accordingly and now forwards traffic destined to the target MAC address to the attacker's host.	■ Prerequisite: DHCP snooping must be enabled. ■ Configure Dynamic ARP Inspection (DAI) and identify trusted ports.
Address spoofing attacks	MAC addresses and IP addresses can be spoofed for a variety of reasons.	■ Prerequisite: DHCP snooping must be enabled. ■ Configure IP Source Guard (IPSG) on trusted ports.
STP manipulation	Attackers attempt to disrupt STP network by introducing rogue switch.	■ Configure PortFast. ■ Configure BPDU guard. ■ Configure root guard.
LAN storms	Also called broadcast storms and are caused by the following: ■ Protocol stack error ■ Misconfiguration ■ DoS attack	■ Configure storm control.

NOTE: This chapter focuses on the Catalyst switch mitigation solutions.

Layer 2 Security Guidelines

■ Use port security where possible for access ports.

■ Set all user ports to nontrunking (unless you are using Cisco VoIP).

■ Disable all unused ports and put them in an unused VLAN.

■ Always use a dedicated native VLAN for trunk ports.

■ Do not use default VLAN 1 for anything.

■ Enable DHCP snooping to mitigate DHCP attacks.

■ Enable Dynamic ARP Inspection (DAI) to mitigate ARP attacks.

■ Enable IP Source Guard (IPSG) to mitigate IP and MAC address spoofing attacks.

■ Manage switches in as secure a manner as possible (for example, Secure Shell [SSH], out-of-band [OOB] access, and permit lists).

- Selectively use Simple Network Management Protocol (SNMP) and treat community strings like root passwords.

- Use Cisco Discovery Protocol only where necessary—it is useful with IP phones.

MAC Address Attacks

MAC address table attack	Enables an attacker to sniff frames by overwhelming a switch MAC address table with fake addresses. Once full, the switch floods all unknown unicast frames. The attacker can then capture all traffic or spoof one of the learned MAC addresses.
MAC address spoofing	Attacker spoofs another interface MAC address and sends a gratuitous Address Resolution Protocol (ARP) request to the target switch in an attempt to make it forward frames back to the attacker host.

NOTE: Configure port security to mitigate MAC address attacks.

Configuring Port Security

To configure port security on an access port, follow these steps:

1. Configure an interface as an access port.

2. Enable port security on the port.

Switch(config-if)# switchport mode access	A required step, this sets the interface to access mode (as opposed to trunk mode). **NOTE:** A port cannot be secured while in the default dynamic auto mode.
Switch(config-if)# switchport port-security	Enable port security and assign the current MAC address to the port. Port-security defaults include the following: <ul><li>Only one MAC address can be assigned.</li><li>Port violation action is shut down.</li></ul> **NOTE:** Defaults can be altered if required.

NOTE: Use the `show port-security` command to view security settings and status and the `show port-security [interface interface-id]` address command to display all secure MAC addresses configured on all switch interfaces.

When a port violation occurs, such as the maximum number of MAC addresses connected is exceeded, error log messages such as `%PM-4-ERR_DISABLE` and `%PORT_SECURITY-2-PSECURE_VIOLATION` are generated and the port status is changed from `Secure-up` to `Secure-shutdown`. When a port is error-disabled, it is effectively shut down, and no traffic is sent or received on the port. The port is error-disabled and must be manually reset by the network administrator using a `shutdown` and `no shutdown` sequence. This should be done after the offending host has been removed; otherwise, the violation will be triggered again.

Fine-Tuning Port Security

If required, you can alter the default maximum number of secure MAC addresses and the port violation action:

`Switch(config-if)# switchport port-security maximum value`	Set the maximum number of secure MAC addresses for the interface. The default is 1, but the range is 1 to 132. **NOTE:** Configure a maximum value of 2 or 3 when connecting an IP phone and host to a switch port. Some switches connecting Cisco IP phones require 3 MAC addresses.
`Switch(config-if)# switchport port-security violation {protect | restrict | shutdown | shutdown vlan}`	Configure the port action when the number of MAC addresses exceeds the defined maximum. Default is `shutdown`. `shutdown` disables the port and generates syslog and SNMP messages. `restrict` drops violating traffic and generates syslog and SNMP messages, while traffic from allowed MAC addresses is permitted to pass normally. `protect` drops violating traffic, while traffic from allowed MAC addresses is permitted to pass normally. `shutdown vlan` drops violating traffic for the offending VLAN instead of shutting down the entire port.

TIP: Configure `shutdown` rather than `restrict` or `protect`.

NOTE: Instead of manually resetting an error-disabled port using the `shutdown` and `no shutdown` sequence, you can implement a dynamic port auto-recovery solution.

Configuring Optional Port Security Settings

Optionally, you can configure the following port security settings:

- Statically assign the secure MAC addresses to the port or enable the switch to dynamically learn the secure MAC addresses and add them to the running configuration.

- Enable the switch to automatically recover an error-disabled port after a specified amount of time.

- Enable address aging (if required).

MAC addresses can be explicitly assigned to the port manually or learned dynamically:

Switch(config-if)# **switchport port-security mac-address** *mac-address*	Manually assign the MAC addresses connecting to the port. Repeat the command for each secure MAC address.
Switch(config-if)# **switchport port-security mac-address sticky**	Enable the switch to dynamically learn the connected MAC addresses until the maximum is reached. Learned MAC addresses are added to the running configuration.

NOTE: Manually entering each secure MAC address is not a scalable solution.

You can also configure a switch to autorecover error-disabled ports after a specified amount of time:

Switch(config)# **errdisable recovery cause psecure-violation**	Enable dynamic error recovery of an error-disabled port. Default is 300 seconds.
Switch(config)# **errdisable recovery interval** *seconds*	Specify how long a port will remain disabled before it is reenabled. **TIP:** Disconnect the offending host; otherwise, the port will remain disabled, and the violation counter will be incremented.

NOTE: Use the **show errdisable recovery** command to display the error-disabled recovery timer information.

By default, when port security is enabled, the first address is added indefinitely as port aging is disabled. If required, you can enable port aging, making the switch periodically refresh the address:

Switch(config-if)# **switchport port-security aging {static | time** *minutes* **| type {absolute | inactivity}}**	Remove secure MAC addresses on a secure port without manually deleting the existing address in the startup-config.
	absolute (default) removes the address after the specified time. Existing addresses are refreshed or new addresses are added.
	inactivity removes the address only if they are inactive for the specified time.

NOTE: You should configure aging only if required. Use the **no switchport port-security aging static** interface configuration command to disable aging.

Configuring Port Security Example

Figure 7-1 shows the topology for the configuring port security example.

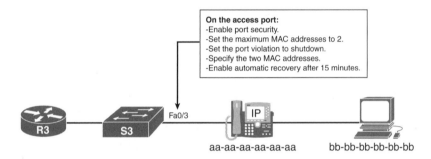

On the access port:
-Enable port security.
-Set the maximum MAC addresses to 2.
-Set the port violation to shutdown.
-Specify the two MAC addresses.
-Enable automatic recovery after 15 minutes.

Fa0/3   IP

R3   S3

aa-aa-aa-aa-aa-aa   bb-bb-bb-bb-bb-bb

Figure 7-1   Network Topology for the Configuring Port Security Example

S3(config)# **interface fa0/3**	Enter interface configuration mode.
S3(config-if)# **switchport mode access**	Configure the port as an access port.
S3(config-if)# **switchport port-security**	Enable port security allowing only one MAC address on the port.
S3(config-if)# **switchport port-security maximum 3**	Change the maximum number of MAC addresses to 3.
S3(config-if)# **switchport port-security violation shutdown**	If a violation occurs, error-disable the port and generate messages.
S3(config-if)# **switchport port-security mac-address aaaa.aaaa.aaaa**	Manually configure the IP phone MAC address.
S3(config-if)# **switchport port-security mac-address bbbb.bbbb.bbbb**	Manually configure the host MAC address.

S3(config)# **errdisable recovery cause psecure-violation**	Enables dynamic error recovery of an error-disabled port.
S3(config)# **errdisable recovery interval 900**	Change the default time to wait from 300 seconds to 900 seconds.

NOTE: Configure MAC address notification using the global configuration command **mac address-table notification** to generate MAC address learning and aging logging messages.

NOTE: Although only a single port is used in this example, port security is typically enabled on all user-facing ports.

VLAN Hopping Attacks

Spoofing DTP messages	Attacker sends spoofed Dynamic Trunking Protocol (DTP) messages in an attempt to establish a trunk link with the switch. If successful, the attacker can send traffic tagged with the target VLAN and have the switch deliver the packets to the destination.
Attach a rogue switch	Attacker connects a rogue switch and attempts to enable trunking with the target switch. If successful, the attacker can then access all the VLANs on the victim switch from the rogue switch.
Double-tagging (double encapsulated) VLAN hopping attack	Attacker embeds a hidden 802.1Q tag inside the already tagged 802.1Q frame. If successful, the frame can go to a VLAN that the original 802.1Q tag did not specify.

NOTE: Secure trunk links, nontrunk links, and unused ports to mitigate VLAN attacks.

Mitigating VLAN Attacks

On the trunk links, explicitly enable trunking and disable DTP:

Switch(config-if)# **switchport mode trunk**	Explicitly enable trunking on the link.
Switch(config-if)# **switchport nonegotiate**	Disable DTP and prevent DTP frames from being generated.

On the trunk links, switch the native VLAN to a dedicated VLAN:

Switch(config-if)# **switchport trunk native vlan** *vlan*	Change the native VLAN to a dedicated VLAN with no other traffic on it.

On the nontrunk links, disable trunking:

Switch(config-if)# **switchport mode access**	Configures port as an access port. This also disables trunking on the interface.

Assign all unused ports to a dedicated unused VLAN and disable the ports:

Switch(config-if)# **switchport mode access**	Configures port as an access port. This also disables trunking on the interface.
Switch(config-if)# **switchport access vlan** *vlan*	Assign the port to an unused VLAN.
Switch(config-if)# **shutdown**	Disable the port.

Mitigating VLAN Attacks Example

Figure 7-2 shows the topology for the mitigating VLAN attacks example.

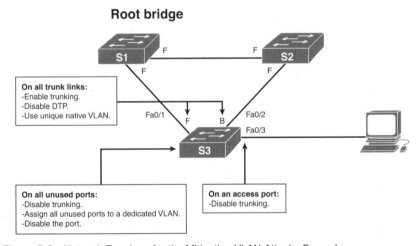

Figure 7-2 Network Topology for the Mitigating VLAN Attacks Example

S3(config)# **interface range Fa0/1 - 2**	Configure the two trunking ports, Fa0/1 and Fa0/2.
S3(config-range-if)# **switchport mode trunk**	Explicitly enable trunking.
S3(config-range-if)# **switchport nonegotiate**	Disable DTP.
S3(config-range-if)# **switchport trunk native vlan 88**	Assign the native VLAN to VLAN 88. VLAN 88 is not used for any other traffic.

S3(config-range-if)# `interface Fa0/3`	Change to interface Fa0/3.
S3(config-if)# `switchport mode access`	Disable trunking.
S3(config)# `interface range Fa0/4 - 24`	Configure all other unused ports.
S3(config-range-if)# `switchport mode access`	Disable trunking on all unused ports.
S3(config-range-if)# `switchport access vlan 999`	Assign the port to an unused VLAN.
S3(config-range-if)# `shutdown`	Disable all unused ports.

DHCP Attacks

DHCP spoofing attack	Attacker connects a rogue DHCP server to the network hoping it provides DHCP addresses to unsuspecting clients.
DHCP starvation attack	Attacker generates multiple DHCP requests using spoofed MAC addresses until the pool is exhausted. Legitimate hosts can no longer get valid DHCP addresses as the pool is exhausted.

NOTE: Configure DHCP snooping to mitigate DHCP attacks.

Mitigating DHCP Attacks

The DHCP snooping feature determines which switch ports can respond to DHCP requests.

Ports are identified as:

- **Trusted ports:** Host a DHCP server or can be an uplink toward the DHCP server and can source all DHCP messages, including DHCP offer and DHCP acknowledgement packets.

- **Untrusted ports:** Can source requests only.

Figure 7-3 identifies trusted and untrusted in a sample topology.

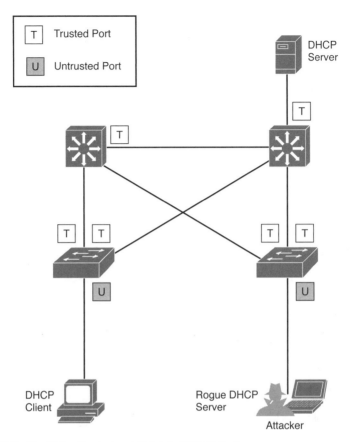

Figure 7-3 Identifying Trusted and Untrusted DHCP Ports

`Switch(config)# ip dhcp snooping`	Globally enable DHCP snooping.
`Switch(config-if)# ip dhcp snooping trust`	Identify trusted ports.
`Switch(config-if)# ip dhcp snooping limit rate rate`	On untrusted ports, limit the number of DHCP messages an interface can receive per second. The range is 1 to 2048.
`Switch(config)# ip dhcp snooping vlan vlan-number [vlan-number]`	Enable DHCP snooping for specific VLANs.

NOTE: Use the `show ip dhcp snooping` command to view DHCP snooping details and the `show ip dhcp snooping binding` to view the content of the DHCP snooping table.

Mitigating DHCP Attacks Example

Figure 7-4 shows the topology for the mitigating DHCP attacks example.

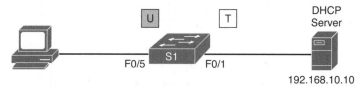

Figure 7-4   Network Topology for the Mitigating DHCP Attacks Example

S1(config)# **ip dhcp snooping**	Globally enable DHCP snooping.
S1(config)# **interface Fa0/1**	Change to interface Fa0/1.
S1(config-if)# **ip dhcp snooping trust**	Identify interface Fa0/1 as a trusted ports.
S1(config-if)# **interface Fa0/5**	Change to interface Fa0/5.
S1(config-if)# **ip dhcp snooping limit rate 10**	Rate limit interface Fa0/5 to 6 DHCP requests per minute.
S1(config)# **ip dhcp snooping vlan 5,10,50-52**	Enable DHCP snooping on VLANs 5, 10, 50, 51, and 52.

ARP Attacks

ARP poisoning attack	The attacker host initiates an ARP poisoning attack with the goal of using ARP spoofing to redirect traffic. An attacker can send a gratuitous ARP message containing a spoofed MAC address to a switch, and the switch would update its CAM table accordingly. Therefore, the attacker's host could claim to be the owner of any IP/MAC they choose.

NOTE: Configure DHCP snooping and Dynamic ARP Inspection (DAI) to mitigate ARP attacks.

Mitigating ARP Attacks

Dynamic ARP inspection (DAI) helps prevent such attacks by not relaying invalid or gratuitous ARP replies out to other ports in the same VLAN. Dynamic ARP inspection intercepts all ARP requests and all replies on the untrusted ports. Each intercepted packet is verified for valid IP-to-MAC binding. ARP replies coming from invalid devices are either dropped or logged by the switch for auditing. DAI can also be rate limited to limit the number of ARP packets, and the interface can be error-disabled if the rate is exceeded.

NOTE: DAI requires DHCP snooping to be enabled because it determines the validity of an ARP packet based on a valid MAC-address-to-IP-address binding in the DHCP snooping database.

`Switch(config)# ip dhcp snooping`	Globally enable DHCP snooping.
`Switch(config-if)# ip dhcp snooping trust`	Identify trusted DHCP ports.
`Switch(config-if)# ip arp inspection trust`	Identify trusted ARP ports.
`Switch(config)# ip arp inspection vlan vlan-range`	Enable DAI on a per-VLAN basis. You can specify a single VLAN identified by VLAN ID number, a range of VLANs separated by a hyphen, or a series of VLANs separated by a comma. The range is 1 to 4094.
`Switch(config)# ip dhcp snooping vlan vlan-number [vlan-number]`	Enable DHCP snooping for specific VLANs.
`S1(config)# ip arp inspection validate { [src-mac] [dst-mac] [ip] }`	Enable DAI to inspect based on the following: `src-mac`: Compare the source MAC address in the Ethernet frame against the sender MAC address in the ARP body. Packets with different MAC addresses are invalid and are dropped. `dst-mac`: Compare the destination MAC address in the Ethernet frame against the target MAC address in ARP body. Packets with different MAC addresses are invalid and are dropped. `ip`: Compare the ARP body for invalid and unexpected IP addresses (e.g., 0.0.0.0, 255.255.255.255, and all IP multicast addresses). Sender IP addresses are compared in all ARP requests and responses. Target IP addresses are checked only in ARP responses.

Mitigating ARP Attacks Example

Figure 7-5 shows the topology for the mitigating ARP attacks example.

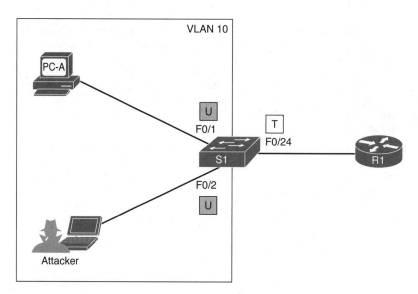

Figure 7-5   Network Topology for the Mitigating ARP Attacks Example

S1(config)# **ip dhcp snooping**	Globally enable DHCP snooping.
S1(config)# **interface Fa0/24**	Change to interface Fa0/24.
S1(config-if)# **ip dhcp snooping trust**	Identify interface Fa0/24 as a trusted port.
S1(config-if)# **ip arp inspection trust**	Identify interface Fa0/24 as a trusted ARP interface.
S1(config)# **ip dhcp snooping vlan 5,10,50-52**	Enable DHCP snooping on VLANs 5, 10, 50, 51, and 52.
S1(config)# **ip arp inspection vlan 5,10,50-52**	Enable DAI on VLANs 5, 10, 50, 51, and 52.
S1(config)# **ip arp inspection validate src-mac dst-mac ip**	Enable DAI to compare frames and packets based on the source MAC address, destination MAC address, or IP addresses.

Address Spoofing Attacks

Address spoofing attack	Attacker uses a MAC address spoofing attack to alter the MAC address of their host to match another known MAC address of a target host. The attacking host then sends a frame with the newly configured MAC address to have the switch update its CAM table entry and forward frames destined for the target host to the attacking host.
	An attacker uses an IP address spoofing attack such as when a rogue PC hijacks a valid IP address of a neighbor, or a uses a random IP address.

NOTE: Configure DHCP snooping and IP Source Guard (IPSG) to mitigate IP and MAC address spoofing attacks.

Mitigating Address Spoofing Attacks

Enable IP Source Guard (IPSG) to mitigate address spoofing attacks. IPSG operates just like DAI, but it looks at every packet, not just ARP packets. The IPSG feature is configured on untrusted interfaces.

NOTE: IPSG requires DHCP snooping to be enabled because it determines the validity of frames and packets based on a valid MAC-address-to-IP-address binding in the DHCP snooping database.

`Switch(config)# ip dhcp snooping`	Globally enable DHCP snooping.
`Switch(config-if)# ip verify source [port-security]`	Enable IP source guard with IP address filtering. Use the `port-security` keyword to enable IP source guard with IP and MAC address filtering.

NOTE: Use the `show ip verify source` command to view the content of the IPSG table.

Mitigating Address Spoofing Attacks Example

Refer to the topology in Figure 7-5 for the mitigating address spoofing attacks example.

`S1(config)# ip dhcp snooping`	Globally enable DHCP snooping.
`S1(config)# interface Fa0/24`	Change to interface Fa0/24.
`S1(config-if)# ip dhcp snooping trust`	Identify interface Fa0/24 as a trusted port.
`S1(config)# ip dhcp snooping vlan 5,10,50-52`	Enable DHCP snooping on VLANs 5, 10, 50, 51, and 52.

| S1(config)# `interface range fa`
`0/1 - 2` | Configure interface FastEthernet 0/1 and 0/2 as untrusted IPSG interfaces. |
| S1(config-if-range)# `ip verify`
`source port-security` | Enable IPSG to filter on IP and MAC address information. |

Spanning Tree Protocol Attacks

Redundant Layer 2 topologies eliminate single points of failure, but they are more susceptible to broadcast storms, multiple frame copies, and MAC address table instability problems.

Spanning Tree Protocol (STP) is a Layer 2 protocol that provides a loop-free redundant network topology by placing certain ports in the blocking state. A hacker could manipulate STP to conduct an attack by changing the topology of a network (for example, by connecting a rogue switch in an attempt to take over as the root and have all traffic for the immediate switched domain flow through it).

NOTE: Configure the STP stability mechanisms to enhance the overall performance of the switches and to reduce the time lost during topology changes.

STP Stability Mechanisms

PortFast	▪ PortFast immediately brings an interface to the forwarding state from a blocking state, bypassing the listening and learning states.
	▪ PortFast should only be configured when there is a host attached to the port, and not another switch.
	▪ Apply to all end-user ports.
BPDU guard	▪ BPDU guard immediately error disables a port that receives a BPDU.
	▪ Typically used on PortFast-enabled ports.
	▪ Apply to all end-user ports.
Root guard	▪ Root guard prevents an inappropriate switch from becoming the root bridge.
	▪ Root guard limits the switch ports out of which the root bridge may be negotiated.
	▪ Apply to all ports that should not become root ports.
Loop guard	Loop guard prevents alternate or root ports from becoming designated ports because of a failure that leads to a unidirectional link.
	Apply to all ports that are or can become nondesignated.

NOTE: Another STP stability mechanism is the BPDU filter feature, which stops the sending and receiving of BPDUs on a port. However, you should not configure this if BPDU guard is enabled.

NOTE: BPDU guard and root guard are similar, but their impact is different. BPDU guard disables the port, and it must be enabled manually. Root guard disables the port but recovers once the offending device ceases to send superior BPDUs.

Configuring STP Stability Mechanisms

Figure 7-6 displays a sample topology indicating where each STP stability feature should be enabled.

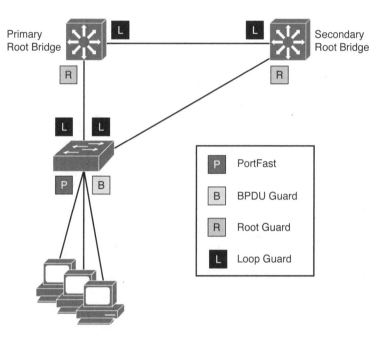

Figure 7-6   Identifying STP Stability Mechanisms Ports

You can enable PortFast globally or individually on an access port:

`Switch(config)# `**`spanning-tree`** **`portfast default`**	Globally enable the PortFast feature on all ports. **NOTE:** You must explicitly disable PortFast on switched ports leading to switches because they may create Layer 2 loops.
`Switch(config-if)# `**`spanning-tree`** **`portfast`**	Enable PortFast on the specified port.

NOTE: Use the `show running-config` `[interface` `interface-id]` command to verify that PortFast is enabled.

You can enable BPDU guard globally or individually on an access port:

`Switch(config)# spanning-tree portfast bpduguard default`	Globally enable BPDU guard on all PortFast-enabled ports.
`Switch(config-if)# spanning-tree bpduguard enable`	Enable BPDU guard on the specified port.

NOTE: Use the `show spanning-tree summary` and the `show spanning-tree summary totals` commands to display STP state information.

You can enable root guard on either an access port or a switch port that connects to another switch (but which should never be the root bridge).

`Switch(config-if)# spanning-tree guard root`	Enable root guard on the specified port.

NOTE: To verify, use the `show spanning-tree inconsistentports` command.

You can also configure a switch to autorecover BPDU guard error-disabled ports after a specified amount of time:

`Switch(config)# errdisable recovery cause bpduguard`	Enable the timer to recover from the BPDU guard error-disabled state.

NOTE: Use the `show errdisable recovery` command to display the error-disabled recovery timer information.

You can enable loop guard on some or all ports to provide additional protection against Layer 2 forwarding loops.

`Switch(config)# spanning-tree loopguard default`	Globally enable loop guard on all point-to-point links.
`Switch(config-if)# spanning-tree guard loop`	Enable loop guard on the specified port.

Configuring STP Stability Mechanisms Example

Figure 7-7 shows the topology for the configuring STP stability mechanisms example.

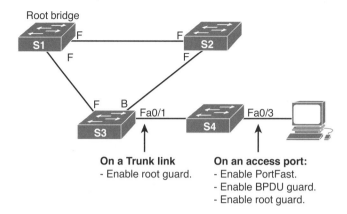

Figure 7-7   Network Topology for the Configuring STP Stability Mechanisms Example

`S3(config)# interface Fa0/1`	Enter interface configuration mode.
`S3(config-if)# spanning-tree guard root`	Enable root guard on this port. This prevents anything connected to this port from ever becoming the root.
`S4(config)# interface Fa0/3`	Enter interface configuration mode.
`S4(config-if)# spanning-tree portfast`	Enable PortFast.
`S4(config-if)# spanning-tree bpduguard enable`	Enable BPDU guard on this port.
`S4(config-if)# spanning-tree guard root`	Enable root guard on this port.
`S4(config)# errdisable recovery cause bpduguard`	Enable the timer to recover from the BPDU guard error-disabled state.
`S4(config)# spanning-tree loopguard default`	Globally enable loop guard on all point-to-point links.

LAN Storm Attacks

A LAN storm occurs when packets flood the LAN, creating excessive traffic and degrading network performance. Causes include errors in the protocol stack implementation, mistakes in network configurations, or users issuing a denial-of-service (DoS) attack.

The storm control feature monitors predefined suppression-level thresholds. When the rising threshold is reached, the port is blocked and only resumes normal forwarding when the traffic rate drops below the falling threshold (if configured) or below the rising threshold.

Configuring Storm Control

You can enable storm control globally or individually on an access port:

`Switch(config-if)#` `storm-control {{broadcast` `| multicast	unicast}` `level {`*`level`* `[`*`level-low`*`]` `| bps` *`bps`* `[`*`bps-low`*`]	pps` *`pps`* `[`*`pps-low`*`]}} {action` `{shutdown	trap}}`	Enable storm control on Layer 2 ports and Etherchannels to monitor the rate of received traffic. Broadcast, multicast, and unicast traffic can be monitored. `level {`*`level`* `[`*`level-low`*`]` specifies the rising and falling suppression levels as a percentage (to two decimal places) of total bandwidth of the port. `level bps {`*`bps`* `[`*`bps-low`*`]` specifies the rising and falling levels in bits per seconds. `level pps {`*`pps`* `[`*`pps-low`*`]` specifies the rising and falling levels in packets per second. The action taken can be ■ `shutdown:` Disables the port during the storm ■ `trap:` Sends an SNMP trap during a storm

NOTE: By default, unicast, broadcast, and multicast storm control are disabled on the switch interfaces; that is, the suppression level is 100 percent.

Configuring Storm Control Example

This example shows how to enable broadcast address storm control on a port to a level of 25 percent. When the broadcast traffic exceeds 25 percent of the total available bandwidth, the switch drops all broadcast traffic until the end of the traffic storm control interval:

`S1(config-if)# storm-control` `broadcast level 25`	Enable storm control on Layer 2 interfaces to monitor the rate of received traffic.

Advanced Layer 2 Security Features

Additional switch security features include the following:

- Access control lists (ACLs) and private VLANs
- Cisco integrated security features
- Secure management plane security features

NOTE: Configuration of these features is beyond the scope of this book.

ACLs and Private VLANs

Port-based ACLs for Layer 2 ports	You can apply security policies on individual switch ports.
Private VLANs	Private VLANs restrict traffic between hosts in a common segment by segregating traffic at Layer 2, turning a broadcast segment into a nonbroadcast multiaccess-like segment.
Private VLAN edge	Private VLAN edge provides security and isolation between switch ports, which helps ensure that users cannot snoop on other users' traffic.

Secure the Switch Management Plane

Just as the management plane is secured on Cisco routers, the Layer 2 switching management plane must also be secured. You can use many of the same tools to secure the management plane on Catalyst switches.

Secure management plane tools include (but are not limited to) the following:

Secure management protocols	SSH and SNMPv3 provide network security by encrypting administrator traffic during SSH and SNMP sessions.
SPAN support	Bidirectional data support on the Switched Port Analyzer (SPAN) port allows Cisco Intrusion Detection System (IDS) to take action when an intruder is detected.
AAA	TACACS+ and RADIUS authentication facilitates centralized control of the switch and restricts unauthorized users from altering the configuration.
RBAC	With role-based access control (RBAC), multilevel security on console access prevents unauthorized users from altering the switch configuration.
MAC notifications	MAC address notification allows administrators to be notified of users added to or removed from the network.
Multidomain authentication	This feature allows an IP phone and a PC to authenticate on the same switch port while placing them on appropriate voice and data VLANs.

CHAPTER 8

Securing the Data Plane in IPv6 Environments

This chapter covers the following topics:

Overview of IPv6

- Comparison Between IPv4 and IPv6
- The IPv6 Header
- ICMPv6
- Stateless Autoconfiguration
- IPv4-to-IPv6 Transition Solutions
- IPv6 Routing Solutions

IPv6 Threats

- IPv6 Vulnerabilities

IPv6 Security Strategy

- Configuring Ingress Filtering
- Secure Transition Mechanisms
- Future Security Enhancements

Overview of IPv6

Comparison Between IPv4 and IPv6

IP Service	IPv4	IPv6
IP header	Consists of a 20-byte field containing multiple fields.	Consists of a 40-byte field containing fewer fields, making it simpler, and provides better routing efficiency.
Addressing range	Requires a 32-bit dotted-decimal address to provide 4.3×10^9 (4.3 billion) addresses.	Requires a 128-bit hexadecimal address to provide 3.4×10^{28} addresses with multiple scopes.
Address types	Includes unicast, multicast, and broadcast addresses.	Includes unicast, multicast, and anycast addresses. No broadcast addresses means that it is not susceptible to broadcast storms.

IP Service	IPv4	IPv6
Autoconfiguration	Supports stateful configuration (Dynamic Host Configuration Protocol, DHCP).	Supports stateless address autoconfiguration (SLAAC) or stateful configuration (DHCPv6).
Security	IPsec must be configured.	IPsec is a mandatory part of the stack, but it still has to be configured.
Mobility	Mobility is not built in, but it supports mobile IP.	Mobile IP is built in, with optimized routing.
Quality of service (QoS)	Supports differentiated service and integrated service.	Supports differentiated service and integrated service, but the header compresses better because of fewer fields.
IP multicast	Heavy application use.	Heavy application and protocol stack use.
ICMP	Mostly used to provide messaging information.	Used extensively to provide messaging and protocol functions.

The IPv6 Header

The IPv6 header is twice as big as the IPv4 header (40 bytes versus 20 bytes). However, IPv6 has fewer fields and is simpler, as shown in Figure 8-1.

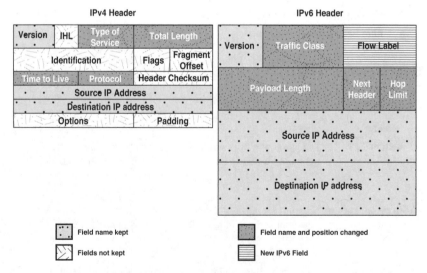

Figure 8-1   IPv4 Versus IPv6 Header

Some IPv4 fields no longer exist in IPv6, although three of these IPv4 fields have kept the same name and are identical in nature. Four fields have had their name and position changed but serve a similar function to IPv4. There is also a new QoS field in IPv6.

Like the IPv4 Protocol field, the IPv6 Next Header identifies the extension header and is not of fixed length. It can contain additional information such as a hop-by-hop list of destinations, routing header (RH), IPsec information, and more. All extension headers are daisy-chained, each header pointing to the next header until they reach the transport layer data. This arrangement allows an IPv6 packet to be customized with features and functionality (for example, TCP, UDP, ICMPv6).

NOTE: Attackers can use these extension headers for malicious purposes.

ICMPv6

Internet Control Message Protocol (ICMP) has a greater role in IPv6.

ICMP Message Type	ICMPv4	ICMPv6
Connectivity checks	✓	✓
Information/error messaging	✓	✓
Fragmentation needed notification	✓	✓
Address assignment		✓
Address resolution		✓
Router discovery		✓
Multicast group management		✓
Mobile IPv6 support		✓

ICMPv6 is used for neighbor and router discovery.

ICMPv6 Message	Type	Description
Neighbor solicitation (NS)	135	Similar to the IPv4 Address Resolution Protocol (ARP), it is sent by a host to determine the link-layer address of a neighbor. Used to verify that a neighbor is still reachable. An NS is also used for duplicate address detection (DAD).
Neighbor advertisement (NA)	136	A response to an NS message. A node may also send unsolicited an NA to announce a link-layer address change.
Router advertisement (RA)	134	RAs contain prefixes that are used for address configuration including a hop limit value, maximum transmission unit (MTU) value, and so on. RAs are sent either periodically or in response to an RS message.
Router solicitation (RS)	133	When a host is booting, it sends out an RS requesting routers to immediately generate an RA rather than wait for their next scheduled time.

NOTE: Attackers may manipulate ICMPv6 for malicious purposes.

Stateless Autoconfiguration

Stateless autoconfiguration enables plug-and-play configuration of an IPv6 device without the use of a server. It uses the Neighbor Discovery Protocol (NDP), which is based on ICMP Version 6 (ICMPv6) protocol messaging. NDP uses the ICMPv6 RS and RA messages.

NOTE: NDP replaces ARP and suffers from the same lack of authentication as ARP and DHCP on IPv4 networks.

IPv4-to-IPv6 Transition Solutions

Many transition mechanisms enable smooth integration of IPv4 and IPv6. Other mechanisms that allow IPv4 nodes to communicate with IPv6 nodes are available. All these mechanisms are applied to different situations.

The three most common techniques to transition from IPv4 to IPv6 are as follows:

Dual stack	A host is configured with an IPv4 and IPv6 network address. As a result, the node and its corresponding routers have two protocol stacks.
Tunneling	**Manual IPv6-over-IPv4 tunneling** is an integration method in which an IPv6 packet is encapsulated within the IPv4 protocol. This method requires dual-stack routers.
	Dynamic 6to4 tunneling is a method that automatically establishes the connection of IPv6 islands through an IPv4 network.
	Intra-Site Automatic Tunnel Addressing Protocol (ISATAP) tunneling is an automatic overlay tunneling mechanism that uses the underlying IPv4 network as a data link layer for IPv6.
	Teredo tunneling is an IPv6 transition technology that provides host-to-host automatic tunneling instead of gateway tunneling.
Proxying and translation (NAT-PT)	This translation mechanism sits between an IPv6 network and an IPv4 network. The job of the translator is to translate IPv6 packets into IPv4 packets and vice versa.

IPv6 Routing Solutions

IPv6 supports static routes, Routing Information Protocol next generation (RIPng), Open Shortest Path First Version 3 (OSPFv3) Protocol, Intermediate System-to-Intermediate System Protocol (IS-IS) for IPv6, Multiprotocol Border Gateway Protocol Version 4 (MP-BGP4), and Enhanced Interior Gateway Routing Protocol (EIGRP) for IPv6. You must configure the **ipv6 unicast-routing** before an IPv6-capable routing protocol or an IPv6 static route will work.

NOTE: Neighbor routers are identified by their next-hop link-local addresses and therefore do not use global unicast addresses.

IPv6 Threats

IPv6 is no more or less secure than IPv4. Many similarities exist between them, and therefore they share similar threats, including the following:

- Attacks against the physical or data link layers
- Attacks against routers and other networking devices
- Application layer attacks
- Denial-of-service (DoS) attacks using IPv6-specific attack tools such as 6tunneldos or 4to6ddos
- Reconnaissance attacks
- Sniffing or eavesdropping using IPv6 tools such as Snort, TCPdump, or Wireshark
- Unauthorized access
- Spoofed packets (that is, forged addresses and fields using Scapy6, sendIP, Packit, or Spak6)
- Man-in-the-middle attacks

Other slightly modified IPv6 threats include the following:

- LAN-based attacks against NDP
- Attacks against DHCP or DHCPv6
- DoS attacks against routers (for example, hop-by-hop extension headers)
- Fragmentation (IPv4 routers performing fragmentation versus IPv6 hosts using a fragment extension header)
- Packet amplification attacks (IPv4 uses broadcast; IPv6 uses multicast.)

Threats that are unique to IPv6 include the following:

- Reconnaissance attacks, although more difficult but possible using IPv6 tools such as Parasit6, Fakeroute6, or Scapy6
- Attacks against ICMPv6
- Extension header (EH) attacks
- Autoconfiguration attacks
- Attacks on transition mechanisms
- Mobile IP attacks
- IPv6 protocol stack attacks

NOTE: IPv6 is a relatively new protocol and therefore is subject to bugs in the stack.

IPv6 Vulnerabilities

New vulnerabilities for IPv6 include the following:

Reliance on multicast and ICMPv6	▪ Multicasting facilitates reconnaissance. (For example, FF02::1 is all hosts; FF02::2 is all routers.) ▪ ICMPv6 is a vehicle for autoconfiguration, subject to spoofing and multiple exploits.
Header extensions	▪ Hosts process routing headers (RHs), which can be exploited (for example, routing header for source routing and reconnaissance). ▪ There already exist RH-based amplification attacks.
Tunneling	▪ Encapsulating IPv6 over IPv4 bypasses firewalls and other inspection systems not ready for IPv6. ▪ Most IPv4/IPv6 transition mechanisms have no authentication built in. ▪ Dual stack is typically automatically enabled on hosts.
DoS amplification attacks	▪ Routing loops are created to consume resources or amplify the packets that are sent to a victim such as when an attacker creates a feedback loop between two routers by spoofing a packet with the RH containing multiple A to B statements. ▪ NDP can be used to amplify a network scan by sending NS messages to all the hosts in the LAN segment, using the FF02 multicast address.
Pivoting attacks	▪ Combines multiple previously mentioned techniques.

IPv6 Security Strategy

IPv6 is mostly IPv4 with larger addresses, and no significant difference exists between IPv4 and IPv6 with respect to security. In some cases, IPv6 is slightly more secure, and in other cases IPv6 is slightly less secure. Security techniques and devices do exist to enforce a security policy for the IPv6 traffic and should be used.

The lack of IPv6 training for network and security staff is probably the biggest threat for operation.

Configuring Ingress Filtering

Deny bogon addresses	Filter bogon addresses because they are commonly found as the source addresses of distributed DoS (DDoS) attacks. The term *bogon addresses* refers to traffic with a source IP address from a reserved IP address space, and it should be filtered by an Internet service provider.
MAC address table attack	Filter multicast packets at your perimeter based on their scope.

Filter incoming traffic	Only receive packets that have a destination address within your allocated block from an Internet service provider and multicast group address or link-local address for NDP.
Filter ICMPv6 messages	Granularly filter ICMPv6 messages at the perimeter. (Remember, ICMPv6 is needed for protocol operations such as NDP.)
Drop packets with unknown extension headers	Drop RH0 packets and unknown extension headers at the perimeter and throughout the interior of the network.

Secure Transition Mechanisms

Secure dual stack	Prefer dual stack as the transition mechanism, but secure IPv4 and IPv6 equally.
Implement IPsec VPN tunnels	When tunnels are used to send sensitive traffic over a public network, they should be secured by adding IPsec authentication and confidentiality that can prevent both the injection/sniffing attacks and unauthorized access.
Do not allow tunnels through perimeter unless required	Terminate tunnels at the edge and do not permit host-to-host tunnels.

Future Security Enhancements

Consider current and future security enhancements:

Secure Neighbor Discovery (SeND)	Combines NDP with crypto features. The SeND protocol enhances NDP with address ownership proof, message protection, and router authorization.
RA-Guard	RA-Guard blocks router advertisement and router redirect ICMP packets from Layer 2 ports.

NOTE: IPv6 security will now be discussed in other chapters.

CHAPTER 9

Endpoint and Content Protection

This chapter covers the following topics:

Endpoint Security

- Endpoint Security
- Data Loss Prevention
- Endpoint Posture Assessment

Cisco Advanced Malware Protection (AMP)

- Cisco AMP Elements
- Cisco AMP for Endpoint
- Cisco AMP for Endpoint Products

Content Security

- Email Threats
- Cisco Email Security Appliance (ESA)
- Cisco Email Security Virtual Appliance (ESAV)
- Cisco Web Security Appliance (WSA)
- Cisco Web Security Virtual Appliance (WSAV)
- Cisco Cloud Web Security (CWS)

Protecting Endpoints

Endpoints such as computers, laptops, and mobile devices are valuable targets. They have to be protected from viruses, malware, data loss, and more. The network should also be protected and only allow hosts with the required and compliant software to connect.

Endpoint Security

Traditionally, endpoint security products such as the following have acted independently to provide endpoint protection:

Antivirus	Typically a software program installed on an endpoint device to prevent, detect, and remove malicious software. For antivirus software to remain effective, it must be updated frequently.

Antispyware	Typically a software program installed on an endpoint to detect and remove spyware. In order for antispyware to remain effective, it must be updated frequently.
Host-based firewalls	Typically a software program installed on an endpoint device to protect the device itself. Most modern operating systems now include integrated personal firewalls.
Host-based IPS	Typically software installed on the local host to monitor and report on the system configuration and application activity and to provide log analysis, event correlation, integrity checking, policy enforcement, rootkit detection, and alerting. Examples include Cisco Security Agent (CSA), which uploads host data to Cisco network IPS devices.

Data Loss Prevention

Endpoints are also susceptible to data theft. For example when a corporate laptop is lost or stolen, how do you protect the files on the device?

The solution is to locally encrypt the disk drive with a strong encryption algorithm (e.g., 256-bit AES). The encrypted disk volumes can only be mounted for normal read/write access with the authorized password. Some operating systems, such as MAC OSX, provide encryption options natively. Windows supports BitLocker, TrueCrypt, Credant, VeraCrypt, and others.

Endpoint Posture Assessment

Windows, Mac OS X, Linux, iOS, and Android endpoints can connect to enterprise sites using the Cisco AnyConnect Secure Mobility Client v4.0. AnyConnect provides VPN access through Secure Sockets Layer (SSL) and also offers enhanced security.

AnyConnect assesses an endpoint's compliance for things like operating system version, antivirus software, and antispyware software installed on the endpoint. You can then restrict network access until the endpoint is compliant.

Enforcing endpoint compliance can be achieved using Cisco AnyConnect and the following:

ASA posture module	This is an AnyConnect module used with the Cisco Adaptive Security Appliance (ASA) to enforce the policy for endpoints that connect to the network via remote access VPN.
	The module performs server-side evaluation where the ASA requests endpoint attributes that AnyConnect gathers and sends. The module also requests personal firewall software data. The ASA evaluates the attributes and determines whether the client is allowed access or quarantined.
	Remediation capabilities enable software that has been disabled, force updates for antivirus and antispyware software, and push firewall policy to the personal firewall software.

ISE posture module	This is an AnyConnect module used with the Cisco Identity Services Engine to enforce policy for internal endpoints that connect via either wired or wireless technology.
	The module performs client-side evaluation where the AnyConnect client receives the posture requirement policy from ISE, performs the posture data collection, compares the results against the policy, and sends the assessment results back to ISE.
	Remediation with ISE is based on quarantining the endpoint. The endpoint is allowed limited connectivity to reach remediation servers where the required software can be obtained. Once the endpoint is compliant, it is allowed normal access to the network.

Cisco Advanced Malware Protection (AMP)

Traditional endpoint security products achieve about 40 percent success in detection. Therefore, advanced malware protection such as the Cisco Advanced Malware Protection (AMP) technology is required. AMP uses integrated controls and a continuous process to detect, confirm, track, analyze, and remediate threats before, during, and after an attack.

The AMP solution can enable malware detection and blocking, continuous analysis, and retrospective alerting with the following:

File reputation	Analyze files inline and block or apply policies. File reputation captures a fingerprint of each file and sends it to AMP's cloud-based intelligence network for a reputation verdict. With these results, AMP can automatically block malicious files, or apply policies.
File sandboxing	Analyze unknown files to understand true file behavior. A sandbox environment makes it possible for AMP to securely determine the files' purpose.
File retrospection	Continue to analyze files for changing threat levels solving the problem of malicious files passing through perimeter defenses but later being deemed a threat.

AMP accesses the collective security intelligence of the Cisco Talos Security Intelligence and Research Group (Talos).

Cisco AMP Elements

Cisco Collective Security Intelligence Cloud	This is where the various detection and analytics engines reside. They use cloud-based detection engines, such as SPERO, which is a machine-learning malware detection engine, and ETHOS, which is a fuzzy logic-based malware detection engine.

AMP for Endpoints (Client Connector)	Windows, Mac, and mobile endpoints run the FireAMP software agent, which enables the device to become a FireAMP connector. The connector communicates with the FirePOWER-enabled devices and the Cisco Collective Security Intelligence Cloud to send and receive file information.
AMP for Networks	Gives FirePOWER devices the capability to query the cloud to obtain file disposition information on files detected by the FirePOWER device.
AMP for Content Security	This is an integrated feature in the Cisco Web and Email Security Appliances, and the Cloud Web Security.

Cisco AMP for Endpoint

Cisco AMP for Endpoints provides the following:

Cloud-based protection	Cisco AMP communicates with the Cisco Collective Security Intelligence Cloud, which performs detection publishing large-scale data processing (big data), decision making performed in real time, and advanced reporting capabilities. The cloud offers rapid detection of known malware, the use of cloud resources to test files with unknown dispositions, and the use of machine learning techniques to constantly keep itself up to date.
Visibility	Cisco AMP for Endpoints can track the file trajectory and file analytics. Trajectory gives you the complete ancestry and lifecycle of a threat on a single device. This historical analysis lets you see, over time, what files did on a system. You can trace back an infection and identify the root cause. It captures the file trajectory, which is the list of hosts that have seen this file and the device trajectory, which shows you what files did on a given host.
Control	AMP for Endpoints enables you to control and block malicious network connections based on security intelligence feeds (IP reputation) and custom IP black lists.

Cisco AMP for Endpoint Products

Capability to provide...	Cisco AMP for Endpoints for Windows	Cisco AMP for Endpoints for Mac	Cisco AMP for Endpoints Mobile
Protection	▪ SHA-256 based disposition check ▪ SPERO and ETHOS detection engine ▪ Advanced analytics ▪ Quarantine	▪ SHA-256 based disposition check ▪ Antivirus signatures ▪ Advanced analytics ▪ Quarantine	▪ SHA-1 based disposition check ▪ Post-installation detection

Visibility	▪ File trajectory ▪ File analytics ▪ Device trajectory	▪ File trajectory ▪ File analytics ▪ Device trajectory	
Control	Simple to advanced custom detection Application blocking IP blacklists	Simple custom detection Application blocking IP blacklists	Simple custom detection

Content Security

Content security systems provide granular control and security on particular network applications. Examples of Cisco content security products include the Cisco Email Security Appliance (ESA) and the Cisco Web Security Appliance (WSA).

Email Threats

Email is a critical business service in most organizations. Failing to protect that service can result in a loss of data and employee productivity.

Email threats include

Spam	A flood of unsolicited and unwanted email that wastes employee time through sheer volume and uses valuable resources like bandwidth and storage.
Malicious email	Email embedded with viruses and malware that perform actions on the end device when clicked, and targeted or directed attacks.
Phishing	Phishing attacks try to mislead employees into releasing confidential information such as credit card numbers, social security numbers, or intellectual property. Phishing attacks can link to malicious websites that distribute additional malware to computer endpoints.

Cisco Email Security Appliance (ESA)

The Cisco ESA is an SMTP firewall and threat monitoring appliance that protects the email infrastructure by filtering unsolicited and malicious email. The Cisco ESA is deployed as the first mail server for email coming from the Internet and the last mail server on the path out to the Internet. The ESA acts as a Mail Transfer Agent (MTA) (or mail relay) within the email-delivery chain and is updated every 3 to 5 minutes by the Cisco cloud-based threat intelligence solution.

Specifically, the ESA provides the following features:

Fights spam	The ESA filters spam and combats phishing attacks using: ■ **Reputation-based filtering:** If a server is a known spam sender, then a file coming from it is more likely spam. Reputation filters look at the source IP address and compare it to the reputation data downloaded from Cisco SenderBase. ■ **Context-based filtering:** These filters inspect the entire mail message analyzing details such as sender identity, message contents, attachments, embedded URLs, and email formatting to identify spam messages without blocking legitimate email.
Fights viruses and malware	The ESA downloads a list of known bad mail servers, called outbreak filters, from the Cisco SenderBase. SenderBase generates these lists by watching global email traffic patterns and looking for anomalies associated with an outbreak. When an email is received from a server on this list, it is kept in quarantine until the antivirus signatures are updated to counter the current threat. The ESA also scans incoming and outgoing email for antivirus signatures.
Email data loss prevention	Data loss prevention for email is content-level scanning of email messages and attachments to detect inappropriate transport of sensitive information. The Cisco ESA's data loss prevention (DLP) features provide rules for identifying classes of data and taking action on the messages as appropriate. Cisco has partnered with RSA to provide integrated DLP technology on Cisco Email Security Appliances.
Advanced Malware Protection	Advanced Malware Protection (AMP) provides malware detection and blocking, continuous analysis, and retrospective alerting to ESA.

NOTE: The ESA is managed using a rich web-based user interface. The interface also provides monitoring and reporting tasks that you will encounter in an email security environment.

Cisco Email Security Virtual Appliance (ESAV)

A less expensive alternative to the dedicated ESA is Cisco ESAV. The Cisco ESAV is a software version of the Cisco ESA and runs on top of a VMware ESXi hypervisor and Cisco Unified Computing System servers. ESAV enables an administrator to create virtual ESA instances where and when they are needed in your network infrastructure.

Cisco Web Security Appliance (WSA)

The Cisco WSA is a device that provides an all-in-one web security solution combining advanced malware protection, application visibility and control, acceptable use policy controls, reporting, and secure mobility. The WSA performs blacklisting, URL-filtering, malware scanning, URL categorization, web application filtering, and TLS/SSL encryption and decryption.

The Cisco WSA is deployed in the path between corporate web users and the Internet. Specifically, the WSA is a web proxy that either forwards or drops web traffic based on reputation filters using the Web-Based Reputation Score (WBRS) or the outcome of inline file scanning using Webroot and McAfee antimalware scanning engines.

When a user initiates a web request, the Cisco ASA firewall redirects the request to the Cisco WSA. The WSA checks the request, replies with denial if the request violates policy, or otherwise initiates a new connection to the destination if the request is acceptable. When the ASA receives the reply from the web server, it forwards the reply to the WSA, which again checks the content for objectionable material. If no issues are found, the reply is forwarded to the initiating host.

Benefits of the WSA include the following:

Single appliance security and control	The WSA offers a single appliance solution to secure and control security risks, resource risks, and compliance risks.
Talos security intelligence	The WSA receives updates every 3 to 5 minutes from the Cisco Talos Security Intelligence and Research Group (Talos). Talos analyzes the telemetry data of billions of web requests and emails and millions of malware samples, open source data sets, and network intrusions. Talos then releases updates to mitigate known threats, emerging threats, and zero-hour attacks.
Enforce acceptable use policies (AUP)	The WSA can enforce an acceptable use web policy to increase the amount of time that employees spend on business-oriented activities while reducing misuse of enterprise networks and bandwidth.
Centralized management and reporting	The WSA provides an easy-to-use, rich web-based user interface. The interface also provides monitoring and reporting tasks that you will encounter in a web security environment.
Roaming-user protection	The WSA integrates with the Cisco AnyConnect Secure Mobility Client to provide a secure VPN tunnel to remote clients. Cisco AnyConnect analyzes traffic in real time before permitting access and integrates with Cisco ISE.

Cisco Web Security Virtual Appliance (WSAV)

A less expensive alternative to the dedicated WSA is Cisco WSAV. The Cisco WSAV is a software version of the Cisco WSA and runs on top of a VMware ESXi hypervisor and Cisco Unified Computing System servers. WSAV enables an administrator to create virtual WSA instances where and when they are needed in your network infrastructure.

Cisco Cloud Web Security (CWS)

The Cisco CWS is a cloud-based security service that uses web proxies in Cisco's cloud environment to scan traffic for malware and policy enforcement. Specifically, it is a cloud-based method of implementing an on-premise WSA. It works with Cisco ISR G2, ASA, WSA, and AnyConnect mobility client.

CHAPTER 10

Configuring ACLs for Threat Mitigation

This chapter covers the following topics:

Access Control Lists

- Mitigating Threats Using ACLs
- ACL Design Guidelines
- ACL Operation

Configuring ACLs

- ACL Configuration Guidelines
- Filtering with Numbered Extended ACLs
- Configuring a Numbered Extended ACL Example
- Filtering with Named Extended ACLs
- Configuring a Named Extended ACL Example

Mitigating Network Attacks with ACLs

- Antispoofing ACLs Example
- Permitting Necessary Traffic through a Firewall Example
- Mitigating ICMP Abuse

Enhancing ACL Protection with Object Groups

- Network Object Groups
- Service Object Groups
- Using Object Groups in Extended ACLs
- Configuring Object Groups in ACLs Example

ACLs in IPv6

- Mitigating IPv6 Attacks Using ACLs
- IPv6 ACLs Implicit Entries
- Filtering with IPv6 ACLs
- Configuring an IPv6 ACL Example

Access Control List

Access control lists (ACLs) provide packet filtering for routers and firewalls to protect internal networks from the outside world and to filter traffic leaving the inside network. ACL criteria could be the source address of the traffic, the destination address of the traffic, the upper-layer protocol, or other information.

CAUTION: Hackers can sometimes successfully evade basic ACLs.

Mitigating Threats Using ACLs

You can use ACLs to mitigate multiple threats, including the following:

- IP address spoofing (inbound and outbound)
- Denial-of-service (DoS) TCP SYN attacks by blocking external attacks
- DoS TCP SYN attacks using TCP intercepts
- DoS smurf attacks
- Filtering Internet Control Message Protocol (ICMP) messages (inbound, outbound, and traceroute)
- Securing vty access

NOTE: This chapter focuses on using ACLs for threat mitigation purposes.

ACL Design Guidelines

- Base the ACL on the security policy.
- Write out what the ACL is required to do and consider potential problems it may cause.
- Build a library of common ACLs.
- Test the ACL in a lab environment and then apply it to the production network.

ACL Operation

ACL statements operate in a sequential, logical, order and evaluate packets from the top down, one statement at a time:

- If a packet header and an ACL statement match, the rest of the statements in the list are skipped and the packet is permitted or denied as determined by the matched statement.
- If a packet header does not match an ACL statement, the packet is tested against the next statement in the list.
- This matching process continues until the end of the list is reached.
- A final implied statement matches all other packets and results in a deny instruction.

NOTE: Each statement in an ACL is referred to as an access control entry (ACE).

ACLs operate in two directions:

Inbound ACLs	Incoming packets are processed before they are routed to an outbound interface.
Outbound ACLs	Incoming packets are routed to the outbound interface, and then they are processed through the outbound ACL.

NOTE: Inbound ACLs are usually more efficient because they do not perform routing lookups on denied packets. Only permitted packets are processed for routing.

Routers support two types of ACLs:

Standard ACL	• Filters IP packets based on source address only.
	• ACLs can be numbered or named.
	• Valid number ranges include 1–99 and 1300–1999.
Extended ACL	• Filters IP packets based on protocol, source and destination addresses, source and destination UDP and TCP ports, and ICMP and Internet Group Management Protocol (IGMP) message types.
	• ACLs can be numbered or named.
	• Valid number ranges include 100–199 and 2000–2699.

NOTE: Numbered ACLs are configured using the `access-list` global configuration command. You cannot edit numbered ACLs using this command. New ACL entries are appended to the end of the ACL.

Standard and extended ACLs can be named. Named ACLs are useful because they provide a hint as to the purpose of the ACL. Names can be alphanumeric but must begin with an alphabetic character. In addition, names cannot contain spaces or punctuation.

NOTE: Named ACLs are configured using the `ip access-list` global configuration command.

TIP: Use uppercase letters to make the named ACL stand out in the configuration.

TIP: You can edit numbered and named ACLs using the `ip access-list` command.

Configuring ACLs

ACL Configuration Guidelines

Three Ps	■ Only one ACL per interface, per protocol (Layer 3), per direction can be configured.
Directional filtering	■ Consider the direction flow of data before creating an ACL.
Order of ACL statements	■ Place the more specific ACE statements at the beginning and generic ACE statements near the end.
Implicit deny	■ Every ACL has a hidden deny all ACE at the end of it. ■ There must be at least one permit ACE; otherwise, all traffic will be denied.
Standard ACL limitation	■ Can only filter by source address. ■ Whenever possible, use an extended ACL instead.
Standard ACL placement	■ Typically place standard ACLs as close to the destination as possible.
Extended ACL placement	■ Typically place extended ACLs as close to the source being filtered.
ACLs are stateless	■ Consider deploying zoned-based policy firewall (ZFW) instead.
Modifying numbered ACLs	■ You can modify numbered ACLs by using the `ip access-list` command.
Router-generated packets	■ Router-generated packets are not subject to ACL filtering on the router generating the packet.

NOTE: This section focuses on extended ACLs.

Filtering with Numbered Extended ACLs

`Router(config)# access-list` `access-list-number {permit	deny}` `protocol source source-wildcard` `[operator port] destination` `destination-wildcard [operator` `port] [established] [log]`	Define an extended ACL. Valid numbers are between 100–199 and 2000–2699. **NOTE:** Parameters will vary depending on the protocol of ACL being configured. **NOTE:** Use caution using the `log` keyword as it could negatively affect the performance of the device.
`Router(config)# interface type` `number`	Specify the interface type and number and enter interface configuration mode.
`Router(config-if)# ip access-group` `access-list-number {in	out}`	Apply the specified extended access list to the interface.

Configuring a Numbered Extended ACL Example

Figure 10-1 displays the network topology for the numbered extended ACL example.

Figure 10-1   Network Topology for Numbered Extended ACL Example

`R1(config)# access-list 100`	Define extended ACL 100.
`R1(config)# access-list 100 remark` `Basic anti-spoofing ACL`	Document the purpose of the ACL.
`R1(config)# access-list 100 deny` `ip 209.165.200.224 0.0.0.31 any`	Deny incoming traffic with the source address the same as the internal subnet.
`R1(config)# access-list 100 permit` `ip any host 209.165.200.254 eq 80`	Permit HTTP web traffic to reach the server.
`R1(config)# interface serial 0/0/0`	Enter interface configuration mode for the serial interface.
`R1(config-if)# ip access-group` `100 in`	Apply ACL 100 incoming on the outside serial interface.

Filtering with Named Extended ACLs

`Router(config)# ip access-list`
`extended {access-list-number |`
`access-list-name}`
	Define a named ACL. The command can also be used to edit a numbered ACL.

`Router(config-ext-nacl)# permit`
`protocol source source-wildcard`
`[operator port] destination`
`destination-wildcard [ operator`
`port ] [ established] [ log]`
	Define the `permit` statement.
	
	NOTE: Parameters will vary depending on the ACL protocol being configured.

`Router(config-ext-nacl)# deny`
`protocol source source-wildcard`
`[ operator port] destination`
`destination-wildcard [ operator`
`port ] [ log]`
	Define the `deny` statement.

`Router(config)# interface type number`	Specify the interface type and number and enter interface configuration mode.
`Router(config-if)# ip access-group` `access-list-name { in | out}`	Apply the specified ACL to the interface.

Configuring a Named Extended ACL Example

`R1(config)# ip access-list extended ACL-IN`	Define an extended ACL named ACL-IN.
`R1(config-ext-nacl)# remark Basic anti-spoofing ACL`	Document the ACL.
`R1(config-ext-nacl)# permit ip 209.165.200.224 0.0.0.31 any eq 80`	Permit HTTP web traffic to reach the server.
`R1(config-ext-nacl)# permit ip any host 209.165.200.254`	Permit traffic to reach the server.
`R1(config-ext-nacl)# interface serial 0/0/0`	Apply ACL-IN to the serial interface.
`R1(config-if)# ip access-group ACL-IN in`	Apply the ACL incoming on the outside interface.

NOTE: To verify the ACLs, use the `show access-lists`, `show ip access-lists`, and `show ip interfaces` commands.

TIP: Append the log keyword at the end of an ACE to generate a system message (106100) every time a flow meets the ACE criteria. Display the number of hits using the `show access-lists` or `show ip access-lists` command.

Mitigating Attacks with ACLs

ACLs can be used to mitigate many network threats including IP address spoofing (inbound and outbound) and DoS attacks. Most DoS attacks use some type of spoofing, which overrides the normal packet creation process by inserting a custom IP header with a different source IP address.

Antispoofing ACLs Example

Attackers can hide their identity by spoofing the source IP address. An administrator should deny these packets from entering an organization's network.

In this example, we are denying all IP packets coming from the Internet containing the following IP addresses in their source field:

- Any local host addresses (127.0.0.0/8)

- Any reserved private addresses (RFC 1918)

- Any addresses reserved for documentation (RFC 5737)

- Any addresses in the IP multicast address range (224.0.0.0/3)

We then only permit inside network users to enter the LAN interface.

Figure 10-2 shows the network topology for the configuring antispoofing ACL example.

Figure 10-2 Network Topology for the Antispoofing ACL Example

`R1(config)# access-list 150 deny` `ip host 0.0.0.0 any`	Define extended ACL 150 denying IP to any host with a source IP address of 0.0.0.0.
`R1(config)# access-list 150 deny` `ip 10.0.0.0 0.255.255.255 any`	Define extended ACL 150 denying IP to any host with a source IP address of 10.0.0.0/8.
`R1(config)# access-list 150 deny` `ip 127.0.0.0 0.255.255.255 any`	Define extended ACL 150 denying IP to any host with a source IP address of 127.0.0.0/8.
`R1(config)# access-list 150 deny` `ip 172.16.0.0 0.15.255.255 any`	Define extended ACL 150 denying IP to any host with a source IP address of 172.16.0.0/12.
`R1(config)# access-list 150 deny` `ip 192.168.0.0 0.0.255.255 any`	Define extended ACL 150 denying IP to any host with a source IP address of 192.168.0.0/16.
`R1(config)# access-list 150 deny` `ip 224.0.0.0 15.255.255.255 any`	Define extended ACL 150 denying IP to any host with a source IP address of 224.0.0.0/3.
`R1(config)# access-list 150 deny` `ip 192.0.2.0 0.0.0.255 any`	Define extended ACL 150 denying IP to any host with a source IP address of 192.0.2.0/24.
`R1(config)# access-list 150 deny` `ip 198.51.100.0 0.0.0.255 any`	Define extended ACL 150 denying IP to any host with a source IP address of 198.51.100.0/24.
`R1(config)# access-list 150 deny` `ip 203.0.113.0 0.0.0.255 any`	Define extended ACL 150 denying IP to any host with a source IP address of 203.0.113.0/24.
`R1(config)# access-list 150 deny` `ip host 255.255.255.255 any`	Define extended ACL 150 denying IP to any host with a source IP address of 255.255.255.255.
`R1(config)# access-list 150 permit` `ip any any`	Define extended ACL 150 permitting everything else.

R1(config)# `interface Serial 0/0/0`	Enter the outside interface Serial 0/0/0 line configuration mode.
R1(config-if)# `ip access-group 150 in`	Apply the extended ACL 150 to the interface in an incoming direction.
R1(config)# `access-list 105 permit` `ip 192.168.1.0 0.0.0.255 any`	Define extended ACL 105 permitting only valid addresses from our internal network. All other traffic will not be permitted.
R1(config)# `interface G0/0`	Enter the inside interface Gigabit Ethernet 0/0 line configuration mode.
R1(config-if)# `ip access-group 105 in`	Apply the extended ACL 105 to the interface in an incoming direction.

Permitting Necessary Traffic through a Firewall Example

A router configured with ACLs must permit some traffic through. For example, DNS, SMTP, and FTP are common services that often must be allowed through a firewall router.

Figure 10-3 shows the network topology for permitting the necessary traffic through a firewall ACL example.

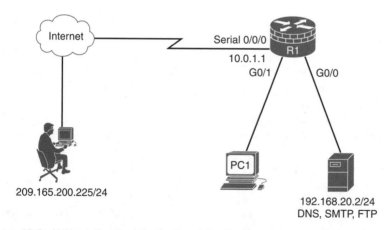

Figure 10-3   Network Topology for the Permitting Traffic ACL Example

R1(config)# `access-list 180 permit`
`udp any host 192.168.20.2 eq`
`domain`
	Define extended ACL 180 permitting DNS traffic from any host to host 192.168.20.2.

R1(config)# `access-list 180 permit` `tcp any host 192.168.20.2 eq smtp`	Define extended ACL 180 permitting SMTP traffic from any host to host 192.168.20.2.

`R1(config)# access-list 180 permit tcp any host 192.168.20.2 eq ftp`	Define extended ACL 180 permitting FTP traffic from any host to host 192.168.20.2.
`R1(config)# access-list 180 permit tcp host 209.165.200.225 host 192.168.20.2 eq 22`	Define extended ACL 180 permitting SSH traffic from 209.165.200.225 to host 192.168.20.2.
`R1(config)# interface Serial 0/0/0`	Enter the outside interface Serial 0/0/0 line configuration mode.
`R1(config-if)# ip access-group 180 in`	Apply the extended ACL 180 to the interface in an incoming direction.

Mitigating ICMP Abuse Example

Hackers use ICMP packets for ping sweeps and DoS flood attacks, and use ICMP redirect messages to alter host routing tables.

Recommended ICMP messages for proper network operation and that should be allowed into the internal network include the following:

Echo reply	Allows users to receive return ping packets from external hosts.
Source quench	Requests that the sender decrease the traffic rate of messages.
Time exceeded	Used by the `traceroute` utility to identify routers in the path between two hosts. Specifically, it informs the source of a discarded packet due to the time-to-live field reaching zero.
Unreachable	Generated for packets administratively denied by an ACL.

Recommended ICMP messages for proper network operation and that should be allowed to exit the network include the following:

Echo	Allows users to ping external hosts.
Parameter problem	Informs the host of packet header problems.
Packet too big	Enables packet maximum transmission unit (MTU) discovery

As a rule, block all other ICMP message types outbound.

Figure 10-4 shows the network topology for the configuring ICMP abuse ACL example.

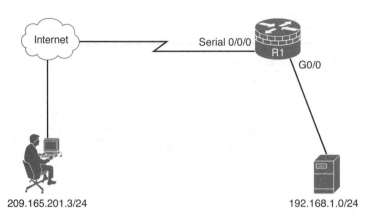

Figure 10-4 Network Topology for the ICMP Abuse ACL Example

`R1(config)# access-list 150 permit icmp any any echo-reply`	Define an extended ACL 150 permitting ICMP Echo Reply traffic.
`R1(config)# access-list 150 permit icmp any any source-quench`	Define an extended ACL 150 permitting ICMP Source Quench traffic.
`R1(config)# access-list 150 permit icmp any any ttl-exceeded`	Define an extended ACL 150 permitting ICMP time exceeded traffic.
`R1(config)# access-list 150 permit icmp any any unreachable`	Define an extended ACL 150 permitting ICMP destination unreachable traffic.
`R1(config)# access-list 150 deny icmp any any`	Define an extended ACL 150 denying all other ICMP traffic.
`R1(config)# access-list 150 permit ip any any`	Define an extended ACL 150 permitting all other traffic.
`R1(config)# interface Serial 0/0/0`	Enter the outside interface Serial 0/0/0 line configuration mode.
`R1(config-if)# ip access-group 150 in`	Apply the extended ACL 150 to the interface in an incoming direction.
`R1(config)# access-list 105 permit icmp 192.168.1.0 0.0.0.255 any echo`	Define an extended ACL 105 permitting ICMP Echo request traffic.
`R1(config)# access-list 105 permit icmp 192.168.1.0 0.0.0.255 any parameter-problem`	Define an extended ACL 105 permitting ICMP parameter problem traffic.
`R1(config)# access-list 105 permit icmp 192.168.1.0 0.0.0.255 any packet-too-big`	Define an extended ACL 105 permitting ICMP packet too big traffic.
`R1(config)# access-list 105 deny icmp any any`	Define an extended ACL 105 denying all other ICMP traffic.
`R1(config)# access-list 105 permit ip any any`	Define an extended ACL 105 permitting all other traffic.

| R1(config)# interface G0/0 | Enter the inside interface GigabitEthernet 0/0 line configuration mode. |
| R1(config-if)# ip access-group 105 in | Apply the extended ACL 105 to the interface in an incoming direction. |

Enhancing ACL Protection with Object Groups

Object grouping is used to bundle addresses and services inside ACLs. ACEs can then refer to the object group instead of having to enter an ACE for each object. Object groups provide a simple and intuitive mechanism for configuring and managing large ACLs that frequently change. It also reduces ACL configuration size and makes ACLs easier to manage. Cisco IOS routers support network and service object groups.

Network Object Groups

A network object group is a group of any of the following objects:

- Hostnames, IP addresses, or subnets

- Ranges of IP addresses

- Existing network object groups

| Router(config)# object-group network network-group-id | Create a network object group. |
| Router(config-network-group)# description description-text \| host {host-address \| host-name} \| network-address {/nn \| network-mask} \| range host-address1 host-address2 \| any \| group-object nested-object-group-name | From network object configuration mode, define the specifics of the network object.

NOTE: Options are optional. |

Here is a command syntax breakdown of the `object-group network` options:

Router(config-network-group)# description description-text	Add a description up to 200 characters.
Router(config-network-group)# host {host-address | host-name}	Identify a host IP address or name of the host.
Router(config-network-group)# network-address {/nn | network-mask}	Identify a subnet object. The default network mask is /32.
Router(config-network-group)# range host-address1 host-address2	Identify a range of host IP addresses.
Router(config-network-group)# any	Identify any host IP address in the range 0.0.0.0–255.255.255.255.

Router(config-network-group)# **group-object** *nested-object-group-name*	Specify a nested (child) object group to be included in the current (parent) object group.

Service Object Groups

A service object group is a group of any of the following objects:

- Top-level protocols (such as TCP, UDP, or ESP)

- Source and destination protocol ports (such as Telnet or SNMP)

- ICMP types (such as echo, echo-reply, or host-unreachable)

- Existing service object groups

Router(config)# **object-group service** *service-group-id*	Create a service object group.
Router(config-service-group)# **description** *description-text* | *protocol* {*protocol-number* | *protocol*} | [**tcp** | **udp** | **tcp-udp** [**source** {{ [**eq**] | **lt** | **gt**} *port1* | **range** *port1* *port2*}] [{ [**eq**] | **lt** | **gt**} *port1* | **range** *port1* *port2*}]] | **icmp** *icmp-type* | **group-object** *nested-object-group-name*	From service object configuration mode, define the specifics of the service object. **NOTE:** Options are optional.

Here is a command syntax breakdown of the **object-group service** options:

Router(config-network-group)# **description** *description-text*	Add a description up to 200 characters.
Router(config-service-group)# *protocol* { *protocol-number* | *protocol*}	Identify an IP protocol number or name.
Router(config-service-group)# **tcp** | **udp** | **tcp-udp** [**source** {{ [**eq**] | **lt** | **gt**} *port1* | **range** *port1* *port2*}] [{ [**eq**] | **lt** | **gt**} *port1* | **range** *port1* *port2*}]	Specify parameters for TCP, UDP, or both.
Router(config-service-group)# **icmp** *icmp-type*	Specify the decimal number or name of an ICMP type.
Router(config-service-group)# **group-object** *nested-object-group-name*	Specify a nested (child) object group to be included in the current (parent) object group.

TIP: To get help with configuration options, use the question mark (?) character.

NOTE: Object groups are not supported in standard ACLs or for use with IPsec but can be used in extended ACLs for quality of service (QoS) match criteria, Cisco IOS firewall features, Dynamic Host Configuration Protocol (DHCP), multicast traffic, and many other features that use extended ACLs.

NOTE: You cannot delete an object group that is being used within an ACL.

Using Object Groups in Extended ACLs

Object groups can be used in most extended ACL operations. On an IPv4 ACL, apply object groups by including the `object-group` command followed by the appropriate object group name:

`Router(config)# ip access-list`
`extended {access-list-number |`
`access-list-name}`
	Define a named ACL. The command can also be used to edit a numbered ACL.

`Router(config-ext-nacl)# permit`
`{protocol | object-group service-`
`object-group-name} [object-group`
`source-network-object-group-name]`
`[object-group destination-network-`
`object-group-name]`
	Define the `permit` statement.

`Router(config-ext-nacl)# deny`
`{protocol | object-group service-`
`object-group-name} [object-group`
`source-network-object-group-name]`
`[object-group destination-network-`
`object-group-name]`
	Define the `deny` statement.

TIP: To get help with configuration options, use the question mark (?) character.

NOTE: The preceding syntax has been simplified to highlight the use of object groups in an extended ACL.

NOTE: An ACE can contain a mixture of object groups and individual objects, such as specific protocols, networks, or services.

NOTE: After an object group is applied to an ACE, the object group cannot be deleted nor emptied. If additional objects are appended to the object group after it has been applied to the ACE, there is no need to reapply the object group to the ACE. The ACE automatically adjusts to include any newly appended objects.

Configuring Object Groups in ACLs Example

In this example, only the outside hosts are allowed web and email access to the two corporate servers. Network object groups are used to identify outside and inside groups of objects, and a service object group identifies the services available. The required access policy is defined using one ACE in an extended ACL.

NOTE: Without object groups, the following configuration would require multiple ACEs instead of one. Additional outside hosts, servers, or services can easily be added without altering the ACE in the ACL.

Figure 10-5 shows the network topology for the using object groups in ACLs example.

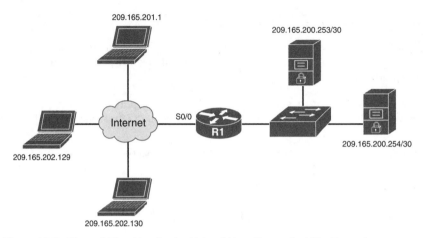

Figure 10-5   Network Topology for the Using Object Groups in ACLs Example

Create a network object group identifying the outside posts.

R1(config)# **object-group network OUTSIDE-HOSTS**	Create a network object group identifying the outside hosts.
R1(config-network-group)# **host 209.165.201.1**	Identify a specific host.
R1(config-network-group)# **range 209.165.202.129 209.165.202.130**	Identify a range of hosts.
R1(config-network-group)# **exit**	Return to global configuration mode.

NOTE: Alternatively, the range of hosts could have been identified using the network subnet 209.165.202.128 /30.

Create a network object group identifying the corporate servers:

R1(config)# **object-group network SERVERS**	Create a network object group identifying the inside servers.
R1(config-network-group)# **209.165.200.252 /30**	Identify a subnet of servers.
R1(config-network-group)# **exit**	Return to global configuration mode.

Create a service object group identifying web and email services:

R1(config)# **object-group service SERVER-APPS**	Create a service object group called SERVER-APPS.
R1(config-service-group)# **tcp www**	Specify HTTP traffic.
R1(config-service-group)# **tcp smtp**	Specify email traffic.
R1(config-service-group)# **exit**	Return to global configuration mode.

Create an extended ACL that combines all the defined objects into one ACE:

R1(config)# **ip access-list extended ACL-IN**	Define an extended ACL named ACL-IN.
R1(config-ext-nacl)# **permit object-group SERVER-APPS object-group OUTSIDE-HOSTS object-group SERVERS**	Permit HTTP and SMTP traffic from the outside hosts to the internal servers.
R1(config-ext-nacl)# **exit**	Return to global configuration mode.

Apply the extended ACL to the outside interface:

R1(config)# **interface serial 0/0**	Enter interface configuration mode for the serial interface.
R1(config-if)# **ip access-group ACL-IN in**	Apply the ACL incoming on the outside interface.

NOTE: To verify the object group, use the **show ip access-list** or **show object-group** commands.

ACLs in IPv6

Packet filtering in IPv6 is similar to packet filtering in IPv4. A strategy to prevent common attacks between the two protocol stacks, such as reconnaissance and spoofing attacks, typically starts with ACLs trying to match malicious traffic.

Mitigating IPv6 Attacks Using ACLs

IPv6 ACLs can help mitigate the following threats, among others:

- Header extension threats; for instance, amplification attacks based on Routing Header (RH)
- Threats based on misuse and abuse of ICMPv6
- Reconnaissance based on multicast IPv6 addresses
- Threats that exploit tunneling solutions such as those used in IPv6 migration environments

NOTE: Some threats require a combined approach using both protocol stacks, specifically those that exploit dual-stack environments.

IPv6 ACLs Implicit Entries

Each IPv6 ACL implicitly appends three lines: two permit entries to enable IPv6 neighbor discovery (ND) and the traditional rule that implements a default deny policy:

```
permit icmp any any nd-na
permit icmp any any nd-ns
deny ipv6 any any
```

CAUTION: It might be desirable to log all implicitly denied packets by explicitly configuring the `deny ipv6 any any log` ACE. A common mistake is to forget the two implicit ND ACEs, which result in ND issues. The solution is to explicitly add all three implicit lines, in the correct order, at the end of the ACL.

Filtering with IPv6 ACLs

`Router(config)# ipv6 access-list` `access-list-name`	Define an IPv6 ACL and enter IPv6 access list configuration mode. IPv6 ACL names cannot contain a space or quotation mark or begin with a numeral.
`Router(config-ipv6-acl)# permit` `protocol {source-ipv6-prefix/nn` `| any	host source-ipv6-address` `| auth} [operator [port-number]]` `{ destination-ipv6-prefix/nn	any` `| host destination-ipv6-address` `| auth} [operator [port-number]]` `[dest-option-type [doh-number |` `doh-type]] [dscp value] [flow-label` `value] [fragments] [log]` `[log-input] [mobility]` `[mobility-type [mh-number |` `mh-type]] [reflect name [timeout` `value]] [routing] [routing-type` `routing-number] [sequence value]` `[time-range name]`	Specify the permit condition for an IPv6 ACL.

`Router(config-ipv6-acl)# deny` `protocol { source-ipv6-prefix/nn` `| any	host source-ipv6-address |` `auth} [operator [port-number]]` `{ destination-ipv6-prefix/nn	any` `| host destination-ipv6-address |` `auth} [operator [port-number]]` `[dest-option-type [doh-number |` `doh-type]] [dscp value]` `[flow-label value] [fragments]` `[log] [log-input] [mobility]` `[mobility-type [mh-number |` `mh-type]] [routing] [routing-type` `routing-number] [sequence value]` `[time-range name] [undetermined-` `transport]`	Specify the deny condition for an IPv6 ACL.
`Router(config)# interface type` `number`	Specify the interface type and number and enter interface configuration mode.
`Router(config-if)# ipv6 traffic-` `filter access-listname { in	out}`	Apply the specified IPv6 access list to the interface.
`Router(config)# line vty 0 4`	Enter line vty mode.
`Router(config-line)# ipv6 access-` `class access-listname { in	out}`	Apply an IPv6 ACL to specify who can access the vty lines.

NOTE: See Cisco.com for more information on the IPv6 ACL parameters.

Configuring an IPv6 ACL Example

Figure 10-6 displays the network topology for the IPv6 ACL example.

Figure 10-6   Network Topology for the IPv6 ACL Example

`R1(config)# ipv6 access-list` `IPV6-ACL-IN`	Define an IPv6 ACL.
`R1(config-ipv6-acl)# remark Basic` `anti-spoofing ACL`	Document the ACL.
`R1(config-ipv6-acl)# deny` `2001:db8:2c80:1000::0/64 any`	Deny incoming traffic with the source address the same as the internal network address.
`R1(config-ipv6-acl)# permit any` `2001:db8:2c80:1000::1/128`	Permit traffic to reach the server.
`R1(config-ipv6-acl)# interface` `serial 0/0`	Enter interface configuration mode for the serial interface.
`R1(config-if)# ipv6 traffic-filter` `IPV6-ACL-IN in`	Apply the IPV6-ACL-IN ACL incoming on the outside interface.

CHAPTER 11

Configuring Zone-Based Firewalls

This chapter covers the following topics:

Firewall Fundamentals

- Types of Firewalls

Firewall Design

- Security Architectures

- Firewall Policies

- Firewall Rule Design Guidelines

- Cisco IOS Firewall Evolution

Cisco IOS Zone-Based Policy Firewall

- Cisco Common Classification Policy Language

- Zone-Based Policy Firewall Design Considerations

- Default Policies, Traffic Flows, and Zone Interaction

- Configuring an IOS ZPF

- Configuring an IOS ZPF Example

Firewall Fundamentals

A firewall is a software or hardware system that acts as a barrier between an internal (trusted) network and an external (untrusted) network.

Specifically, firewalls must

- Be resistant to attacks

- Be the only transit point between two networks

- Enforce the security policy access control

Types of Firewalls

There are different types of firewalls, including the following:

Network Address Translation (NAT) firewall	Hides inside (usually private) IP addresses by translating them to outside (usually public) IP addresses.

Packet-filtering firewall	Filters packets at Layer 3 (and 4). Filtering is stateless, which means it does not keep track of traffic flows. This also makes them vulnerable to spoofing attacks.
Stateful firewall	Performs the same function as packet-filtering firewalls but also keeps track of the state of network connections (that is, TCP and UDP sequence numbers) traveling across it.
Application gateway firewall (proxy firewall)	Typically a server filtering information at Layers 3, 4, 5, and 7. It can adapt if a protocol requires additional dynamic ports (for example, FTP, H.323).
Next Generation Firewall	This is the Cisco Adaptive Security Appliance (ASA) integrated with Sourcefire's FirePOWER services. The Cisco ASA with FirePOWER services is an adaptive, threat-focused firewall designed with advanced malware protection to provide defense before, during, and after attacks.

NOTE: Other firewall solutions exist, including host-based (server and personal) firewalls; Layer 2 transparent firewalls; and hybrid firewalls, which are a combination of the various firewall types.

NOTE: Stateful packet filtering is the focus of this chapter.

Firewall Design

Best practices for firewall design include the following:

- Position firewalls at security boundaries to separate security domains.

- Use firewalls as a key security control, but not the only one.

- Implement a variety of firewall technologies to provide comprehensive, multilayer access control.

- Ensure that physical access to the firewall is controlled.

- Regularly monitor firewall logs and implement an event management strategy.

- Practice change management for firewall rule creation and configuration changes.

Security Architectures

Modularize networks into security zones connecting similar endpoints and governed by the same network policy. Traffic is only allowed between zones if it complies with the policy enforced by these systems.

Common security zones include the following:

Inside	Also called the "private" network, this is a zone populated by inside hosts that must be protected from outside hosts. The traffic from the inside is typically permitted to traverse the firewall to the outside with little or no restrictions, whereas traffic returning from the outside that is associated with traffic originating from the inside is permitted to traverse from the untrusted interface to the trusted interface.
Outside	Also called the "public" network, this zone is not to be trusted as it connects to the outside of our network. Traffic originating from the outside is generally blocked entirely or very selectively permitted.
Demilitarized zone (DMZ)	This zone typically connects to servers providing access and services to outside users. For example, hosting a web server, email server, and more.
Self zone	This is a system-defined zone that does not have any interfaces as members. It applies to traffic directed to the router (e.g., SSH, HTTPS, SNMP) or traffic generated by the router (e.g., Syslog, SNMP traps).

Firewall Policies

Access rules are typically implemented using access control lists (ACLs). When defining access rules, you can use multiple criteria as a starting point:

Rules based on service control	Determines the types of Internet services that can be accessed, inbound or outbound. The firewall may filter traffic based on IP address and TCP port number. It may provide proxy software that receives and interprets each service request before passing it on. It may host the server software itself, such as a web or mail service.
Rules based on direction control	Determines the direction in which particular service requests may be initiated and allowed to flow through the firewall.

Rules based on user control	Controls access to a service according to which user is attempting to access it. This feature is usually applied to users inside the firewall perimeter (local users). It may also be applied to incoming traffic from external users. The latter requires some form of secure authentication technology, such as that provided in IP Security (IPsec).
Rules based on behavior control	Controls how particular services are used. For example, the firewall may filter email to eliminate spam, or it may enable external access to only a portion of the information on a local web server.

NOTE: Firewall rule design usually follows a hybrid approach, combining all these criteria and following a restrictive-access approach.

Firewall Rule Design Guidelines

When creating firewall rules, use the following guidelines:

- Use a restrictive approach for all interfaces and all directions of traffic to permit the required traffic flows and deny everything else.

- Be paranoid and assume that malicious traffic could come from any security domain, even the most trusted ones.

- Balance access control, performance, and rule maintenance. Specific and granular rules provide more control but also result in longer rule sets and increased change management and maintenance challenges.

- Exercise care with the use of **any** keywords matching sources, destinations, and ports because they may allow unwanted traffic.

- For a given access requirement, more specific rules should be at the top, and more generic rules should be at the bottom. The top-down processing order demands this approach to prevent shadow rules when creating exceptions to a given access policy.

- Filtering impossible packets is a common practice. An example is antispoofing rules that are aimed at blocking private IPv4 address spaces in the source address of inbound Internet packets.

- Auditing and change management are crucial. Obsolete rules tend to clutter the rule set and cause breaches to the access policy.

Cisco IOS Firewall Evolution

Firewall technology has evolved as follows:

- Packet filtering using ACLs

- Context-Based Access Control (CBAC) (also referred to as Classic Firewall)

- Cisco IOS Zone-Based Policy Firewall (ZPF)

NOTE: The focus of this chapter is on ZPF.

Cisco IOS Zone-Based Policy Firewall

A ZPF assigns interfaces to zones. An inspection policy is applied to traffic moving between the zones using the Cisco Common Classification Policy Language (C3PL). Zones establish the security borders where traffic is subjected to policy restrictions as it crosses to another region of your network.

NOTE: The C3PL structure is similar to the modular quality of service (QoS) CLI (MQC) structure.

Cisco Common Classification Policy Language

To create firewall policies, complete the following tasks:

Task	Specifics
Define match criteria (class map).	Contains multiple `match` statements to filter traffic based on an access group (ACL), Layer 4 protocol (for example, TCP, UDP, and ICMP), Layer 7 protocol (HTTP, SMTP, FTP), or another nested class map.
Associate actions to the match criteria (policy map).	Contains class maps that are evaluated in order of configuration and assigned actions of inspect, permit, drop, or drop and log. All unclassified traffic matches the default class, known as class-default, with a default action to drop traffic.
Attach the policy map to a zone pair (service policy).	Identify the source and destination zone pair and assign a service policy to it.

ZPF Design Considerations

- The default policy between zones is to deny all.
- Interfaces belonging to the same zone permit access between them.
- A zone pair permits a unidirectional firewall policy between a source and destination zone.
- An interface can be assigned to one zone only.
- An interface pair can be assigned only one policy.

Default Policies, Traffic Flows, and Zone Interaction

The following rules govern interface behavior for the traffic moving between zone member interfaces:

- A zone must be configured before you can assign interfaces to the zone.

- You can assign an interface to only one security zone.

- All active interfaces should be a member of a zone.

- By default, traffic is implicitly allowed to flow between interfaces in the same zone.

- Traffic cannot flow between a zone member interface and any interface that is not a zone member. To permit traffic to and from a zone member interface, a policy allowing or inspecting traffic must be configured between that zone and any other zone.

- You can apply the following actions between two zones.

Pass	Traffic is allowed to flow. Analogous to the ACL `permit` statement.
Drop	Traffic is not allowed to flow. Analogous to the ACL `deny` statements. A `log` option is available to log rejected packets.
Inspect	Performs stateful packet inspection (SPI).

NOTE: Interfaces that have not been assigned to a zone function as classical router ports and might still use classical stateful inspection (CBAC) configuration.

NOTE: If you do not want an interface to be part of the ZPF, assign it to a "pass all" policy between it and any other target zone.

The following rules govern interface behavior when the self zone (that is, to/from the router) is involved in the traffic flow:

- All traffic to and from a given interface is implicitly blocked when the interface is assigned to a zone, except traffic to or from other interfaces in the same zone and traffic to any interface on the router.

- All the IP interfaces on the router are automatically made part of the self zone when a ZPF is configured. The self zone is the only exception to the default deny-all policy. All traffic to any router interface is allowed until traffic is explicitly denied.

- The only exception to the deny-by-default approach is the traffic to and from the router itself. This traffic is permitted by default. You can configure an explicit policy to restrict such traffic.

NOTE: Interface ACLs are still relevant and are applied before a ZPF when they are applied inbound. Interface ACLs are applied after a ZPF when they are applied outbound.

Configuring an IOS ZPF

To configure basic interzone policies using the IOS command-line interface (CLI), follow these steps:

1. Create security zones.

2. Create a Layer 3/4 or Layer 7 class map and match traffic.

3. Create the policy map, identify the class map, and associate an action.

4. Identify zone pairs and assign a service policy.

5. Assign interfaces to zones.

NOTE: LAN and WAN configurations must be completed before configuring the ZPF.

Create the security zones:

`Router(config)# zone security` `zone-name`	Create a security zone.

Create a Layer 3 and Layer 4 inspection type class map:

`Router(config)# class-map type` `inspect {match-any	match-all}` `class-map-name`	Create a Layer 3 and Layer 4 inspect type class map.
`Router(config-cmap)# match` `access-group {access-group	name` `access-group-name}`	Configure the match criteria on the basis of a preconfigured ACL.
`Router(config-cmap)# match` `protocol protocol`	Configure the match criteria on the basis of a specified protocol.
`Router(config-cmap)# match` `service {any	text-chat}`	Configure the match criteria for any supported instant messenger protocol.
`Router(config-cmap)# match` `class-map class-map-name`	Nest traffic classes within one another.

NOTE: You can also use the `description` command to document the zone.

(Optionally) Create a Layer 7 inspect type class map:

`Router(config)# class-map type`
`inspect protocol-name { match-any |`
`match-all} class-map-name`
	Create a Layer 7 (application-specific) inspect type class map.
	
	NOTE: Command parameters will vary depending on the protocol.

`Router(config-cmap)# match` `protocol-parameters`	**NOTE:** The `match` parameters will vary depending on the protocol.

Configure an action using a policy map:

`Router(config)# policy-map type inspect` *policy-map-name*	Create a Layer 3 and Layer 4 inspect type policy map.
`Router(config-pmap)# class type inspect` *class-map-name*	Identify the class map. **NOTE:** You can also configure `class class-default`.
`Router(config-pmap-c)# {drop	inspect	pass}`	Assign an action. **NOTE:** `drop` denies the traffic matching the traffic class. **NOTE:** `inspect` permits and statefully tracks the sessions of the traffic class. **NOTE:** `pass` statelessly permits packets between zones.

Identify zone pairs and assign a service policy:

`Router(config)# zone-pair security` *zone-pair-name* `source {`*source-zone-name* `| self	default}`  `destination {`*destination-zone-name* `| self	default}`	Create a zone pair that permits a unidirectional firewall policy between a pair of security zones. **NOTE:** `self` specifies the system-defined zone. Indicates whether traffic will be going to or from a router. **NOTE:** `default` specifies the name of the default security zone. Interfaces without configured zones belong to the default zone.
`Router(config-sec-zone-pair)# service-policy type inspect` *policy-map-name*	Assign the service policy to the zone pair.

Assign interfaces to zones:

`Router(config)# interface` *type number*	Specify the interface type and number.
`Router(config-if)# zone-member security` *zone-name*	Attach the interface to the specified security zone.

Configuring an IOS ZPF Example

Figure 11-1 displays the network topology for the IOS ZPF example.

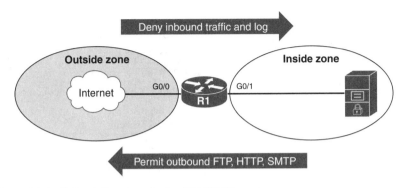

Figure 11-1   Network Topology for the IOS ZPF Example

R1(config)# **zone security PRIVATE**	Create the inside security zone called PRIVATE.
R1(config-sec-zone)# **exit**	Return to global configuration mode.
R1(config)# **zone security INTERNET**	Create the inside security zone called INTERNET.
R1(config-sec-zone)# **exit**	Return to global config mode.
R1(config)# **class-map type inspect match-any TRAFFIC**	Create a class map called TRAFFIC.
R1(config-cmap)# **match protocol http**	Match HTTP services.
R1(config-cmap)# **match protocol smtp**	Match SMTP services.
R1(config-cmap)# **match protocol ftp**	Match FTP services.
R1(config-cmap)# **exit**	Return to global configuration mode.
R1(config)# **policy-map type inspect MY-POLICY**	Create a service policy called MY-POLICY.
R1(config-pmap)# **class type inspect TRAFFIC**	Identify the class map TRAFFIC.
R1(config-pmap-c)# **inspect**	Inspect all traffic.
R1(config-pmap-c)# **exit**	Return to policy-map configuration mode.
R1(config-pmap)# **exit**	Return to global configuration mode.
R1(config)# **zone-pair security IN-TO-OUT source PRIVATE destination INTERNET**	Create a zone pair identifying the source (PRIVATE) and destination (INTERNET) zones.
Router(config-sec-zone-pair)# **service-policy type inspect MY-POLICY**	Assign the service policy MY-POLICY for all traffic travelling from the source to the destination.
R1(config-sec-zone-pair)# **exit**	Return to global configuration mode.

R1(config)# **int G0/0**	Enter interface G0/0 configuration mode.
R1(config-if)# **zone-member security INTERNET**	Assign the interface to be a member of the INTERNET zone.
R1(config-if)# **exit**	Return to global configuration mode.
R1(config)# **int G0/1**	Enter interface G0/1 configuration mode.
R1(config-if)# **zone-member security PRIVATE**	Assign the interface to be a member of the PRIVATE zone.

NOTE: Use the **show zone security** and the **show zone-pair security** commands to verify the configuration.

CHAPTER 12

Configuring Cisco IOS IPS

This chapter covers the following topics:

IDS and IPS Fundamentals

- Types of IDS and IPS Sensors
- Types of Signatures
- Types of Alarms

Intrusion Prevention Technologies

- IPS Attack Responses
- IPS Anti-Evasion Techniques
- Managing Signatures
- Cisco IOS IPS Signature Files
- Implementing Alarms in Signatures
- IOS IPS Severity Levels
- Event Monitoring and Management
- IPS Recommended Practices

Configuring IOS IPS

- Creating an IOS IPS Rule and Specifying the IPS Signature File Location
- Tuning Signatures per Category
- Configuring IOS IPS Example

IDS and IPS Fundamentals

An intrusion detection system (IDS) sensor captures packets in real time, processes them, and can respond to threats, but it works on copies of data traffic to detect suspicious activity by using signatures. An IDS allows malicious traffic to pass before it can respond.

An intrusion prevention system (IPS) sensor works in line in the data stream to provide protection from malicious attacks in real time. An IPS responds immediately and does not allow malicious traffic to pass.

NOTE: This chapter focuses on IPS.

Types of IPS Sensors

IPS sensors can be deployed as follows:

Cisco IPS 4300 Sensor	As a dedicated IPS appliance available in multiple form factors
Cisco FirePower 7000 and 80000 Series Appliances	A dedicated high-performance platform for the Cisco FirePOWER next-generation intrusion prevention system (NGIPS) solution
Network modules	As a network module installed in an Integrated Services Router (ISR), an Adaptive Security Appliance (ASA), or a high-end Catalyst switch
Cisco IOS IPS	Integrated in the IOS of an ISR and some Layer 3 switches
Virtual Next-Generation IPS (NGIPSv) for VMware	Virtualized offering of Cisco FirePOWER NGIPS solution

Types of Signatures

IDS and IPS technologies use signatures to detect the following general patterns of misuse:

Atomic pattern	An attempt is made to access a specific port on a specific host, and malicious content is contained in a single packet.
Composite pattern	A sequence of operations that are distributed across multiple hosts over an arbitrary period (event horizon).

Types of Alarms

Attacks can generate the following four types of alarms:

True positive	Occurs when an IDS or IPS signature is correctly fired and an alarm is generated when offending traffic is detected
True negative	Occurs when the sensor does not fire an alarm when it captures and analyzes network traffic that is normal
False positive	Alarm that is triggered by normal traffic or a benign action
False negative	Occurs when an alarm is not triggered when offending traffic is detected

NOTE: True positives and true negatives are expected IDS and IPS alarms.

CAUTION: False positives must be tuned; false negatives must be corrected.

Intrusion Prevention Technologies

Multiple detection technologies are typically used to provide an effective intrusion detection architecture:

Signature-based IPS	■ Signatures are a set of rules installed on an IPS sensor. ■ As sensors scan network packets, they use signatures to detect known attacks and respond with predefined actions. ■ Sensors can modify existing signatures and define new ones.
Policy-based IPS	■ Policies are created and configured on the IPS sensor based on the network security policy. ■ Any traffic detected outside the policy will generate an alarm and/or will be dropped.
Anomaly-based IPS (profile-based detection)	■ Sensors generally look for network traffic that deviates from the norm. ■ Statistical baselining is when normal behavior is defined based on traffic patterns, traffic and protocol mix, traffic volumes, and other criteria. ■ Protocol anomaly baselining focuses on traffic that deviates from protocol standards.
Reputation-based IPS	■ Technique uses reputation analysis for various traffic descriptors, such as IP addresses, URLs, Domain Name System (DNS) domains, and others. ■ This usually translates into reputation filters that round up a signature-based system by filtering known malicious sources, destinations, or application components. ■ The approach generally requires communication between the sensor and the source of the reputation information. ■ Sources can be local to the device, enterprise knowledge, and even global knowledge.

NOTE: There are advantages and disadvantages to each intrusion detection technique. It is recommended to strike a balance between these methods and combine them to improve the accuracy, sensitivity, relevancy, and precision of your IPS.

IPS Attack Responses

When an IPS sensor detects malicious activity, it can choose from any or all of the following actions:

Deny attacker inline	■ Action terminates the current packet and future packets from the attacker address for a specified period. ■ The sensor maintains a list of the attackers currently being denied by the system, and these entries can be manually removed from the list or wait for the sliding timer to expire.
Deny connection inline	■ Action terminates the current packet and future packets on this TCP flow.
Deny packet inline	■ Action terminates the packet.
Log attacker packets	■ Action starts IP logging on packets that contain the attacker address and sends an alert to the Event Store, even if the Produce Alert action is not selected.
Log pair packets	■ Action starts IP logging on packets that contain the attacker and victim address pair and sends an alert to the Event Store, even if the Produce Alert action is not selected.
Log victim packets	■ Action starts IP logging on packets that contain the victim address and sends an alert to the Event Store, even if the Produce Alert action is not selected.
Produce alert	■ Action writes the event to the Event Store as an alert.
Produce verbose alert	■ Action includes an encoded dump of the offending packet in the alert and is written to the Event Store.
Request block connection	■ Action sends a request to a blocking device to block this connection.
Request block host	■ Action sends a request to a blocking device to block this attacker host.
Request SNMP trap	■ Action sends a Simple Network Management Protocol (SNMP) notification and an alert to the Event Store, even if the Produce Alert action is not selected.
Reset TCP connection	■ Action sends TCP resets to hijack and terminate the TCP flow.

NOTE: You can use the reset TCP connection action with deny packet and deny connection actions. However, deny packet and deny flow actions do not automatically cause TCP reset actions to occur.

NOTE: Cisco IOS IPS does not support all of these actions.

IPS Anti-Evasion Techniques

Attackers use multiple IPS evasion techniques to allow them to deploy exploits using a stealth approach that often renders IPS sensors unable to detect and prevent intrusion.

Evasion Method	Evasion Description	Anti-Evasion Feature
Traffic fragmentation	Attacker fragments malicious traffic, hoping to avoid detection or filtering by confusing the network IPS sensor reassembly methods, bypassing the network IPS sensor if it does not perform any reassembly at all, or reordering split data if the network IPS sensor does not correctly order it in the reassembly process.	Complete session reassembly in string and service engines
Traffic substitution and insertion	Attacker substitutes payload data with other data in a different format but with the same meaning.	Data normalization (de-obfuscation) in service engines
Protocol-level misinterpretation	Attacker causes the IPS sensor to misinterpret the end-to-end meaning of network protocols. Consequently, the sensor either ignores traffic that should not be ignored or vice versa.	IP Time to Live (TTL) analysis TCP checksum validation
Timing Attacks	Attacker evades detection of correlating signatures by performing their actions more slowly, to not exceed the event horizon.	Increase configurable intervals or use third-party for correlation
Encryption and tunneling	Attacker has already established a secure session with the target network or host. The sensor captures the encrypted data but is unable to decrypt it and cannot perform meaningful analysis.	Generic routing encryption (GRE) tunnel inspection
IPS resource exhaustion	Attacker uses specialized tools to create a tremendous number of alarms that consume the resources of the IPS device and prevent attacks from being logged.	Smart dynamic event summarization

NOTE: The mitigation techniques vary depending on the IPS sensor.

Managing Signatures

Cisco IPS relies on signature micro-engines to support IPS signatures. All the signatures in a signature micro-engine are scanned in parallel, which increases efficiency and results in higher throughput. Each signature micro-engine does the following:

- Categorizes a group of signatures with a set of acceptable ranges or sets of values
- Uses router memory to compile, load, and merge signatures

Signature Micro-Engine	Description
ATOMIC-IP Engine	Signatures that examine simple packets, such as Internet Control Message Protocol (ICMP) and User Datagram Protocol (UDP). The ATOMIC engine does not store persistent protocol-based state data across packets; instead, it can trigger a signature from the analysis of the header (Layers 3 and 4) of a single packet.
Service engines	Signatures that examine the many services that are attacked.
STRING engines	STRING engines are generic pattern-matching inspection engines for ICMP, TCP, and UDP protocol packets. They use a regular expression engine that can combine multiple patterns into a single pattern-matching table, allowing for a single search through the data.
MULTI-STRING engine	Inspects Layer 4 protocol packets in a flexible pattern-matching manner.
Other	Internal engine to handle miscellaneous signatures.

Cisco IOS IPS Signature Files

The Cisco IOS IPS signature files must be downloaded from Cisco.com (CCO login required). Two versions of signature files are available, and the file required depends on whether IPS is configured using the command-line interface (CLI) or using Cisco Configuration Professional (CCP). Specifically, if configuring IPS using

- **CLI:** Download IOS-S*xxx*-CLI.pkg (*xxx* = signature version number).
- **CCP:** Download sigv5-SDM-S*xxx*.zip.

You must also download the realm-cisco.pub.key.txt file because it must be used to generate an RSA crypto key and load the public signature on the router for signature decryption.

Implementing Alarms in Signatures

Consider the following when implementing signatures:

- The level assigned to the signature determines the alarm severity level.
- The alarm severity levels are informational, low, medium, and high.

- Make the severity level of the signature the same as the severity level of the alarm.

- Tune your signatures to recognize intrusion patterns out of character with your network traffic patterns.

IOS IPS Severity Levels

Informational	Activity that triggers the signature is not considered an immediate threat, but the information provided is useful information.
Low	Abnormal network activity is detected that could be perceived as malicious, but an immediate threat is not likely.
Medium	Abnormal network activity is detected that could be perceived as malicious, and an immediate threat is likely.
High	Attacks used to gain access or cause a denial-of-service (DoS) attack are detected, and an immediate threat is extremely likely.

Event Monitoring and Management

Consider the following when implementing event monitoring and management:

- The two key functions of event monitoring and management are to provide real-time event monitoring and management and for analysis based on archived information (reporting).

- Multiple protocols are available for alarm generation, including Security Device Event Exchange (SDEE), syslog, and SNMP.

- Event monitoring and management can be hosted on a single server or on separate servers for larger deployments.

- Archiving is important for forensics and compliance.

- A hierarchical approach of local, enterprise, and global event management is recommended.

NOTE: SDEE is an application-level communication protocol used to exchange IPS messages between IPS clients and IPS servers. SDEE is always running, but it does not receive and process events from IPS unless SDEE notification is enabled. If SDEE notification is not enabled and a client sends a request, SDEE responds with a fault response message, indicating that notification is not enabled.

Local correlation	Device-level correlation is accomplished with products such as CCP, IPS Device Manager, or IPS Manager Express.
Enterprise intelligence	Gathered using Cisco Security Manager (CSM). Third-party Security Information and Event Management (SIEM) systems (for example, ArcSight, netForensics, Splunk) can be used for more specialized event management and forensics capabilities.

Global intelligence	Global security intelligence correlation is the responsibility of the Cisco Security Intelligence Operations (SIO) cloud-based service that connects global threat information, reputation-based services, and sophisticated analysis to Cisco network security devices to provide stronger protection with faster response times.

For event management, you can use the SDEE protocol and a syslog-based approach to send Cisco IOS IPS alerts. The sensor generates an alarm when an enabled signature is triggered. Alarms are stored on the sensor. A host can pull the alarms from the sensor using SDEE. Pulling alarms from a sensor allows multiple hosts to subscribe to the event "feed" to allow a host or hosts to subscribe on an as-needed basis.

IPS Recommended Practices

- Use a combination of detection technologies.
- Take advantage of multiple form factors to deploy a distributed and cost-effective IPS architecture.
- Plan the IPS architecture carefully, using a "places in the network" approach and considering the different levels of risk for the different assets you are trying to protect.
- Enable anti-evasion techniques.
- Take advantage of local, enterprise, and global correlation.
- Use a risk-based approach to improve accuracy and simplify management.
- When deploying a large number of sensors, automatically update signature packs instead of manually upgrading every sensor.
- Place the signature packs on a dedicated FTP server within the management network.
- Tune the IPS architecture on a regular basis.

NOTE: IPS capabilities vary depending on the IPS form factor. Refer to the proper documentation for each IPS sensor product for specific platform details.

Configuring IOS IPS

To configure basic IPS using the IOS CLI, complete these steps:

1. Create an IOS IPS configuration directory in flash.
2. Copy the Cisco IOS IPS signature package to flash.
3. Configure an IOS IPS crypto key.
4. Create an IPS rule and specify the location of the IPS signature file.
5. Enable SDEE and logging event notification.
6. Modify signature categories.
7. Assign the IPS rule to an interface.

NOTE: Download the latest signature package (IOS-S*xxx*-CLI.pkg) and crypto file (realm-cisco.pub.key.txt), the latter of which contains the public key from Cisco.com (CCO login is required).

Create an IOS IPS directory in flash:

Router# **mkdir flash:***dir-name*	Create a directory in flash. **NOTE:** You could specify other locations.

Copy the Cisco IOS IPS signature package to flash using one of the following methods:

Router# **copy ftp:**//*myuser:my-pass@* *ftp-server*/**IOS-S***xxx***-CLI.pkg** **flash:***dir-name* **idconf**	Copy from an FTP server to the directory in flash.
Router# **copy tftp:**//*tftp-server*/ **IOS-S***xxx***-CLI. pkg flash:***dir-name* **idconf**	Copy from a TFTP server to the directory in flash.
Router# **copy usbflash0:/IOS-S***xxx***-CLI. pkg flash:***dir-name* **idconf**	Copy from the USB drive to the directory in flash.

NOTE: Add the **idconf** parameter at the end to initiate the compiling process after the copy is complete.

NOTE: The preceding list shows only common examples. Other methods are available.

To create the RSA crypto key, copy and paste the following:

- Open the **realm-cisco.pub.key.txt** text file and select the entire contents.
- Copy the text and paste it in global configuration mode.

NOTE: The router executes all the commands from the text file and creates the RSA key. Use the **show running-config | section crypto key pubkey-chain rsa** command to verify the configuration.

Creating an IOS IPS Rule and Specifying the IPS Signature File Location

Router(config)# **ip ips name** *ips-name* [**list** *acl*]	Create an IPS rule name. **list** *acl* is optional and specifies an extended or standard ACL to filter the traffic that will be scanned. All traffic that is permitted by the ACL is subject to inspection by the IPS. Traffic that is denied by the ACL is not inspected by the IPS.

Router(config)# `ip ips config location flash:`*dirname*	Specify the IPS signature file location. The IPS signature file location is used to restore the IPS configuration in cases such as router reboots or IPS becoming disabled or reenabled. Files, such as signature definitions, signature-type definitions, and signature category information, are written in Extensible Markup Language (XML) format, compressed, and saved to the specified IPS signature location.

NOTE: The IPS does not load the signatures until the rule is applied to an interface.

Enable SDEE and logging event notification:

Router(config)# `ip http server`	Enable the HTTP server (required).
Router(config)# `ip ips notify sdee`	Enable IPS SDEE event notification.
Router(config)# `ip ips notify log`	Enable logging.

Tuning Signatures per Category

Router memory and resource constraints prevent a router from loading all Cisco IOS IPS signatures. Therefore, only load a selected set of signatures defined by the categories.

TIP: The larger the number of signatures, the larger the amount of memory consumed. Therefore, retire signatures that are irrelevant to your network to save router memory.

All signatures are pregrouped into categories; the categories are hierarchical. An individual signature can belong to more than one category. Top-level categories help to define general types of signatures.

TIP: Because the categories are applied in a top-down order, you should first retire all signatures, followed by unretiring specific categories.

Router(config)# `ip ips signature-category`	Enter IPS category configuration mode to tune Cisco IOS IPS signature parameters on the basis of a signature category.
Router(config-ips-category)# `category {all	ios ips [basic	advanced] }`	Specify the signature category to change, and enter IPS category action mode. **NOTE:** Many other categories and subcategories exist (for example, `attack, dos, ddos email, p2p`). For a list of supported top-level categories, use the router CLI help (?). **NOTE:** IOS IPS processes `category` commands in the order listed in the configuration.

`Router(config-ips-category-action)#` **`retired {false	true}`**	Specify whether a signature or signature category definition should be saved in the router memory. `false` unretires all signatures within a given category. `true` retires all signatures within a given category. **NOTE:** Retired signatures are not scanned by Cisco IOS IPS and therefore do not fire alarms. **NOTE:** To return to the default action, use the `no retired` command.
`Router(config-ips-category-action)#` **`event-action`** *action*	Change router actions for a specified signature category. Actions include the following: ■ `deny-attacker-inline` ■ `deny-connection-inline` ■ `deny-packet-inline` ■ `produce-alert` ■ `reset-tcp-connection` **NOTE:** Event actions associated with a category can be entered separately or on a single line. **NOTE:** To verify the event-action configuration, use the `show ip ips signatures` command.
`Router(config-ips-category-action)#` **`alert-severity {high	medium |`** **`low	informational}`**	(Optional) Change the alert severity rating for a given signature or signature category. **NOTE:** To return to the default action, use the no `alert-severity` command.
`Router(config-ips-category-action)#` **`fidelity-rating`** *rating*	(Optional) Change the signature fidelity rating for a signature given category.
`Router(config-ips-category-action)#` **`exit`**	Return to IPS category mode.

`Router(config-ips-category)# exit`
`Do you want to accept these`
`changes? [confirm]`
	After signature-based changes are complete, you are prompted to confirm whether the changes are acceptable.
	
	Confirming the changes instructs IOS IPS to compile the changes for the signature and modify memory structures to reflect the change and save the changes to the IPS location specified.

CAUTION: Do not unretire the `all` category because it contains all the signatures in a signature release. The IOS IPS cannot compile and use all the signatures at one time; if it were to do so, it would run out of memory.

NOTE: Use the `show ip ips` command to display IPS configuration information. Use the `show ip ips signature-category` [config] command to display IPS signature parameters by signature category.

Apply the IPS rule to a desired interface and specify the direction:

`Router(config-if)# ip ips` `ips-name {in	out}`	Apply the IPS rule to an interface. The router loads the signatures and builds the signature engines when IPS is applied to the first interface: `in` inspects only incoming traffic. `out` inspects only outgoing traffic. **NOTE:** The command can be repeated to configure incoming and outgoing traffic.

NOTE: The router prompt disappears while the signatures are loading and the signature engines are building. It reappears after these tasks are complete.

NOTE: Building the signature engine can take several minutes depending on the router platform and how many signatures are being loaded. It is recommended that you enable logging messages so you can monitor the engine building status.

NOTE: The process creates six files in the IPS directory: router-sigdef-default. xml, which contains all the factory default signature definitions; router-sigdef-delta. xml, which contains signature definitions that have been changed from the default; router-sigdef-typedef.xml, which is a file that has all the signature parameter definitions; router-sigdef-category.xml, which has all the signature category information, such as category ios_ips basic and advanced; router-seap-delta.xml, which contains changes made to the default Signature Event Action Processor (SEAP) parameters; and router-seap-typedef.xml, which contains all of the SEAP parameter definitions.

(Maintenance) To periodically update the signature package after the IPS has been configured, use this command:

Router# `copy url idconf`	Load a signature package to the identified IPS directory. `url` specifies the location from which the router loads the signature file (for example, FTP, TFTP, USB, rcp).

NOTE: Use the `clear ip ips configuration` to remove all IPS configuration entries and release dynamic resources. Use the `clear ip ips statistics` command to reset statistics on packets analyzed and alarms sent.

NOTE: Configure automatic signature updates using the `ip ips auto-update` command. Updates can be configured to run on the basis of a preset time.

Configuring IOS IPS Example

1. Create an IOS IPS configuration directory called **IPS-DIR** in flash.

2. Copy the Cisco IOS IPS signature package from a USB drive to flash.

3. Configure an IOS IPS crypto key.

4. Create an IPS rule called **MY-IPS** and specify the location of the IPS file.

5. Enable SDEE event notification.

6. Retire the **all** signature category and then unretire the **ios-basic** and the **ids_evasion** categories. Change the **ids_evasion** default event notification.

7. Assign the IPS rule to inspect inbound traffic on the Gigabit Ethernet 0/0 interface.

Figure 12-1 shows the network topology for the IOS IPS example.

Figure 12-1 Network Topology for the IOS IPS Example

R1# `mkdir IPS-DIR` Create directory filename [IPS-DIR]? Created dir flash:/IPS-DIR	Create a directory to store the IPS signature file.
R1# `copy usbflash0:/IOS-S614-CLI.pkg flash:/` `IPS-DIR idconf` Destination filename [/IPS-DIR/IOS-S614-CLI.pkg]? Copy in progress... CCCCCCCCCCCCCCCCCCCCCCCCCCCCCC CCCCCCCCCCCCCCC CCCCCCCCCCCCCCCCCCCCCCCCCC \<Output omitted\> 14219010 bytes copied in 35.528 secs (400220 bytes/sec)R1#	Copy the signature from the USB drive to the IPS-DIR directory.

Configure the IOS IPS RSA crypto key. Copy the contents of the realm-cisco.pub.key. txt file to global configuration.

Create an IOS IPS rule and specify the IPS signature file location:

R1(config)# `ip ips name MY-IPS`	Create an IPS rule name.
R1(config)# `ip ips config location flash:IPS-DIR`	Specify the IPS signature file location.
R1(config)# `ip http server`	Enable the HTTP server service.
R1(config)# `ip ips notify sdee`	Send events to SDEE.
R1(config)# `ip ips signature-category`	Enter IPS category configuration mode.
R1(config-ips-category)# `category all`	Change signature parameters for the all category.
R1(config-ips-category-action)# `retired true`	Retire the all category.
R1(config-ips-category-action)# `exit`	Return to IPS category configuration mode.
R1(config-ips-category)# `category ios_ips basic`	Change signature parameters for the ios_ips basic category.
R1(config-ips-category-action)# `retired false`	Unretire the signatures.
R1(config-ips-category-action)# `exit`	Return to IPS category configuration mode.
R1(config-ips-category)# `category attack ids_evasion`	Change signature parameters for the ids_evasion category.
R1(config-ips-category-action)# `event-action produce-alert`	Write the event to the Event Store as an alert.
R1(config-ips-category-action)# `event-action deny-packet-inline`	Terminate the packet.
R1(config-ips-category-action)# `event-action reset-tcp-connection`	Terminate the TCP flow.
R1(config-ips-category-action)# `end` Do you want to accept these changes? [confirm] **y**	Exit IPS configuration mode and confirm the signature changes.
R1(config-ips-category-action)# `interface G0/0`	Move to interface configuration mode.
R1(config-if)# `ip ips MY-IPS in`*Jan 14 17:16:02.319: %IPS-6-ENGINE_ BUILDS_STARTED: 12:16:02 Ne <output omitted>	Apply the IPS rule MY-IPS to inbound traffic on the Gigabit Ethernet 0/0 interface. **NOTE:** You could also apply the MY-IPS IPS rule inbound on the inside interface.

NOTE: The preceding is a simple example for implementing IOS IPS.

CHAPTER 13

VPNs and Cryptology

This chapter covers the following topics:

Virtual Private Networks

- VPN Deployment Modes

Cryptology = Cryptography + Cryptanalysis

- Historical Cryptographic Ciphers

- Modern Substitution Ciphers

- Encryption Algorithms

- Cryptanalysis

Cryptographic Processes in VPNs

- Classes of Encryption Algorithms

- Symmetric Encryption Algorithms

- Asymmetric Encryption Algorithm

- Choosing an Encryption Algorithm

- Choosing an Adequate Key Space

Cryptographic Hashes

- Well-Known Hashing Algorithms

- Hash-Based Message Authentication Code

Digital Signatures

Virtual Private Networks

A virtual private network (VPN) is as an encrypted connection between private networks over a public network such as the Internet.

VPN solutions may be classified based on the following:

Deployment mode	■ Site-to-site VPN
	■ Remote-access VPN

OSI layer	<ul><li>Layer 2 VPN (legacy protocols such as Frame Relay or ATM)</li><li>Layer 2 VPN (Multiprotocol Label Switching [MPLS] VPN)</li><li>Layer 3 VPN (IP Security [IPsec] and Multiprotocol Label Switching [MPLS] Layer 3 VPN)</li><li>Layer 7 VPN (Secure Sockets Layer [SSL] VPN)</li></ul>
Underlying technology	<ul><li>IPsec VPN</li><li>SSL VPN</li><li>MPLS VPN</li><li>Other Layer 2 technologies such as Frame Relay or ATM</li><li>Hybrid VPNs combining multiple technologies</li></ul>

NOTE: This book focuses on site-to-site IPsec VPNs using Cisco IOS Integrated Services Routers (ISR) and on remote-access SSL VPNs using the Adaptive Security Appliance (ASA).

VPN Deployment Modes

Site-to-site VPNs	<ul><li>Connects entire networks to each other.</li><li>VPN hosts do not require VPN client software.</li><li>VPNs send and receive normal TCP/IP traffic through a VPN "gateway" such as a Cisco ISR or an ASA.</li><li>The VPN gateway is responsible for encapsulating and encrypting outbound traffic over the Internet to a peer VPN gateway.</li><li>Upon receipt, the peer VPN gateway decrypts the content and relays the packet toward the target host inside its private network.</li></ul>
Remote-access VPNs	<ul><li>VPN securely connects telecommuters, mobile users, and extranet users over the Internet.</li><li>Hosts may require a preinstalled VPN client (for example, Cisco VPN Client or Cisco AnyConnect) or access the target site using Hypertext Transfer Protocol Secure (HTTPS).</li><li>The client encapsulates and encrypts that traffic and sends it over the Internet to the target VPN gateway.</li><li>The VPN gateway behaves as it does for site-to-site VPNs.</li></ul>

NOTE: VPNs implement cryptographic protocols to secure the VPN network traffic.

Cryptology = Cryptography + Cryptanalysis

Cryptology is the science of creating and breaking secret codes. It consists of the following:

Cryptography	■ The science of creating secret codes to ensure confidentiality
	■ Involves encryption and hashing, which provides authentication/integrity
Cryptanalysis	■ The science of breaking (cracking) secret codes

Historical Cryptographic Ciphers

Cryptography uses ciphers to secure data. A cipher is an algorithm for performing encryption and decryption using a series of well-defined steps that are followed as a procedure. Ciphers are commonly classified as transposition or substitution based.

In transposition-based ciphers, characters are "permuted" or rearranged. A simple example is encrypting HELLO by reversing the letters to produce OLLEH. Other examples include the Scytale, Rail Fence, and Grilles ciphers.

NOTE: Some modern algorithms, such as the Data Encryption Standard (DES) and the Triple Data Encryption Standard (3DES), still use transposition as part of the algorithm.

Substitution ciphers include the following:

Substitution (monoalphabetic)	■ Substitute one character for another (for example, A=C, B=D, C=E).
	■ Examples: Caesar cipher, Affine cipher, Atbash cipher.
Polyalphabetic	■ Based on substitution, using multiple substitution alphabets.
	■ Examples: Vigenère cipher, Autokey cipher.
One-time pads	■ A substitution cipher that combines the text letter with a special key material character.
	■ For example, the Vernam cipher key must be random, as long as the data can only be used once.
	■ Key distribution is challenging because the source and destination must have the same key.
	■ One-time pads are no longer practical, but the concept still applies in modern encryption algorithms such as DES and AES.

NOTE: Another type of substitution cipher is the polygraphic cipher (for example, Playfair cipher).

Modern Substitution Ciphers

Modern substitution ciphers are categorized by the process they follow to encrypt text:

Block ciphers	■ Referred to as "block-by-block cipher" because it operates on large blocks of digits with a fixed, unvarying transformation.
	■ Padding is used to keep the data size a multiple of the block size.
	■ The ciphertext is generally longer than the plaintext.
	■ The block size varies by algorithm. (DES has 8 bytes.)
	■ Examples: DES, 3DES, AES, Twofish.
Stream ciphers	■ Referred to as "bit-by-bit cipher," in which each plaintext digit is encrypted one at a time with the corresponding digit of the key stream, to give a digit of the ciphertext stream.
	■ Stream ciphers operate on smaller units of plaintext (bits).
	■ The size of the message does not typically change.
	■ The transformation of smaller plaintext units varies depending on encryption requirements.
	■ Examples: RC4, SEAL.

Encryption Algorithms

Encryption is the process of disguising a message in such a way as to hide its original contents. Plaintext (that is, the readable message) is converted to ciphertext (the unreadable, "disguised" message).

Encryption provides confidentiality because only authorized entities can read the original message.

> **NOTE:** Historically, confidentiality was provided by the secrecy of the algorithm (method) used. Secrecy in modern encryption lies in the secrecy of the key used, not in the algorithm.

Encryption can provide confidentiality at various OSI layers, such as the following:

- Encrypt data link layer data using proprietary link-encrypting devices.
- Encrypt network layer data using protocols such as those in the IPsec protocol suite.
- Encrypt session layer data using a protocol such as SSL or Transport Layer Security (TLS).
- Encrypt application layer data, such as secure email, secure database sessions (Oracle SQL*Net), and secure messaging (Lotus Note's sessions).

NOTE: Both IPsec and SSL are used to set up a VPN. An IPsec VPN is application independent and requires a specialized IP stack on the end system or in the packet path that includes IPsec. An SSL-based VPN supports only web-based applications, but the SSL software is included with all Internet browsers.

Cryptanalysis

Cryptanalysis is the practice of breaking codes to obtain the meaning of encrypted data. One of the following methods may be used to decrypt ciphertext:

Brute-force attack	▪ Attacker tries every possible key with the decryption algorithm knowing that eventually one of the keys will work. ▪ All encryption algorithms are vulnerable to this attack. ▪ On average, a brute-force attack succeeds about 50 percent of the way through the keyspace (the set of all possible keys). ▪ Choose a keyspace large enough so that it takes too much time (and money) to accomplish a brute-force attack.
Ciphertext-only attack	▪ Attacker obtains several ciphertext messages. ▪ Attacker uses statistical analysis to deduce the key used to encrypt the messages. ▪ These kinds of attacks are no longer practical today because modern algorithms are resistant to statistical analysis.
Known-plaintext attack	▪ Attacker obtains several ciphertext messages and also knows something about the plaintext underlying that ciphertext. ▪ Attacker uses a brute-force attack to try keys until decryption with the correct key produces a meaningful result. ▪ Modern algorithms with enormous keyspaces make it unlikely for this attack to succeed.
Chosen-plaintext attack	▪ Attacker chooses the data and observes the ciphertext output. ▪ A chosen-plaintext attack is more powerful than a known-plaintext attack because the attacker gets to choose the plaintext blocks to encrypt, allowing the attacker to choose plaintext that might yield more information about the key. ▪ This attack might not be very practical because it is often difficult or impossible to capture both the ciphertext and plaintext.

Chosen-ciphertext attack	■ Attacker chooses the ciphertext and observes the cleartext output. ■ This attack might not be very practical because it is often difficult or impossible to capture both the ciphertext and plaintext.
Man-in-the-middle attack	■ Attacker knows a portion of the plaintext and the corresponding ciphertext. ■ The plaintext is encrypted with every possible key, and the results are stored. ■ The ciphertext is then decrypted by using every key until one of the results matches one of the stored values.

Cryptographic Processes in VPNs

Cryptography provides key services to VPN technologies and solutions:

Confidentiality	■ The assurance that no one can read a particular piece of data except the receivers explicitly intended
Integrity	■ The assurance that data has not been altered in transit, intentionally or unintentionally
Authentication	■ The assurance the other entity is who he, she, or it claims to be
Key management	■ The generation, exchange, storage, safeguarding, use, vetting, and replacement of keys

VPN services use a combination of cryptographic technologies and algorithms to accomplish their goals. For example, in site-to-site VPNs, IP packets use the following:

■ Symmetric encryption algorithms to encrypt the payload, with keys negotiated by key management protocols

■ Asymmetric encryption algorithms to create digital signatures and authenticate the VPN peers

■ Hashing functions to provide checksum-type integrity checks

NOTE: This combination of algorithms and cryptographic methods negotiates the security settings to accomplish confidentiality, integrity, and authentication.

Classes of Encryption Algorithms

There are two classes of encryption algorithms, which differ in their use of keys:

Symmetric encryption algorithms	▪ Referred to as *private-key* or *secret-key* encryption.
	▪ A sender and receiver must share a secret key.
	▪ Typical key-length range is 40–256 bits.
	▪ They are usually quite fast (wire speed).
	▪ Algorithms are based on simple mathematical operations.
	▪ Encryption techniques include block ciphers, stream ciphers, and message authentication codes (MAC).
	▪ Examples: DES, 3DES, AES, and RC.
Asymmetric encryption algorithms	▪ Referred to as *public-key* encryption.
	▪ Use different keys to encrypt and decrypt data.
	▪ Typical key length is 512–4096 bits.
	▪ These algorithms are relatively slow because they are based on difficult computational algorithms.
	▪ Examples: RSA, ElGamal, ECDH, and DH.

Symmetric Encryption Algorithms

Well-known symmetric encryption algorithms include the following:

Data Encryption Standard (DES)	▪ Block cipher that encrypts 64-bit data blocks.
	▪ Fixed-length 64-bit key. (Only 56 bits are used for encryption.)
Triple Data Encryption Standard (3DES)	▪ Applies DES three times using three different keys.
	▪ Key 1 (56 bits) encrypts data.
	▪ Key 2 (56 bits) decrypts data.
	▪ Key 3 (56 bits) encrypts data.
	▪ Key sizes of 168 bits and 112 bits (if key 1 = key 3).
Advanced Encryption Standard (AES)	▪ Block cipher with variable block and key lengths.
	▪ It is stronger, faster, and more efficient than 3DES and is suitable for high-throughput, low-latency environments.
	▪ Key sizes of 128-, 192-, or 256-bit keys.
Software-optimized Encryption Algorithm (SEAL)	▪ Designed in 1993, it is a stream cipher that uses a 160-bit encryption key.
	▪ Lower impact on the CPU compared to other software-based algorithms.

Rivest ciphers	■ Widely deployed family of algorithms, including the following: ■ RC2: Designed as alternative to DES. ■ RC4: Popular algorithm used in SSL. ■ RC6: Designed as alternative to AES. ■ Variable block and key sizes.

Specifics	DES	3DES	AES	SEAL
Description	Data Encryption Standard	Triple DES	Advanced Encryption Standard	Software-Optimized Encryption Algorithm
Timeline	Standardized 1976	Standardized 1977	Standardized 2001	Published in 1994 but current version is 3.0 (1997)
Key size in bits	56 bits	112 and 168 bits	128, 192, and 256	160
Speed	Medium	Low	High	High
Resource consumption	Medium	Medium	Low	Low
Time to crack	Days	4.6 billion years with current technology	149 trillion years	Unknown but considered very safe
Note	Avoid. Legacy! Do not use.	Legacy. If used, then implement using very short key lifetimes.	Considered to be next generation encryption.	Not popular.

Asymmetric Encryption Algorithm

Asymmetric algorithms are substantially slower than symmetric algorithms. Their design is based on computational problems, such as factoring extremely large numbers or computing discrete logarithms of extremely large numbers.

Because they lack speed, asymmetric algorithms are typically used in low-volume cryptographic mechanisms, such as digital signatures and key exchange. However, the key management of asymmetric algorithms tends to be simpler than that of symmetric algorithms because usually one of the two encryption or decryption keys can be made public.

NOTE: Asymmetric encapsulation is covered later in more detail.

Choosing an Encryption Algorithm

Two main criteria to consider when selecting an encryption algorithm are as follows:

Is the algorithm trusted by the cryptographic community?	▪ Most new algorithms are broken very quickly.
	▪ Algorithms that have resisted attacks for a number of years are preferred.
	▪ Examples: DES, 3DES, AES, IDEA, and RC4.
Does the algorithm adequately protect against brute-force attacks?	▪ If the algorithm is trusted, no shortcut exists to break it, and the attacker must search through the keyspace to guess the correct key.
	▪ Use adequate key lengths to satisfy the confidentiality requirements of the organization.

Choosing an Adequate Keyspace

	Symmetric Key	Asymmetric Key	Hash
Protection up to 3 years	80	1248	160
Protection up to 10 years	96	1776	192
Protection up to 20 years	112	2342	224
Protection up to 30 years	128	3248	256
Protection against quantum computers	256	15424	512

NOTE: Notice the comparatively short symmetric key lengths. However, do not directly compare the key length of asymmetric and symmetric algorithms; the underlying design of the two algorithm families differs greatly.

NOTE: An 80-bit symmetric key is considered equal to a 1024-bit key using the RSA algorithm. A 112-bit symmetric key is considered equal to a 2048-bit key using the RSA algorithm. A 128-bit symmetric key is considered equal to a 3072-bit key using the RSA algorithm.

Cryptographic Hashes

Cryptographic hashes are based on one-way functions used for integrity assurance. They hash arbitrary data into a fixed-length digest known as a fingerprint.

NOTE: Hashing alone does not add security to the message. It only prevents the message from being changed accidentally, such as by a communication error.

Well-Known Hashing Algorithms

Message digest algorithm 5 (MD5)	<ul><li>Popular, ubiquitous hashing algorithm but is now considered a security risk.</li><li>Collision-resistant one-way function, which means that two messages with the same hash are very unlikely to occur.</li><li>128-bit message digest.</li></ul>
Secure Hash Algorithm 1 (SHA-1)	<ul><li>Although slower than MD5, it is the stronger algorithm but is now considered a security risk.</li><li>160-bit message digest.</li></ul>
Secure Hash Algorithm 2 (SHA-2)	<ul><li>Available as SHA-224, SHA-256, SHA-384, and SHA-512.</li><li>SHA-256, SHA-384, and SHA-512 are considered to be next-generation algorithms and should be used whenever possible.</li><li>Adopted by U.S. federal government as a secure hash standard.</li></ul>

Hash-Based Message Authentication Codes

Hash-based Message Authentication Codes (HMAC) use existing hash functions and add a secret key as input to the hash function to provide integrity assurance and authentication. Only parties who have access to that secret key can compute the digest of an HMAC function.

NOTE: HMACs defeat man-in-the-middle attacks.

Cisco technologies use two well-known HMAC functions:

- Keyed MD5, based on the MD5 hashing algorithm
- Keyed SHA-1, based on the SHA-1 hashing algorithm

Cisco products use hashing for entity authentication, data integrity, and data authenticity purposes, such as the following:

- IPsec gateways and clients use MD5 and SHA-1 in HMAC mode to provide packet integrity and authenticity.
- Cisco IOS images use MD5 to verify the integrity of downloaded images and router passwords.
- Cisco routers use hashing with secret keys to add authentication to routing protocols.

Digital Signatures

Digital signatures are commonly used in the following situations:

- To provide a unique proof of the data source, which can only be generated by a single party, such as with contract signing in e-commerce environments

- To authenticate a user by using the private key of that user and the signature it generates

- To prove the authenticity and integrity of public key infrastructure (PKI) certificates

- To provide a secure time stamp, such as with a central trusted time source

Digital signatures provide three basic security services in secure communications:

Authenticity of digitally signed data	Digital signatures authenticate a source, proving that a certain party has seen and has signed the data in question.
Integrity of digitally signed data	Digital signatures guarantee that the data has not changed from the time it was signed.
Nonrepudiation of the transaction	The recipient can take the data to a third party, and the third party accepts the digital signature as a proof that this data exchange did take place. The signing party cannot repudiate that it has signed the data.

To achieve these goals, digital signatures have the following properties:

The signature is authentic.	The signature convinces the recipient of the document that the signer signed the document.
The signature is not forgeable.	The signature is proof that the signer, and no one else, signed the document.
The signature is not reusable.	The signature is a part of the document and cannot be moved to a different document.
The signature is unalterable.	After a document is signed, it cannot be altered.
The signature cannot be repudiated.	The signature and the document are physical things. Signers cannot claim later that they did not sign it.

NOTE: The next chapter discusses digital signatures.

CHAPTER 14

Asymmetric Encryption and PKI

This chapter covers the following topics:

Asymmetric Encryption

- Public Key Confidentiality and Authentication
- RSA Functions

Public Key Infrastructure

- PKI Terminology
- PKI Standards
- PKI Topologies
- PKI Characteristics

Asymmetric Encryption

Asymmetric algorithms are based on complex mathematical formulas, and therefore computation takes more time than symmetric algorithms.

Examples of public key encryption algorithms are the Rivest, Shamir, and Adleman (RSA) algorithm; Digital Signature Algorithm (DSA); Diffie-Hellman (D-H); ElGamal; and elliptic curve cryptography (ECC).

Public Key Confidentiality and Authentication

Asymmetric algorithms use a public key and a private key. Both keys are capable of encryption. However, the complementary matched key is required for decryption.

For example, if a public key encrypts the data, the matching private key decrypts the data. The opposite is also true. If a private key encrypts the data, the corresponding public key decrypts the data.

Asymmetric cryptography is used to accomplish confidentiality and authentication.

Public Key Confidentiality	Confidentiality = Public Key (Encrypt) + Private Key (Decrypt)
	■ The public key is used to encrypt; the corresponding private key is used to decrypt.
	■ Because the private key is only present on one system, confidentiality is achieved in communicating with that system.
	■ This scenario is often used for key exchange.
Public Key Authentication	Authentication = Private Key (Encrypt) + Public Key (Decrypt)
	■ The private key is used to encrypt; the corresponding public key is used to decrypt.
	■ Because the private key is only present on one system, authentication is ensured when its public key decrypts the message.

RSA Functions

RSA is one of the most common asymmetric algorithms because it is easy to implement. It is flexible because it has a variable key length that allows speed to be traded for the security of the algorithm if necessary. An RSA key is usually 512–2048 bits long. The security of RSA is based on the difficulty of factoring very large numbers, which is breaking large numbers into multiplicative factors. RSA is substantially slower than Digital Encryption Standard (DES) and is typically used only to protect small amounts of data within the context of confidentiality.

RSA is mainly used for two services:

■ To ensure confidentiality of data by performing encryption, usually for small amounts of data such as session keys

■ To perform authentication of data or nonrepudiation of data, or both, by generating digital signatures

Public Key Infrastructure

A public key infrastructure (PKI) ensures confidentiality, integrity, and authentication in an enterprise and is based on the fundamentals of asymmetric encryption. PKI solutions are based on digital certificates and a trusted third-party trust model.

PKI uses the power of private and public keys, digital signatures, and trust models that are derived from asymmetric encryption. PKI provides services that include identity management, software code signing, encrypted file systems, email, virtual private networks (VPNs), and others.

The PKI is a set of technical, organizational, and legal components. Those components are needed to establish a system that enables large-scale use of public key cryptography to provide authenticity, confidentiality, integrity, and nonrepudiation services.

PKI Terminology

Public key infrastructure (PKI)	■ A service framework needed to support large-scale public key-based technologies.
Certificates	■ Electronic document that binds a name of a user or an organization to a public key certificate (digital certificate).
	■ Digital certificates are digitally signed by a CA.
	■ The certificate can be used to verify that a public key belongs to an individual or organization.
Certificate authority (CA)	■ A certificate authority (that is, a trusted third party) binds public keys with respective user identities.
	■ It digitally signs and publishes the public keys associated with an organization.
	■ Commercial CAs (for example, VeriSign) charge for services and are trusted by most web browsers.
	■ Some service providers provide public CAs and do not charge for services.
	■ CAs can also be implemented by an organization or a government for its users.
Registration authority (RA)	■ PKI servers that help CAs by performing key management tasks and therefore offloading the CA.
	■ They are like proxies of the CA.
	■ They minimize CA exposure to the network.

NOTE: Certificates are commonly used at the application layer for Secure Sockets Layer (SSL), Transport Layer Security (TLS), Secure MIME (S/MIME), and Pretty Good Privacy (PGP). Cisco devices can use certificates for the initial key exchange (IKE) in IPsec VPNs and in 802.1x authentication using Extensible Authentication Protocol-TLS (EAP-TLS).

PKI Standards

PKI requires interoperability with other technologies from different PKI vendors. The Internet Engineering Task Force (IETF) has formed the PKIX Working Group dedicated to promoting and standardizing PKI for the Internet.

Solutions include the following:

X.509	• A well-known ITU-T standard that defines basic PKI standard formats for public key certificates and certificate revocation lists (CRL).
	• X.509 Version 3 (X.509v3) defines the digital certificate format used extensively in SSL website authentication, email agents, and IPsec VPNs for initial key exchange.
Public-Key Cryptography Standards (PKCS)	• RSA standards that define formats for the secure exchange of data, including the following:
	• PKCS #1: RSA Cryptography Standard
	• PKCS #3: DH Key Agreement Standard
	• PKCS #7: Cryptographic Message Syntax Standard
	• PKCS #8: Private-Key Information Syntax Standard
	• PKCS #10: Certification Request Syntax Standard
	• PKCS #12: Personal Information Exchange Syntax Standard
	• PKCS #13: Elliptic Curve Cryptography Standard
	• PKCS #15: Cryptographic Token Information Format Standard

PKI Topologies

Simple (single-root) PKI	• Issues all the certificates to the end users.
	• The benefit in such a setup is simplicity.
	• VPNs that are managed by a single organization often use this topology.
Hierarchical CA topology	• Involves multiple hierarchical CAs within an organization.
	• CAs can issue certificates to end users and to subordinate RAs, which in turn issue their certificates to end users or other CAs.
	• The main benefits are increased scalability and manageability.
	• Trust decisions can now be hierarchically distributed to smaller branches.
Cross-certified CAs	• Involves multiple flat, single-root CAs that establish trust relationships horizontally by cross-certifying their own CA certificates.

PKI Characteristics

- To authenticate each other, users have to obtain the digital certificate of the CA and their own digital certificate. These steps require the out-of-band verification of the processes.

- Public key systems use public and private asymmetric keys. Whatever is encrypted using one key can only be decrypted using the other key providing nonrepudiation.

- Key management is simplified because two users can freely exchange the certificates, and the validity of the received certificates is verified using the public key of the CA, which the users already have in their possession.

- Because of the strength of the algorithms, you can set a long lifetime for the certificates, typically measured in years.

This chapter covers the following topics:

IPsec Protocol

- IPsec Protocol Framework
- Encapsulating IPsec Packets
- Transport Versus Tunnel Mode
- Confidentiality Using Encryption Algorithms
- Data Integrity Using Hashing Algorithms
- Peer Authentication Methods
- Key Exchange Algorithms
- NSA Suite B Standard

Internet Key Exchange

- IKE Negotiation Phases
- IKEv1 Phase 1 (Main Mode and Aggressive Mode)
- IKEv1 Phase 2 (Quick Mode)
- IKEv2 Phase 1 and 2
- IKEv1 Versus IKEv2

IPv6 VPNs

IPsec Protocol

The IP Security (IPsec) protocol is an open standard that provides the following:

Confidentiality	<ul><li>Confidentiality is provided using encryption algorithms.</li><li>Data encryption prevents third parties from reading the data transmitted over public or wireless networks.</li><li>Encryption algorithms: Digital Encryption Standard (DES), Triple DES (3DES), Advanced Encryption Standard (AES), or Software-optimized Encryption Algorithm (SEAL).</li></ul>

Data integrity	■ Data integrity is provided using hashing algorithms.
	■ Hashing algorithms validate that the received data has not been altered.
	■ Hashing algorithms: message digest algorithm 5 (MD5) or Secure Hash Algorithm (SHA).
Authentication	■ Authentication is defined by the Internet Key Exchange (IKE) protocol.
	■ IKE authenticates users and devices.
	■ Authentication methods: pre-shared keys (PSK) or digital certificates.
Antireplay protection	■ Antireplay verifies that each packet is unique and not duplicated.

IPsec Protocol Framework

IPsec identifies the framework to support secure network communication over a virtual private network (VPN). Figure 15-1 illustrates the IPsec framework and optional algorithms.

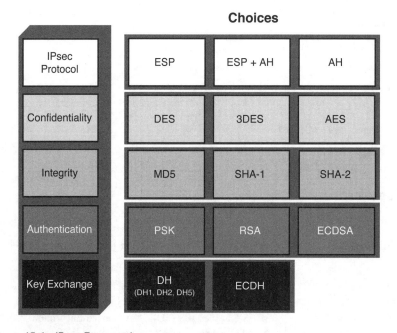

Figure 15-1   IPsec Framework

Encapsulating IPsec Packets

There are two main IPsec framework protocols:

Authentication Header (AH)	■ AH provides data authentication and integrity.
	■ However, it does not provide confidentiality.
	■ AH provides integrity and authentication of the payload using either HMAC-MD5 or HMAC-SHA-1.
	■ AH is IP protocol 51.
Encapsulating Security Payload (ESP)	■ ESP provides confidentiality by encrypting the payload using DES, 3DES, or AES.
	■ ESP can also provide integrity and authentication of the payload using either HMAC-MD5 or HMAC-SHA-1.
	■ ESP can also enforce antireplay protection by requiring that a receiving host set the replay bit in the header to indicate that the packet has been seen.
	■ ESP is IP protocol number 50.

NOTE: This chapter focuses on ESP, along with other important IPsec protocols.

Transport Versus Tunnel Mode

ESP and AH can be used in two different modes:

Transport mode	■ Security is provided only for the transport layer and above.
	■ Transport mode protects the payload of the packet but leaves the original IP address in the clear.
	■ ESP transport mode is used between hosts.
Tunnel mode	■ Tunnel mode provides security for the complete IP packet.
	■ The original packet is encrypted and then encapsulated in another IP packet.
	■ ESP tunnel mode is used between a host and a security gateway or between two security gateways.

NOTE: The focus in this book is on tunnel mode.

Confidentiality Using Encryption Algorithms

The following are some of the encryption algorithms and key lengths that IPsec can use:

Data Encryption Standard (DES) algorithm	■ DES uses a 56-bit symmetric key cryptosystem. ■ Legacy protocol. Do not use.
Triple Data Encryption Standard (3DES) algorithm	■ 3DES is a symmetric key cryptosystem. ■ A variant of DES that processes blocks of data three times, each time with an independent 56-bit encryption key. ■ Legacy protocol. If used, then configure short key lifetimes.
Advanced Encryption Standard (AES)	■ Recommended encryption algorithm and considered to be next-generation. ■ AES is a symmetric key cryptosystem that provides stronger security than DES and is computationally more efficient than 3DES. ■ It offers key lengths of 128 bits, 192 bits, and 256 bits.
Software-optimized Encryption Algorithm (SEAL)	■ SEAL is a stream cipher that uses a 160-bit key for encryption.
Rivest, Shamir, and Adleman (RSA)	■ RSA is an asymmetrical key cryptosystem. ■ It uses a key length of 512 bits, 768 bits, 1024 bits, or larger. ■ It is not used for data encryption but instead is used during the peer-authentication phase.

NOTE: SEAL and RSA algorithms are beyond the scope of this chapter.

Data Integrity Using Hashing Algorithms

The following are some of the Hash-based Message Authentication Code (HMAC) algorithms and key lengths that IPsec can use:

HMAC-Message Digest 5 (HMAC-MD5)	■ HMAC-MD5 uses a 128-bit shared-secret key. ■ The message and 128-bit shared-secret key are combined and run through the HMAC-MD5 hash algorithm. ■ The hash is appended to the original message and is forwarded to the remote end. ■ Avoid using as it is now considered to be a security risk.

HMAC-Secure Hash Algorithm 1 (HMAC-SHA-1)	<ul><li>HMAC-SHA-1 uses a 160-bit secret key.</li><li>The message and the 160-bit shared-secret key are combined and run through the HMAC-SHA-1 hash algorithm.</li><li>The hash is appended to the original message and is forwarded to the remote end.</li><li>Avoid using as it is now considered to be a security risk.</li></ul>
HMAC-Secure Hash Algorithm 2 (HMAC-SHA-2)	<ul><li>The SHA-2 family is based on SHA-1.</li><li>SHA-256, SHA-384, and SHA-512 are considered to be next-generation algorithms and should be used whenever possible.</li></ul>

Peer Authentication Methods

Pre-shared keys (PSK)	<ul><li>Peers authenticate each other by comparing preconfigured secret keys.</li><li>The PSK is combined with other information to create the authentication key.</li></ul>
RSA signatures	<ul><li>Peers authenticate each other using digital certificates.</li><li>The sending peer creates an encrypted hash using their private key, attaches it to a message, and forwards it.</li><li>The remote peer decrypts the hash using the public key and compares it with a recomputed hash.</li></ul>
RSA encrypted nonces	<ul><li>Peers authenticate each other using RSA-generated random numbers (called nonces).</li><li>Public keys must be manually copied to each peer as part of the configuration process.</li><li>This method is the least popular.</li></ul>
Elliptical Curve Digital Signature Algorithm (ECDSA)	<ul><li>ECDSA is the method used for the Digital Signature Standard (DSS).</li><li>ECDSA improves the communication efficiency:<ul><li>It is quicker than similar-strength RSA operations.</li><li>It is smaller than RSA signatures.</li></ul></li></ul>

Key Exchange Algorithms

Encryption algorithms require a symmetric shared-secret key to perform encryption and decryption. These algorithms are used within IKE to establish session keys. The following public key exchange methods are available in Cisco IOS software:

Diffie-Hellman (DH)	■ Provides a way for two peers to establish a shared-secret key, which only they know, even though they are communicating over an unsecure channel.
	
	■ Examples:
	
	  ■ For DES, use DH1 (768-bit key).
	
	  ■ For 3DES, use DH2 (1024-bit key).
	
	  ■ For AES, use DH5 (1536-bit key), DH14 (2048-bit key), DH15 (3072-bit key), or DH16 (4096-bit key).

ECDH	■ A variant of the DH protocol using elliptic curve cryptography (ECC). ■ For ECDH, use DH19 (256-bit ECDH key), DH20 (384-bit ECDH key), or DH24 (2048-bit ECDH key).

NOTE: DH groups determine the strength of the key used in the key exchange process. Higher group numbers are more secure, but they require additional time to compute the key.

NSA Suite B Standard

The National Security Agency (NSA) as part of its Cryptographic Modernization Program has identified a globally recognized set of cryptography standards referred to as Suite B. As described in RFC 4869, Suite B cryptography secures information traveling over networks using four well-established, public-domain cryptographic algorithms:

- Encryption uses AES with 128-bit or 256-bit keys.
- Hashing (digital fingerprinting) uses SHA-2.
- Digital signatures use the ECDSA.
- Key exchange uses the Elliptic Curve Diffie-Hellman (ECDH) method.

Internet Key Exchange

IPsec requires the IKE protocol to negotiate security associations (SA), which are agreements between two peers engaging in an IPsec exchange. IKE is also responsible for the automatic key generation and key refresh.

There are two versions of the IKE protocol: IKEv1 and IKEv2.

IKEv2 was created to overcome some of the limitations of IKEv1. It is more reliable, flexible, and simpler than IKEv1 because it requires fewer transactions to establish SAs. It also provides mobility, allowing mobile users to roam without disconnecting their IPsec session.

IKE Negotiation Phases

To establish an IPsec VPN tunnel, IKEv1 and IKEv2 both require two negotiation phases.

IKE Phase 1	<ul><li>Goal is to establish an IKE SA.</li><li>Phase can be completed in *main mode* or in *aggressive mode*.</li><li>Two IPsec peers perform the initial negotiation of SAs.</li><li>SA negotiations are bidirectional; data may be sent and received using the same encryption key.</li></ul>
IKE Phase 2	<ul><li>Goal is to establish an IPsec SA.</li><li>Phase is also called *quick mode*.</li><li>SAs are negotiated by the IKE process Internet Security Association and Key Management Protocol (ISAKMP).</li><li>In this phase, the SAs that IPsec uses are unidirectional, and therefore a separate key exchange is required for each data flow.</li></ul>

IKEv1 Phase 1 (Main Mode and Aggressive Mode)

The basic purpose of IKEv1 Phase 1 is to negotiate IKE policy sets, authenticate the peers, and set up a secure channel between the peers.

IKEv1 Phase 1 operates in either main mode or aggressive mode:

Main mode	<ul><li>Negotiation exchanges six messages between peers.</li><li>These exchanges define what encryption and authentication protocols are acceptable, how long keys should remain active, and whether perfect forward secrecy (PFS) should be enforced.</li></ul>
Aggressive mode	<ul><li>Negotiation exchanges three messages between peers.</li><li>The initiator passes all data that is required for the SA.</li><li>The responder sends the proposal, key material, and ID and authenticates the session in the next packet.</li><li>The initiator replies by authenticating the session.</li></ul>

NOTE: Main mode protects the identity of the peers, whereas aggressive mode does not. The use of main mode or aggressive mode is a tradeoff between performance and security.

IKE Phase 1 main mode includes three, two-message exchanges:

First message exchange	<ul><li>Peers negotiate and agree upon the algorithms and hashes that will be used to secure the subsequent IKE exchanges.</li><li>The responder chooses the best-suited proposal and then sends that proposal to the initiator.</li></ul>
Second message exchange	<ul><li>Peers use the DH key exchange algorithm to generate a shared-secret key used to encrypt all the other encryption and authentication keys.</li><li>This negotiation results in a single bidirectional ISAKMP SA.</li></ul>
Third message exchange	<ul><li>The third exchange authenticates an ISAKMP session.</li><li>The peer is authenticated using PSK, digital signature, or public key encryption.</li></ul>

IKEv1 Phase 2 (Quick Mode)

The purpose of IKE Phase 2 is to negotiate (and renegotiate) the IPsec security parameters (called transform sets) and establish IPsec SAs. It also periodically renegotiates IPsec SAs. IKE Phase 2 has one mode, called quick mode.

After IKE Phase 1 is complete, quick mode uses three messages to negotiate a shared IPsec transform, derives shared-secret keying material that the IPsec security algorithms will use, and establishes IPsec SAs. Quick mode also exchanges nonces that are used to generate new shared-secret key material and prevent replay attacks from generating false SAs.

IKEv2 Phase 1 and 2

IKE Phases 1 and 2 are enhanced by IKEv2. IKEv2 simplifies the initial exchange of messages, thus reducing latency and increasing the connection establishment speed. IKEv2 includes all the functionality of IKEv1, including the two negotiation phases:

IKEv2 Phase 1	<ul><li>Negotiation exchanges four messages between peers.</li><li>The first two messages flow in the clear on the network while the other two messages are encrypted.</li></ul>
IKEv2 Phase 2	<ul><li>Negotiation exchanges two messages between peers.</li><li>The Phase 2 SA contains the keys used to encrypt and decrypt IPsec packets on the host, authenticate IPsec packets on the host, or both.</li></ul>

IKEv1 Versus IKEv2

Fewer RFCs	■ IKEv1 is defined in five RFCs.
	■ IKEv2 is defined in RFC 5996.
Simplified message exchange	■ IKEv1 exchanges nine messages (Phase 1 = 6, Phase 2 = 3).
	■ IKEv2 exchanges six messages (Phase 1 = 4, Phase 2 = 2).
Security	■ IKEv1 may be susceptible to denial-of-service (DoS) attacks.
	■ IKEv2 is more immune to DoS attacks because it does not process a request until it determines the requester.
NAT traversal	■ The encapsulation of IKE and ESP in UDP port 4500 enables these protocols to pass through a device or firewall performing Network Address Translation (NAT).
Reliability	■ IKEv2 uses sequence numbers and acknowledgments and mandates some error-processing logistics and shared state management.
Support for EAP	■ IKEv2 can leverage existing authentication infrastructure and credential databases such as Extensible Authentication Protocol (EAP).
Mobility	■ IKEv2 can implement MOBIKE (Mobility and Multihoming Protocol), which allows for Layer 3 roaming by changing the peer's IP address without reestablishing all SAs with the VPN gateway.

IPv6 VPNs

IPsec is native to IPv6. However, IPv6 does not mandate that IPsec be used for all IPv6 communications. In IPv4, AH and ESP were IP protocol headers. IPv6 uses the extension header approach, and therefore ESP uses the next-header value of 50 and AH uses the next-header value of 51.

IPv6 supports the latest cryptography suites (Suite B and beyond), and the mobility enhancements found in IKEv2 are key.

CHAPTER 16

Configuring Site-to-Site VPNs

This chapter covers the following topics:

Site-to-Site IPsec VPNs

- IPsec VPN Negotiation Steps
- Planning an IPsec VPN
- Cipher Suite Options

Configuring IOS Site-to-Site VPNs

- Verifying the VPN Tunnel
- Configuring a Site-to-Site IPsec VPN

Site-to-Site IPsec VPNs

Organizations of all kinds often deploy site-to-site virtual private networks (VPNs) when implementing a corporate network across public and private networks. Internet-based VPN environments and Multiprotocol Label Switching (MPLS) VPN environments benefit from the flexibility of deployment and standards-based implementation of cryptographic mechanisms.

The choice of device-terminating VPNs becomes a key factor in implementing site-to-site VPNs. Organizations benefit from leveraging their existing network elements and using an integrated approach to VPN deployments. This lesson highlights the use of Cisco IOS routers as site-to-site VPN termination points in IP Security (IPsec) environments.

IPsec VPN Negotiation Steps

IPsec VPN negotiation can be broken down into five steps, including Phase 1 and Phase 2 of Internet Key Exchange (IKE):

1. An IPsec tunnel is initiated when a host sends "interesting" traffic to a destination host. Traffic is considered interesting when it travels between the IPsec peers and meets the criteria defined in the crypto ACL.

2. The interesting traffic initiates IKE Phase 1 between the peer routers. The IPsec peers negotiate the established IKE security association (SA) policy. Once the peers are authenticated, a secure tunnel is created by using Internet Security Association and Key Management Protocol (ISAKMP).

3. The peers then proceed to IKE Phase 2. The IPsec peers use the authenticated and secure tunnel to negotiate IPsec SA transforms. The negotiation of the shared policy determines how the IPsec tunnel is established.

4. The IPsec tunnel is created, and data is transferred between the IPsec peers based on the IPsec parameters configured in the IPsec transform sets.

5. The IPsec tunnel terminates when the IPsec SAs are deleted or when their lifetime expires.

Planning an IPsec VPN

When planning to deploy a site-to-site IPsec VPN, remember the following:

Verify connectivity between peers.	Ensure that IP protocols 50 (ESP) and 51 (AH) and UDP port 500 (ISAKMP) traffic are permitted and not blocked by an access control list (ACL).
Define interesting traffic.	Define which traffic will trigger a VPN session (interesting traffic) and which traffic will travel outside the tunnel (noninteresting traffic).
Determine the cipher suite requirements.	Choose a cipher that suits the network security policy of the organization.
Manage monitoring, troubleshooting, and change.	Consider all three areas in the planning process.

Interesting traffic is defined by crypto ACLs in site-to-site IPsec VPN configurations. Crypto ACLs perform these functions:

Outbound	Selects outbound traffic that IPsec should protect. Traffic not selected is sent in plaintext.
Inbound	If you want, you can create inbound ACLs to filter and discard traffic that should have been protected by IPsec.

NOTE: Traffic matching a permit action in the ACL is protected and sent through the VPN. Traffic matching a deny action in the ACL is sent outside the VPN in cleartext.

Cipher Suite Options

The following compares weaker options to stronger options:

Parameter	Weakest	Strongest
Encryption algorithm	Digital Encryption Standard (DES)	Advanced Encryption Standard (AES)
Hash algorithm	Message digest algorithm 5 (MD5)	Secure Hash Algorithm 2 (SHA-256, SHA384, and SHA512)
Authentication method	Pre-share key (PSK)	Rivest, Shamir, Adleman (RSA) Signature
Key exchange	Diffie-Hellman (DH) group 1	DH group 24
IKE SA lifetime	86,400 seconds	< 86,400 seconds

Configuring IOS Site-to-Site VPNs

To configure a site-to-site VPN using IOS, complete the following steps:

1. Create an IKE policy and configure the required Phase 1 parameters.

2. Specify the PSK and identify the peer address (or hostname).

3. Create the IPsec policy required for Phase 2.

4. Create the crypto map and configure crypto map specifics.

5. Identify interesting traffic using an extended ACL.

6. Apply the crypto map to an interface.

7. Verify the tunnel.

NOTE: Some of these steps can be done out of order.

Create an IKE policy.

`Router(config)# crypto isakmp policy `*`priority`*	Define an IKE policy to specify the parameters to be used during an IKE negotiation to create the IKE SA.
	`priority` uniquely identifies the IKE policy and assigns a priority to the policy. Use an integer from 1 to 10,000, with 1 being the highest priority and 10,000 the lowest.

NOTE: You can configure multiple IKE policies. When the IKE negotiation begins, it tries to find a common policy configured on both peers, starting with the highest-priority policies as specified on the remote peer.

NOTE: Use the `show crypto isakmp policy` command to verify the IKE settings.

Configurable IKE parameters include the following:

- Hash (default = SHA-1)

- Authentication (default = RSA signatures)

- Group (DH default = 768-bit DH)

- Lifetime (default = 86400 seconds [1 day])

- Encryption (default = 56-bit DES)

NOTE: Use the mnemonic **HAGLE** to remember the five policy parameters to configure hash, authentication, group, lifetime, and encryption.

Configure IKE policy Phase 1 parameters:

Router(config-isakmp)# hash {md5 | sha | sha256 | sha384 | sha512}	Set the hashing algorithm for the IKE policy. **NOTE:** sha specifies SHA-1 (HMAC variant) as the hash algorithm.
Router(config-isakmp)# authentication {pre-share | rsa-encr | rsa-sig}	Set the authentication method for the IKE policy.
Router(config-isakmp)# group {1 | 2 | 5 | 14 | 15 | 16 | 19 | 20 | 21 | 24}	Set the DH group to use for the IKE policy.
Router(config-isakmp)# lifetime seconds	Configure the maximum amount of time an IKE SA can exist before it expires. Time values are from 60 to 86400 seconds (1 minute to 24 hours).
Router(config-isakmp)# encryption {des | 3des | aes aes-bit}	Set the encryption algorithm for the IKE policy. **NOTE:** Encryption options may vary depending on IOS image.

NOTE: If a parameter is not configured, the default value will be used for that parameter.

Specify the PSK and identify the peer address (or hostname):

Router(config)# crypto isakmp key pre-shared-key {address address | hostname hostname}	Set the PSK for the remote peer and identify the peer by IP address or hostname. (Domain Name System [DNS] must be enabled.)

NOTE: This PSK must be identical on both peers.

NOTE: Use the show crypto isakmp key command to list PSKs.

Create the IPsec policy required for Phase 2:

Router(config)# crypto ipsec transform-set transform-name transform1 [transform2] [transform3] [transform4]	Define the IPsec transform set and settings. A transform set specifies one or two IPsec security protocols (either Authentication Header [AH], Encapsulation Security Protocol [ESP], or both) and specifies which algorithms to use with the selected security protocol.

You may specify up to four *transforms*:

- ESP encryption transform set options include `esp-des`, `esp-3des`, `esp-aes`, or `esp-seal`.

- ESP authentication transform set options include `esp-md5-hmac`, `esp-sha-hmac`, `esp-sha256-hmac`, `esp-sha384-hmac`, or `esp-sha512-hmac`.

- (Optional) AH options transform set includes `ah-md5-hmac`, `ah-sha-hmac`, `ah-sha256-hmac`, `ah-sha384-hmac`, or `ah-sha512-hmac`.

- (Optional) IP compression transform set option is `comp-lzs`.

NOTE: You can specify just an ESP encryption transform set or the ESP encryption transform set and an ESP authentication transform set.

NOTE: When configuring AES encryption options, you can also specify a key length (128 bits, 192 bits, or 256 bits).

NOTE: After you issue the `crypto ipsec transform-set` command, you are put into the crypto transform configuration mode. While in this mode, you can change the mode to tunnel or transport. (Tunnel is the default.)

NOTE: Changes to transform sets are not applied to existing SAs but are used in subsequent negotiations to establish new SAs. To force the settings sooner, clear all or part of the SA database by using the `clear crypto sa` command.

NOTE: Use the `show crypto ipsec transform-set` command to verify the IPsec settings.

Create the crypto map specifics:

`Router(config)# `**`crypto map`** `map-name sequence-number` **`ipsec-isakmp`**	Define the site-to-site IPsec VPN crypto map settings.

NOTE: Other options are available, but the focus of this chapter is on IPsec and ISAKMP crypto map definitions.

Configurable site-to-site VPN crypto map parameters include the following:

- Identify the remote peers.
- Identify the transform set to use.
- Identify interesting traffic.
- Identify the lifetime of the IPsec SA.
- Identify the DH group to use.

NOTE: Other options can be configured, but these are typical for site-to-site VPNs.

Configure crypto map specifics:

`Router(config-crypto-map)#` **`description`** `description`	Add the description to the crypto map.
`Router(config-crypto-map)#` **`set peer`** `peer-ip`	Specify an IPsec peer. **NOTE:** You can identify multiple peers using separate commands.
`Router(config-crypto-map)#` **`set transform-set`** `transform-name1` `[transform-name2 ...` `transformname6]`	Specify which transform sets can be used with the crypto map entry. **NOTE:** You can identify up to six transform sets in one command.
`Router(config-crypto-map)#` **`match address`** `crypto-acl`	Assign an extended access list to a crypto map entry that will be used by IPsec to determine which traffic should be protected by crypto and which traffic does not need crypto protection. **NOTE:** Traffic that is permitted by the access list will be protected. Traffic that is denied by the access list will not be protected in the context of the corresponding crypto map entry.
`Router(config-crypto-map)#` **`set security-association lifetime`** {**`days`** `days` | **`kilobytes`** `bytes` | **`seconds`** `seconds`}	Identify how long the IPsec SA will remain in effect before having to renegotiate.
`Router(config-crypto-map)#` **`set pfs`** [**`group1`** | **`group2`** | **`group5`** | **`group14`** | **`group15`** | **`group16`** | **`group19`** | **`group20`** | **`group21`** | **`group24`**]	Identify the DH group to use.

Identify interesting traffic using an extended access control list (ACL). The ACL identifies when source traffic going to a destination network should enable the VPN tunnel. The extended ACL can be numbered or named.

NOTE: The extended ACLs between peers should be reciprocal (for example, on Peer-A, source-A to destination-B and on Peer-B, source-B to destination-A).

Apply the crypto map to an interface:

`Router(config)#` **`interface`** `type` `number`	Specify the interface type and number.
`Router(config-if)#` **`crypto map`** `crypto-map-name`	Apply a previously defined crypto map set to an interface.

Verifying the VPN Tunnel

To verify the site-to-site VPN configuration, use the following commands.

To verify IKE phase status, use these commands:

Router# **show crypto isakmp policy**	Display configured IKE policies.
Router# **show crypto isakmp sa** [**active**]	Display the status of the IKE phase 1 SAs.

> **NOTE:** The **show crypto isakmp sa** command displays the state and status of Phase 1. A state of QM_IDLE is considered normal for an established Phase 1 tunnel.

To verify IKE Phase 2 status, use these commands:

Router# **show crypto isakmp transform-set**	Display configured IPsec transform sets.
Router# **show crypto map**	Display configured crypto maps.
Router# **show crypto ipsec sa**	Display established IPsec tunnels.

To test a tunnel, complete these steps:

1. Clear the IPsec SAs using the **clear crypto sa** command.

2. Issue the **show crypto ipsec sa** command to verify that the counters have been cleared.

3. Create interesting traffic using an extended ping such as **ping** *destination-network-ip* **source** *source-network-ip*.

4. Issue the **show crypto ipsec sa** command to verify that the counters have increased.

Configuring a Site-to-Site IPsec VPN

This example establishes a site-to-site VPN between R1 and R3, protecting traffic that travels between the two LAN segments. A strong cipher suite is required, using PSKs, AES, and SHA-2.

Figure 16-1 shows the network topology for the site-to-site VPN example.

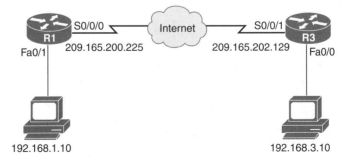

Figure 16-1 Network Topology for Site-to-Site IPsec VPN Example

Create IKE policy 1 and configure the required Phase 1 parameters:

`R1(config)# crypto isakmp policy 1`	Define the IKE policy settings.
`R1(config-isakmp)# hash sha256`	Set the hashing algorithm for the IKE policy.
`R1(config-isakmp)# authentication pre-share`	Set the authentication method for the IKE policy.
`R1(config-isakmp)# group 24`	Set the DH group to use for the IKE policy.
`R1(config-isakmp)# lifetime 3600`	Set the IKE SA expiration timer to 1 hour.
`R1(config-isakmp)# encr aes`	Set the encryption algorithm for the IKE policy.
`R1(config-isakmp)# exit`	Return to global configuration mode.

Specify the PSK and identify the peer address (or hostname):

`R1(config)# crypto isakmp key cisco123 address 209.165.202.129`	Set the PSK for the R3 peer.

Create the IPsec policy required for Phase 2:

`R1(config)# crypto ipsec transform-set R1-to-R3-SET esp-aes esp-sha-hmac`	Define the IPsec transform set and settings.
`R1(cfg-crypto-trans)# exit`	Return to global configuration mode.

Create the crypto map specifics:

`R1(config)# crypto map R1-to-R3-MAP 1 ipsec-isakmp`	Define the site-to-site IPsec VPN crypto map settings.
`R1(config-crypto-map)# description Create a site-to-site VPN when going from R1 LAN to R3 LAN`	Document the crypto map.
`R1(config-crypto-map)# set transform-set R1-to-R3-SET`	Identify the transform set to use with this crypto map.
`R1(config-crypto-map)# set peer 209.165.202.129`	Identify the peer to use with this crypto map.
`R1(config-crypto-map)# match address VPN-ACL`	Identify the crypto ACL to use with this crypto map.
`R1(config-crypto-map)# set pfs group24`	Identify the DH group.
`R1(config-crypto-map)# set security-association lifetime seconds 900`	Identify the crypto map lifetime.
`R1(config-crypto-map)# exit`	Return to global configuration mode.

Create the crypto ACL to identify interesting traffic:

R1(config)# **ip access-list extended VPN-ACL**	Create a named extended ACL.
R1(config-ext-nacl)# **remark IPSec Rule**	Provide ACL documentation.
R1(config-ext-nacl)# **permit ip 192.168.1.0 0.0.0.255 192.168.3.0 0.0.0.255**	Identify the interesting traffic.
R1(config-ext-nacl)# **exit**	Return to global configuration mode.

Apply the crypto map to an interface:

R1(config)# **interface s0/0/0** R1(config-if)# **crypto map R1-to-R3-MAP**	Specify the interface type and number.

CHAPTER 17

Introduction to the ASA

This chapter covers the following topics:

Adaptive Security Appliance

- ASA Models

- Routed and Transparent Firewall Modes

- ASA Licensing

Basic ASA Configuration

- ASA 5505 Front and Back Panel

- ASA Security Levels

- ASA 5505 Port Configuration

- ASA 5505 Deployment Scenarios

- ASA 5505 Configuration Options

Adaptive Security Appliance

Cisco offers firewall solutions using a firewall-enabled Integrated Services Router (ISR) or using the Cisco Adaptive Security Appliance (ASA) with FirePOWER services comprehensive firewall solution. The ASA with FirePOWER are next-generation firewall (NGFW) devices that deliver integrated threat defense across the entire attack continuum. They combine proven ASA firewalls with Sourcefire threat and advanced malware protection in a single device.

The Cisco Adaptive Security Appliance (ASA) with FirePOWER services combines the following features into one platform:

Stateful firewall	<ul><li>An ASA provides stateful firewall services tracking the TCP or UDP network connections traversing it.</li><li>Only packets matching a known active connection are allowed by the firewall; others are rejected.</li></ul>
VPN concentrator	<ul><li>The ASA supports IPsec and Secure Sockets Layer (SSL) remote access and IPsec site-to-site virtual private network (VPN) features.</li></ul>
Next-generation Intrusion Prevention System (NGIPS)	<ul><li>ASA with FirePOWER services can provide NGIPS, the industry-leading contextual awareness, full visibility and control for users, devices, applications, and content, and industry-leading threat prevention.</li></ul>

Virtualization	▪ A single ASA can be partitioned into multiple virtual devices called security contexts. ▪ Each context is an independent device, with its own security policy, interfaces, and administrators. ▪ Most IPS features are supported except VPN and dynamic routing protocols.
High availability	▪ Two ASAs can be paired into an active/standby failover configuration to provide device redundancy. ▪ One ASA is the primary (active) device, while the other is the secondary (standby) device. ▪ Both ASAs must have identical software, licensing, memory, and interfaces.
Identity firewall	▪ The ASA can provide access control using Windows Active Directory login information. ▪ Identity-based firewall services allow users or groups to be specified instead of being restricted by traditional IP address-based rules.
AMP	▪ The ASA with FirePOWER services provides industry-leading ability to discover, understand, stop, and when necessary remediate malware and emerging threats missed by other security layers.
Reputation-based URL filtering	▪ The ASA with FirePOWER services can block high-risk web addresses. ▪ Spam, URL-based viruses, phishing attacks, and spyware can direct users to malicious URLs. ▪ Cisco accurately analyzes URLs and associates a reputation score for each one, enabling users to avoid high-risk web addresses.

NOTE: This section focuses on the ASA firewall and remote-access VPN features.

ASA Models

There are several ASA models addressing the needs of various organizations. The choice of ASA model depends on an organization's requirements, such as maximum throughput, maximum connections per second, and budget:

ASA 5505	▪ Small business, branch office, and enterprise teleworker solution providing a maximum of 150-Mbps throughput.
ASA 5506-X ASA 5508-X ASA 5512-X ASA 5515-X ASA 5516-X	▪ Small business, branch office, and enterprise teleworker solutions providing stateful inspection maximum throughputs of 750 Mbps to 1.8 Gbps.

ASA 5525-X ASA 5545-X ASA 5555-X	■ Medium to large business Internet edge solutions providing stateful inspection maximum throughputs of 2 Gbps to 4 Gbps.
ASA 5585-X SSP10 ASA 5585-X SSP20 ASA 5585-X SSP40 ASA 5585-X SSP60	■ Large enterprise and data center solution. ■ The Cisco ASA with Cisco FirePOWER Security Services Processor (SSP) provides stateful inspection maximum throughputs of 4 Gbps to 15 Gbps.
ASAv5 Cisco ASAv10 Cisco ASAv30	■ The Cisco Adaptive Security Virtual Appliance (ASAv) brings the power of ASA appliances to the virtual domain. ■ The Cisco ASAv5 and ASAv10 require up to 2 GB of memory and deliver maximum throughputs of 100 Mbps and 1 Gbps, respectively. ■ The Cisco ASAv30 requires up to 8 GB of memory and delivers up to 2 Gbps of throughput.

NOTE: For the Cisco ASA 5505, the default DRAM memory is 256 MB (upgradable to 512 MB), and the default internal flash memory is 128 MB.

NOTE: This section focuses on the ASA 5505.

Routed and Transparent Firewall Modes

Two firewall modes of operation are available on ASA devices:

Routed mode	■ The traditional mode for deploying a firewall. ■ Two or more interfaces that separate Layer 3 networks. ■ The ASA is a router hop in the network and can perform Network Address Translation (NAT) between connected networks. ■ Routed mode supports multiple interfaces, and each interface is on a different subnet and requires an IP address on that subnet.
Transparent mode	■ The ASA functions like a Layer 2 device. ■ Also referred to as a *bump in the wire* or a *stealth firewall*. ■ The ASA requires only one management IP address configured in global configuration mode. ■ Transparent mode does not support dynamic routing protocols, VPNs, quality of service (QoS), or Dynamic Host Control Protocol (DHCP) Relay.

NOTE: This section focuses on routed mode.

ASA Licensing

The ASA 5505 security appliance comes preinstalled with either a Base license
or a Security Plus license, the latter supporting a higher connection capacity, full
demilitarized zone (DMZ) capabilities, VLAN trunking, and high-availability features.

You can verify license information using the **show activation-key** or the **show
version** command:.

```
ciscoasa# show version


<Output omitted>


Licensed features for this platform:
Maximum Physical Interfaces      : 8              perpetual
VLANs                            : 3              DMZ Restricted
Dual ISPs                        : Disabled       perpetual
VLAN Trunk Ports                 : 0              perpetual
Inside Hosts                     : 10             perpetual
Failover                         : Disabled       perpetual
VPN-DES                          : Enabled        perpetual
VPN-3DES-AES                     : Enabled        perpetual
AnyConnect Premium Peers         : 2              perpetual
AnyConnect Essentials            : Disabled       perpetual
Other VPN Peers                  : 10             perpetual
Total VPN Peers                  : 25             perpetual
Shared License                   : Disabled       perpetual
AnyConnect for Mobile            : Disabled       perpetual
AnyConnect for Cisco VPN Phone   : Disabled       perpetual
Advanced Endpoint Assessment     : Disabled       perpetual
UC Phone Proxy Sessions          : 2              perpetual
Total UC Proxy Sessions          : 2              perpetual
Botnet Traffic Filter            : Disabled       perpetual
Intercompany Media Engine        : Disabled       perpetual


This platform has a Base license.


Serial Number: JMX15364077


Running Permanent Activation Key: 0x970bc671 0x305fc569 0x70d21158
0xb6ec2ca8 0x8a003fb9
```

```
Configuration register is 0x41 (will be 0x1 at next reload)

Configuration last modified by enable_15 at 10:03:12.749 UTC Fri Nov 13
2015

ciscoasa#
```

> **NOTE:**   Additional optional licenses (for example, AnyConnect Premium license) or time-based licenses (for example, Botnet Traffic Filter license) can be purchased.

> **NOTE:**   Preinstalled licenses combined with additional licenses create a permanent license that needs to be activated using the `activation-key` command. The product activation key is purchased from a Cisco account representative.

Basic ASA Configuration

ASA 5505 Front and Back Panel

Figure 17-1 shows the front panel of the ASA 5505.

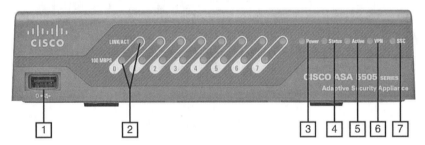

Figure 17-1   ASA 5505 Front Panel

The front panel of the ASA 5505 features as numbered in Figure 17-1 are as follows:

1	USB port	▪ Can be used to enable additional services and capabilities.
2	Speed and link activity LEDs	▪ When the 100-Mbps LED is a solid green, it indicates 100 Mbps; otherwise, it indicates 10 Mbps. ▪ A solid LINK/ACT LED indicates an established network link, and a blinking LED indicates network activity.
3	Power LED	▪ Solid green indicates that the appliance is powered on.

4	**Status LED**	■ A blinking green LED indicates that the system is booting and power-up tests are running. ■ Solid green indicates that the system tests passed and the system is operational. ■ Solid amber indicates that the system tests failed.
5	**Active LED**	■ Green indicates that the Cisco ASA is providing failover.
6	**VPN LED**	■ Solid green indicates that a VPN tunnel is active.
7	**SSC LED**	■ Solid green indicates that a Security Services Card (SSC) is present in the SSC slot.

Figure 17-2 shows the back panel of the ASA 5505.

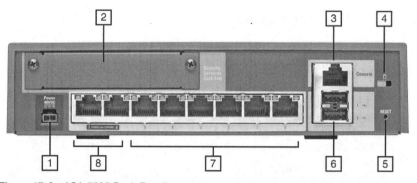

Figure 17-2   ASA 5505 Back Panel

The back panel of the ASA 5505 features as numbered in Figure 17-2 are as follows:

1	**Power connector**	■ Requires a 48 VDC adapter.
2	**SSC slot**	■ Can add IPS features using the Cisco Advanced Inspection and Prevention Security Services Card (AIP-SSC).
3	**Console port**	■ To initially configure the appliance.
4	**Lock slot**	■ To physically secure the appliance.
5	**Reset button**	■ The Reset button is disabled by default.
6	**USB ports**	■ A total of three USB ports can be used to enable additional services and capabilities (two USB ports on the back and one on the front).
7 – 8	**Eight-port Fast Ethernet switch**	■ Each port can be grouped to create up to three separate VLANs (or zones) to support network segmentation and security. ■ Ports 6 and 7 are Power over Ethernet (PoE) ports.

ASA Security Levels

The building blocks of ASA security are assigning interfaces to security levels to distinguish between inside (trusted) and outside (untrusted) networks:

- Security levels define the level of trustworthiness of an interface.

- The higher the level, the more trusted the interface.

- The security level numbers range between 0 (untrustworthy) to 100 (very trustworthy).

- Each operational interface must have a name and a security level from 0 (lowest) to 100 (highest) assigned.

Figure 17-3 illustrates the default ASA security policy.

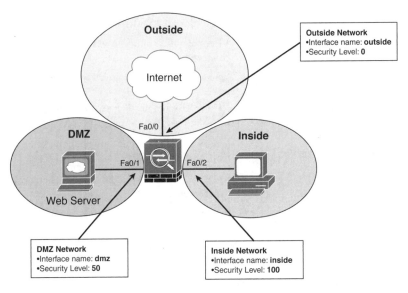

Figure 17-3   Default ASA Security Policy

The default security policy on an ASA 5505 is as follows:

- Traffic sourced from the Inside network (security level 100) and going into either the DMZ (security level 50) or the Outside network (security level 0) is allowed and inspected. Return traffic is allowed due to the stateful packet inspection.

- Traffic sourced from the DMZ network and going into the Inside network is denied.

- Traffic sourced from the Outside network and going into either the DMZ or the Inside network is denied by default.

NOTE: Any exception to this default behavior requires the configuration of access control lists (ACLs) to explicitly permit traffic from an interface with a lower security level to an interface with a higher security level (for example, Outside to DMZ).

ASA 5505 Port Configuration

The ASA 5505 is configured differently than higher models because it does not have any Layer 3 interfaces. It comes with an integrated eight-port Layer 2 Fast Ethernet switch. Each port is individually assigned to a specific VLAN. All Layer 3 parameters (that is, IP address, interface name, and security level) must be configured for the VLAN interface also known as a switch virtual interface (SVI). Switch ports on the same VLAN can communicate with each other using hardware switching.

ASA 5505 Deployment Scenarios

The ASA 5505 is commonly used as an edge security device that connects a small business to an ISP to access the Internet. It can be deployed as follows:

Small branch deployment	▪ The ASA 5505 can be deployed with two security zones:
	  ▪ VLAN 1 with security level 100 for inside hosts
	  ▪ VLAN 2 with security level 0 for the Internet connection

Small business deployment	▪ The ASA 5505 can be deployed with three security zones:
	  ▪ VLAN 1 for the inside network connecting workstations
	
	  ▪ VLAN 2 for the outside network connecting to the Internet
	
	  ▪ VLAN 3 for the DMZ connecting to a company web servers

Enterprise deployment	▪ The ASA 5505 can be used by telecommuters and home users to connect to a centralized location using a VPN.

ASA 5505 Configuration Options

ASA devices can be configured and managed using either the

- ▪ Command-line interface (CLI) required for initial ASA deployment and maintenance
- ▪ Adaptive Security Device Manager (ASDM) GUI

NOTE: ASDM simplifies the deployment and maintenance of an ASA.

CHAPTER 18

Introduction to ASDM

This chapter covers the following topics:

Adaptive Security Device Manager

- Accessing ASDM
- Factory Default Settings
- Resetting the ASA 5505 to Factory Default Settings
- Erasing the Factory Default Settings
- Setup Initialization Wizard

Installing and Running ASDM

- Running ASDM

ASDM Wizards

- The Startup Wizard
- VPN Wizards
- Advanced Wizards

Adaptive Security Device Manager

Cisco Adaptive Security Device Manager (ASDM) is a Java-based GUI tool that facilitates the setup, configuration, monitoring, and troubleshooting of Cisco Adaptive Security Appliances (ASA).

NOTE: ASDM is now preloaded in flash memory on any ASA Versions 7.0 and later.

ASDM can be

- Run from a browser as a Java Web Start application dynamically downloaded from the ASA flash, allowing an administrator to configure and monitor that ASA device
- Downloaded from flash and installed locally on a host as an application, allowing an administrator to use ASDM to configure and manage multiple ASA devices

Accessing ASDM

ASDM access requires connecting to a management interface that has some minimal configurations to communicate over the network.

The management interface depends on the model of ASA:

- On an ASA 5505, the management switch port can be any port, except for Ethernet 0/0.

- On other ASA models the management interface is Management 0/0. However, another Fast Ethernet interface can also be used.

The minimal configuration can be provided on an ASA 5505 using any of the following methods:

Restore factory default settings	- The ASA can be reset to provide a basic configuration that is sufficient for a small office/home office (SOHO) deployment. - The configuration includes two preconfigured VLAN networks, Dynamic Host Configuration Protocol (DHCP), and Network Address Translation (NAT) services.
Setup Initialization Wizard	- The ASA interactively guides an administrator to configure the basic security settings to access ASDM. - Additional HTTP settings must be configured to access the ASDM.
CLI configuration	- Configure all parameters using the command-line interface (CLI).

NOTE: The next chapter covers the CLI configuration method.

Factory Default Settings

The ASA 5505 with a Base license ships with the following default factory settings:

- A default hostname of **ciscoasa**.

- Console or enable passwords, which are blank.

- An inside VLAN 1 interface that includes the Ethernet 0/1 through 0/7 switch ports. The VLAN 1 IP address and mask are 192.168.1.1 and 255.255.255.0.

- An outside VLAN 2 interface that includes the Ethernet 0/0 switch port. VLAN 2 derives its IP address from the ISP using DHCP.

- The default route derived from DHCP.

- All inside IP addresses to be translated when accessing the outside using interface Port Address Translation (PAT).

- The HTTP server to support ASDM access.

- An internal DHCP server to provide addresses between 192.168.1.5 and 192.168.1.36 for hosts that connect to a VLAN 1 interface.

NOTE: You can change these settings manually using the CLI or interactively using either the CLI Setup Initialization Wizard or by using the ASDM Startup Wizard.

NOTE: The Reset button on the ASA 5505 is disabled and inoperable by default.

Resetting the ASA 5505 to Factory Default Settings

You can restore the ASA to its factory default configuration by using the following:

ciscoasa# **config t**	Enter global configuration mode.
ciscoasa(config)# **config factory-default**	Reset the ASA to factory default settings. **NOTE:** A warning appears stating that the boot system configuration (startup configuration) will be cleared. **NOTE:** The ASA loads a default configuration into the running configuration.
ciscoasa(config)# **reload save-config noconfirm**	Save the configuration and then reload the ASA without asking for confirmation.

Erasing the Factory Default Settings

ciscoasa# **write erase**	Erase the startup-configuration file.
ciscoasa(config)# **reload noconfirm**	Reload the ASA without confirmation.

Setup Initialization Wizard

When the default factory settings are erased and an ASA is reloaded, the ASA Setup Initialization Wizard prompts eventually appear asking Pre-configure Firewall now through interactive prompts [yes]?

Answering no cancels the Setup Initialization Wizard, and the ASA displays its default prompt. In this case, you must manually configure the ASA via the CLI.

Pressing **Enter** accepts the default [yes], and the ASA interactively guides an administrator to configure basic ASA features, including the following:

- Firewall mode
- Enable password
- Enable password recovery
- Time and date settings
- Inside IP address and mask
- ASA device name
- Domain name

NOTE: The security appliance displays the default values in brackets ([ ]) before prompting the user to accept or change them. To accept the default input, press **Enter**.

When the interactive portion of the Setup Initialization Wizard completes, the security appliance displays the summary of the new configuration and prompts the user to save or reject the settings:

- Answering **yes** saves the configuration and displays the configured hostname prompt.

- Answering **no** restarts the Setup Initialization Wizard. Any changes previously made become the new default settings enabling an administrator to correct a misconfigured setting.

The Setup Initialization Wizard provides most of the settings for ASDM. However, the HTTP service must be enabled.

To allow access to ASDM, enable HTTPS connections from any host on the inside network:

ciscoasa(config)# **http server enable**	Enable HTTP services.
ciscoasa(config)# **http** *ip-address* *network-mask interface-name*	Identify a host or hosts that can access the ASA HTTP server using ASDM.

NOTE: To remove and disable the ASA HTTP server service, use the global configuration command **clear configure http**.

Installing and Running ASDM

The ASDM interface can be accessed from any workstation with an IP address included in the HTTP trusted network list.

TIP: Before attempting to establish a secure ASDM connection to the ASA, verify that IP connectivity exists between the workstation and the Cisco ASA.

With a factory default configuration

- A host on the 192.168.1.0/24 network can connect to the ASA default management IP address of 192.168.1.1 using ASDM.

- The host must establish a connection through a browser to the inside interface IP address using the HTTPS protocol.

A security certificate window may appear. Depending on the browser settings, select **Yes** or click on **Continue to This Website** to continue to the ASDM launcher window.

The ASDM launcher appears, as shown in Figure 18-1.

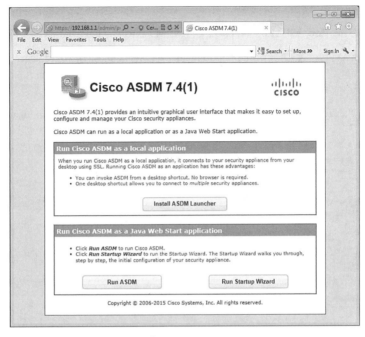

Figure 18-1   Cisco ASDM Launcher Screen

The ASDM launcher window provides three choices:

Install ASDM Launcher and Run ASDM	▪ Install ASDM as an application on the Windows host.
	▪ The advantage is that the application can be used to manage several ASA devices.
	▪ An Internet browser will no longer be required to start ASDM.
Run ASDM	▪ Run ASDM as a Java Web Start application.
	▪ The advantage is that the ASDM is not locally installed.
	▪ An Internet browser is required to establish a connection.
Run Startup Wizard	▪ Run the ASDM Startup Wizard.
	▪ Similar to the Setup Initialization Wizard, it provides step-by-step windows to help initially configure the ASA.

NOTE: The recommended choice is to install ASDM locally on the host. For security reasons, you might want to simply run ASDM.

Running ASDM

Selecting the **Run ASDM** option opens an ASDM authentication window.

If you are starting ASDM for the first time after running a Startup Wizard, leave the fields empty. If Secure Shell (SSH) has been configured, a local database username and password should be used.

When authentication is successful, the ASDM Home page appears, as shown in Figure 18-2.

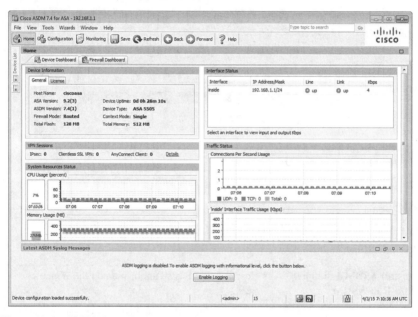

Figure 18-2   ASDM Home Page

The Cisco ASDM Home page is updated every 10 seconds and provides a quick view of the operational status of the ASA. The ASDM GUI includes the following elements:

Menu bar	■ Provides quick access to files, tools, wizards, and help.
Toolbar	■ Provides easy navigation of Cisco ASDM.
	■ From the toolbar, an administrator can access the Home, Configuration, and Monitoring views and can save, refresh, navigate between views, and access Help.

Device List button	■ Opens a dockable page that lists other ASA devices.
	■ Use this page to switch to another device running the same version of ASDM.
	■ When managing only one ASA device, the Device List page is hidden and must be opened using the Device List button.
Status bar	■ Displays the time, connection status, user, memory status, running configuration status, privilege level, and SSL status at the bottom of the application window.

The Home page also displays two to four tabs:

Device Dashboard	■ (Default) Provides a view of important information about the ASA, such as the status of interfaces, the OS version, licensing information, and performance-related information.
Firewall Dashboard	■ (Default) Provides security-related information about traffic that passes through the ASA, such as connection statistics, dropped packets, and scan and syn attack detection.
Intrusion Prevention	■ Appears only if an Intrusion Prevention System (IPS) module or card is installed.
	■ The additional tab displays status information about the IPS software.
Content Security	■ Appears only if a Content Security and Control Security Services Module (CSC-SSM) is installed in the ASA.
	■ The Content Security tab displays status information about the CSC-SSM software.

The Configuration and Monitoring views also feature a dockable navigation pane that you can maximize, restore, or make float so that it can be moved, hidden, or closed. The navigation pane of the Configuration view displays the following tabs:

- ■ Device Setup
- ■ Firewall
- ■ Remote-Access VPN
- ■ Site-to-Site VPN
- ■ Device Management

The navigation pane of the Monitoring view displays the following tabs:

- Interfaces
- VPN
- Routing
- Properties
- Logging

NOTE: The options listed in the navigation pane vary depending on the view and tab selected.

ASDM Wizards

Cisco ASDM offers several wizards to help simplify the configuration of the appliance:

- Startup Wizard
- Virtual private network (VPN) wizards
- Advanced wizards

The Startup Wizard

The Startup Wizard guides the administrator through the initial configuration of the ASA and helps to define basic settings.

Choose either **Wizards > Startup Wizard** or **Configuration > Device Setup > Startup Wizard** to open the configuration Startup Wizard screen (see Figure 18-3).

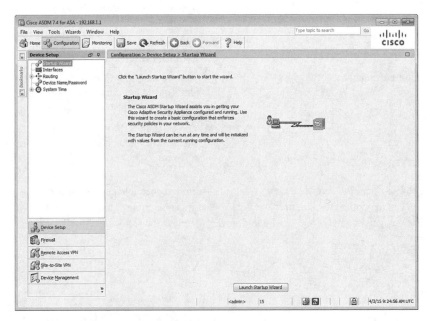

Figure 18-3   Configuration Startup Wizard Screen

After the Startup Wizard page appears, click the **Launch Startup Wizard** button.

NOTE: The actual number of steps in the wizard may vary depending on the specific ASA model and modules installed. However, most ASA models can be configured in a nine-step process.

After the Startup Wizard has been launched, follow these steps:

1. The Starting Point window (also referred to as the Welcome window) is displayed and provides a choice to Modify an Existing Configuration or to Reset the Configuration to Factory Defaults.

2. In the Basic Configuration window, complete the basic ASA management configuration consisting of a hostname, domain name, and privileged EXEC password. Optionally, this step also allows the administrator to deploy the ASA for a remote worker.

3. In the Interface Selection window, create the VLAN switch interfaces. This and other VLAN-related steps are specific to the ASA 5505 model. The Startup Wizard for the ASA 5510 and later models provides steps to configure the Fast Ethernet routed interfaces as needed without the need for VLANs.

4. In the Switch Port Allocation window, map the physical Layer 2 switch ports to the logically named VLANs in the previous step. By default, all switch ports are assigned to VLAN 1 (Inside).

5. In the Interface IP Address Configuration window, identify the inside and outside IP addresses for the defined VLANs. Note that these addresses could also be created using DHCP or PPPoE.

6. The DHCP window allows the administrator to enable the DHCP service for inside hosts. All DHCP-related options are defined in this window.

7. The Address Translation (NAT/PAT) window allows the administrator to enable PAT or NAT.

8. In the Administrative Access window, specify which host or hosts are allowed to access the ASA using HTTPS/ASDM, SSH, or Telnet.

9. The final window is the Startup Wizard Summary. Review the proposed configuration. You can make changes by clicking the **Back** button or save by clicking the **Finish** button.

VPN Wizards

The various VPN wizards enable an administrator to configure basic site-to-site and remote-access VPN connections and assign either pre-shared keys or digital certificates for authentication.

To launch a VPN wizard from the menu bar, click **Wizards** and choose **VPN Wizards** (see Figure 18-4).

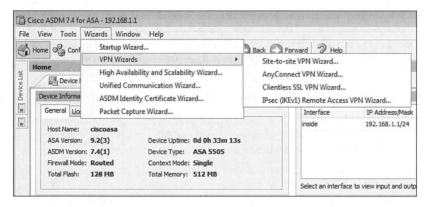

Figure 18-4 Available VPN Wizards

Advanced Wizards

Three other wizards are available in ASDM:

High Availability and Scalability Wizard	■ Guides an administrator to configure failover with high availability and VPN cluster load balancing. ■ VPN cluster mode requires two ASA devices establishing VPN sessions to the same destination network and performing load balancing.
Unified Communication Wizard	■ Used to configure the ASA to support the Cisco Unified Communications Proxy feature.
Packet Capture Wizard	■ Used to configure and run captures for troubleshooting errors and for validating a NAT policy. ■ The captures can use access lists to limit the type of traffic captured, the source and destination addresses and ports, and one or more interfaces. ■ The wizard runs one capture on each of the ingress and egress interfaces. ■ Captures can be saved to a host and examined in a packet analyzer.

NOTE: These three wizards are beyond the scope of this chapter and so are not explored further.

CHAPTER 19

Configuring Cisco ASA Basic Settings

This chapter covers the following topics:

ASA Command-Line Interface

- Differences Between IOS and ASA OS

Configuring Basic Settings

- Configuring Basic Management Settings
- Enabling the Master Passphrase

Configuring Interfaces

- Configuring the Inside and Outside SVIs
- Assigning Layer 2 Ports to VLANs
- Configuring a Third SVI

Configuring the Management Plane

- Enabling Telnet, SSH, and HTTPS Access
- Configuring Time Services

Configuring the Control Plane

- Configuring a Default Route

Basic Settings Example

- Configuring Basic Settings Example Using the CLI
- Configuring Basic Settings Example Using ASDM
- Configuring Interfaces Using ASDM
- Configuring the System Time Using ASDM
- Configuring Device Management Access Using ASDM

ASA Command-Line Interface

The Adaptive Security Appliance (ASA) command-line interface (CLI) is a proprietary OS that has a similar look and feel to the router IOS. Like a Cisco IOS router, the ASA recognizes the following:

- Abbreviation of commands and keywords
- Using the Tab key to complete a partial command
- Using the help key (**?**) after a command to view additional syntax

Differences Between IOS and ASA OS

Unlike an ISR, the ASA

- Can execute any ASA CLI command regardless of the current configuration mode prompt and does not require or recognize the `do` IOS CLI command

- Can provide additional help listing a brief command description and syntax by using the EXEC command `help` followed by the CLI command (for example, `help reload`)

- Interrupts `show` command output by simply using the letter `Q` (unlike the **Ctrl+C** (**^C**) IOS CLI key sequence)

Although the ASA CLI uses many of the same commands as IOS, there are also many different ASA commands. The following partial list highlights common IOS router commands and the equivalent ASA CLI command:

IOS Router Command	Equivalent ASA Command
`enable secret` *password*	`enable password` *password*

`line vty 0 4`
`password` *password*
`login`
	`passwd` *password*

`ip route`	`route outside`
`show ip interfaces brief`	`show interfaces ip brief`
`show ip route`	`show route`
`show vlan`	`show switch vlan`
`show ip nat translations`	`show xlate`
`copy running-config startup-config`	`write [memory]`
`erase startup-config`	`write erase`

NOTE: The listed IOS router commands are not available on an ASA device.

Configuring Basic Settings

To configure settings on an ASA 5505, follow these steps:

1. Configure basic management settings (that is, hostname, domain name, and enable password).

2. Enable the master passphrase.

3. Configure the Inside and Outside switch virtual interfaces (SVIs).

4. Assign Layer 2 ports to VLANs.

5. Enable Telnet, SSH, and HTTPS access.

6. Configure time services.

7. Configure a default route.

NOTE: Assume that the ASA startup configuration file has been erased and the device has been reloaded.

Enter privileged EXEC and then global configuration mode:

`Pre-configure Firewall now through interactive prompts [yes]?` **`no`**	At the Setup Initialization Wizard prompt, enter no to exit the wizard.
`ciscoasa>` **`enable`** `Password:`	Enter privilege EXEC mode. When prompted for the password, press **Enter**. **NOTE:** The default is no enable password. **NOTE:** If the ASA device is booted using the default factory settings, the password is cisco.
`ciscoasa#` **`configure terminal`**	Enter ASA global configuration mode.

NOTE: The first time global configuration mode is accessed, a message prompting you to enable the Smart Call Home feature appears. This feature offers proactive diagnostics and real-time alerts on select Cisco devices.

Configuring Basic Management Settings

Configure hostname, domain name, and privileged EXEC password:

`ciscoasa(config)#` **`hostname`** `ASA-hostname`	Configure the ASA hostname.
`ciscoasa(config)#` **`domain-name`** `ASA-domain-name`	Configure a domain name.
`ciscoasa(config)#` **`enable password`** `password`	Configure the privileged EXEC mode password. **NOTE:** There is no secret option.
`ciscoasa(config)#` **`banner motd`** `string`	Provide legal notification. However, unlike the IOS version of the command, there is no delimiter. To configure a banner with several lines, enter the command multiple times. To remove a line(s), use the `no banner motd` message command.

Enabling the Master Passphrase

The master passphrase must be configured and enabled to encrypt all user passwords:

ciscoasa(config)# **key config-key password-encryption** [*new-passphrase* [*old-passphrase*]]	Create or change an existing master passphrase. **NOTE:** The passphrase must be 8–128 characters in length, and all characters except a backspace and double quote are accepted. **NOTE:** If a new passphrase is not included in the command, the ASA prompts for it. **NOTE:** To change the passphrase, you must first enter the old passphrase.
ciscoasa(config)# **password encryption aes**	Enable password encryption.

NOTE: To determine whether password encryption is enabled, use the **show password encryption** command.

NOTE: Interfaces must be configured before Telnet, SSH, HTTPS, and static routes are configured.

Configuring Interfaces

Similar to the Integrated Services Router (ISR), the ASA models have routed Ethernet interfaces directly configured with IP configurations. However, the ASA 5505 has an integrated eight-port Layer 2 switch, and therefore IP configurations are accomplished by

- Configuring the inside and outside SVIs by assigning interface name, security level, and IP address

- Assigning Layer 2 ports to the inside and outside SVI VLANs

- (Optional) Configuring a third SVI if required

Configuring the Inside and Outside SVIs

ciscoasa(config)# **interface vlan** *vlan-id*	Create an SVI.
ciscoasa(config-if)# **nameif** {**inside** | **outside** | *name*}	Assign a name to the SVI interface. **NOTE:** Using the name **inside** automatically assigns a security level of 100. **NOTE:** Using the name **outside** automatically assigns a security level of 0.

ciscoasa(config-if)# **security-level** *level*	Assign or change the SVI security level. **NOTE:** All SVIs must be assigned a security level value. **NOTE:** Security levels are automatically assigned for inside and outside interfaces.
ciscoasa(config-if)# **ip address** *ip-address netmask*	Assign an IP address and mask to the SVI. **NOTE:** The ASA could also obtain its IP address and default route if it is configured as a Dynamic Host Configuration Protocol (DHCP) client or PPP over Ethernet (PPPoE) client.

NOTE: By default, an SVI is active and does not require the **no shutdown** command.

Assigning Layer 2 Ports to VLANs

The Layer 2 ports must be assigned to a VLAN.

NOTE: By default, all ports are members of VLAN 1.

Therefore, to change the default VLAN assignment, you must configure the Layer 2 port with the following commands:

ciscoasa(config)# **interface** *interface/number*	Specify a Layer 2 physical port.
ciscoasa(config-if)# **switchport** **access vlan** *vlan-id*	Change the VLAN assignment of the port from the default of VLAN 1.
ciscoasa(config-if)# **no shutdown**	Enable physical port.

NOTE: The Layer 2 port must be enabled and therefore requires the **no shutdown** command.

NOTE: To verify VLAN settings, use the **show switch vlan** command. To verify interface settings, use the **show interface** or **show int ip brief** command.

NOTE: ASA Fast Ethernet interfaces are designated as Ethernet x/x (for example, E0/0).

Configuring a Third SVI

An ASA 5505 with the Security Plus license automatically supports the creation of additional VLANs to create other zones such as a demilitarized zone (DMZ). However, an ASA 5505 with a Base license only supports a third, *restricted* SVI that is limited from initiating contact to another specified VLAN.

Use the following to configure a third VLAN SVI on an ASA 5505 with a Base license:

`ciscoasa(config)# interface` `interface/number`	Specify a Layer 2 physical port.

`ciscoasa(config-if)# no`
`forward interface vlan`
`vlan-id`
	Limit the interface from initiating contact to another VLAN.
	
	NOTE: The `vlan-id` argument specifies the VLAN ID to which this VLAN interface cannot initiate traffic.
	
	NOTE: You must configure this command before the interface is named.
	
	NOTE: Configure this command on the third SVI after the inside and outside VLAN interfaces have been configured.

Configuring the Management Plane

Enabling Telnet, SSH, and HTTPS Access

The ASA can be configured to accept Telnet connections from a single host or a range of hosts on the inside network. Use the following commands to enable the Telnet service:

`ciscoasa(config)# passwd` `password`	Configure the Telnet/SSH password.

`ciscoasa(config)# telnet`
`ip-address subnet-mask`
`interface-name`
	Identify which inside hosts can telnet to which ASA interface.

`ciscoasa(config)# telnet` `timeout minutes`	Alters the default EXEC timeout of 5 minutes.

Alternatively, Telnet can be configured to use authentication, authorization, and accounting (AAA) authentication:

`ciscoasa(config)# username` `name password password`	Create a local database entry.

`ciscoasa(config)# aaa`
`authentication telnet`
`console LOCAL`
	Configure Telnet to refer to the local database for authentication.

Secure Shell (SSH) is also supported, but it requires AAA authentication to be enabled. Use the following commands to enable SSH support:

`ciscoasa(config)# username` `name password password`	Create a local database entry.
`ciscoasa(config)# aaa authen-` `tication ssh console LOCAL`	Configure SSH to refer to the local database for authentication. **NOTE:** The LOCAL keyword is case sensitive and is a predefined server tag.
`ciscoasa(config)# crypto key` `generate rsa modulus modulus`	Generates the RSA key required for SSH encryption. **NOTE:** Valid modulus values include 512, 768, 1024, and 2048. Higher modulus values are recommended.

`ciscoasa(config)# ssh`
`ip-address subnet-mask`
`interface-name`
	Identify which inside hosts can SSH to which ASA interface.

`ciscoasa(config)# ssh version` `{1 | 2}`	Enable SSH version 1 or 2. Use the no ssh version command to reset to the default version 1 and 2.
`ciscoasa(config)# ssh timeout` `minutes`	Alters the default privilege EXEC timeout of 5 minutes.

NOTE: To verify the SSH configuration, use the show ssh command.

Enable HTTPS services on the ASA:

`ciscoasa(config)# http server` `enable`	Enable the ASA HTTP server.

`ciscoasa(config)# http`
`ip-address network-mask`
`interface-name`
	Identify a host or hosts that can access the ASA HTTP server using ASDM.

NOTE: To remove and disable the ASA HTTP server service, use the clear configure http global configuration command.

Configuring Time Services

To configure the local system clock, use the following command:

`ciscoasa(config)# clock set` `hh:mm:ss month day year`	Manually sets the clock via the CLI.

NOTE: To verify the clock setting, use the show clock command.

Alternatively, you can configure the ASA to use Network Time Protocol (NTP) services. Use the following global configuration commands to securely configure and enable NTP:

ciscoasa(config)# ntp server ip-address [key key-number]	Identify the NTP server address.
ciscoasa(config)# ntp authentication-key key-number md5 password	Configure the NTP key and password.
ciscoasa(config)# ntp trusted-key key-number	Identify the trusted key.
ciscoasa(config)# ntp authenticate	Enable NTP authentication.

NOTE: To verify the NTP configuration and status, use the show ntp status and show ntp associations commands.

Configuring the Control Plane

Configuring a Default Route

If an ASA is configured as a DHCP or PPPoE client, it most probably is getting a default route provided by the upstream device. Otherwise, the ASA requires a default static route to be configured:

ciscoasa(config)# route interface-name 0.0.0.0 0.0.0.0 next-hop-ip-address	Create a default static route.

NOTE: To verify the route entry, use the show route command.

Basic Settings Example

In this example, you

- Configure basic management settings.
- Configure and enable the master passphrase.
- Create the inside network SVI (VLAN 1) and assign it an IP address, create the outside network SVI (VLAN 2) and assign it an IP address, and create a limited DMZ network SVI (VLAN 3) and assign it an IP address and a security level.
- Assign interface Ethernet 0/1 to VLAN 1, E0/0 to VLAN 2, and E0/2 to VLAN 3.
- Enable Telnet, SSH, and HTTPS access and NTP time services.
- Configure a default route to the ISP.

Figure 19-1 shows the network topology for the ASA basic settings example.

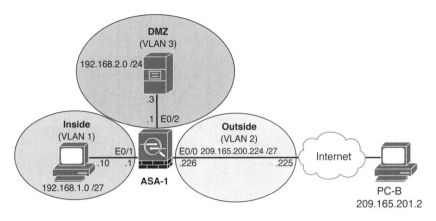

Figure 19-1   Network Topology for the ASA Basic Settings Example

Configuring Basic Settings Example Using the CLI

`ciscoasa(config)# hostname ASA-1`	Name the ASA.
`ASA-1(config)# domain-name ccnas.com`	Configure the domain name.
`ASA-1(config)# enable password` `cisco123`	Configure the privileged EXEC password.
`ASA-1(config)# key config-key` `password-encryption cisco123`	Configure the master passphrase key.
`ASA-1(config)# password encryption` `aes`	Enable the master passphrase.
`ASA-1(config)# interface vlan 1`	Define the inside SVI (VLAN 1).

`ASA-1(config-if)# nameif inside`
`INFO: Security level for "inside"`
`set to 100 by default.`
	Name the inside SVI. It defaults to a security level of 100.

`ASA-1(config-if)# ip address` `192.168.1.1 255.255.255.0`	Assign the inside interface IP address.
`ASA-1(config-if)# interface vlan 2`	Define the outside SVI (VLAN 2).

`ASA-1(config-if)# nameif outside`
`INFO: Security level for "outside"`
`set to 0 by default.`
	Name the outside SVI. It defaults to a security level of 0.

`ASA-1(config-if)# ip address` `209.165.200.226 255.255.255.248`	Assign the outside interface IP address.
`ASA-1(config-if)# interface vlan 3`	Define the DMZ SVI (VLAN 3).
`ASA-1(config-if)# no forward` `interface vlan 1`	Disable forwarding to interface VLAN 1, denying the DMZ server the ability to communicate with the inside users. **NOTE:** Required because of the Base license restriction.

`ASA-1(config-if)# nameif dmz`
`INFO: Security level for "dmz"`
`set to 0 by default.`
	Name the DMZ SVI. It defaults to a security level of 0.

`ASA-1(config-if)# security-level 70`	Change the security level to 70.
`ASA-1(config-if)# ip address` `192.168.2.1 255.255.255.0`	Assign the DMZ interface an IP address.
`ASA-1(config-if)# exit`	Return to global configuration mode.
`ASA-1(config)# interface e0/1`	Configure interface Ethernet 0/1.
`ASA-1(config-if)# switchport` `access vlan 1`	Assign it to VLAN 1.
`ASA-1(config-if)# no shut`	Enable the physical port.
`ASA-1(config-if)# interface e0/0`	Configure interface Ethernet 0/0.
`ASA-1(config-if)# switchport` `access vlan 2`	Assign it to VLAN 2.
`ASA-1(config-if)# exit`	Enable the physical port.
`ASA-1(config-if)# interface e0/2`	Configure interface Ethernet 0/2.
`ASA-1(config-if)# switchport` `access vlan 3`	Assign it to VLAN 3.
`ASA-1(config-if)# exit`	Return to global configuration.
`ASA-1(config)# password cisco123`	Create a Telnet/SSH password.
`ASA-1(config)# telnet 192.168.1.10` `255.255.255.255 inside`	Identify which inside host can connect to the ASA using Telnet.
`ASA-1(config)# telnet timeout 4`	Change the default EXEC timeout from 5 minutes to 4 minutes.
`ASA-1(config)# username admin` `password cisco123`	Create a local database entry.
`ASA-1(config)# aaa authentication` `ssh console LOCAL`	Enable AAA authentication for SSH using the local database.
`ASA-1(config)# crypto key` `generate rsa modulus 1024`	Create the crypto key required for SSH.
`ASA-1(config)# ssh 192.168.1.10` `255.255.255.255 inside`	Identify which inside host can connect to the ASA using SSH.
`ASA-1(config)# ssh timeout 4`	Change the default EXEC timeout from 5 minutes to 4 minutes.
`ASA-1(config)# http server enable`	Enable the HTTP server services.
`ASA-1(config)# http 192.168.1.10` `255.255.255.255 inside`	Identify which inside host can connect to the ASA using HTTP.
`ASA-1(config)# ntp server` `209.165.200.225`	Identify the authoritative NTP source.
`ASA-1(config)# ntp authentication-key` `51 md5 cisco123`	Specify the key number and password.
`ASA-1(config)# ntp trusted-key 51`	Identify which key to trust.
`ASA-1(config)# ntp authenticate`	Enable NTP authentication.

`ASA-1(config)# route outside` `0.0.0.0 0.0.0.0 209.165.200.225`	Create a default route to the ISP router.
`ASA-1(config)# exit`	Return to privileged EXEC.

`ASA-1# copy running-config`
`startup-config`
 	
`Source filename [running-config]?`
 	
`Cryptochecksum: 2ffaa172`
`764cb357 91204306 c9a552e4`
 	
`1579 bytes copied in 1.300 secs`
`(1579 bytes/sec)`
 	
`ASA-1#`
	Save the running configuration.

Configuring Basic Settings Example Using ASDM

To configure the hostname, domain name, enable, and Telnet passwords, choose **Configuration > Device Setup > Device Name/Password**.

It is important to note that most configuration changes are not implemented unless they are exclusively applied. Therefore, configuration screens typically have an **Apply** button at the bottom of the screen to enable the configured settings.

The Device Name/Password screen is shown in Figure 19-2.

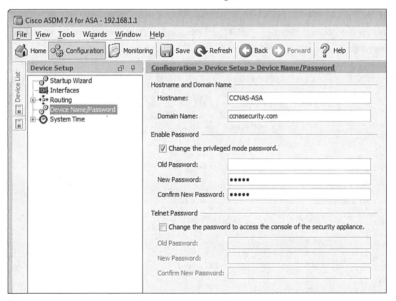

Figure 19-2   Device Name/Password Screen

From this screen, you can configure the following:

- The hostname (appears in the command-line prompt and is also used in system messages)
- The domain name (appended as a suffix to unqualified names)

- The Telnet password (sets the login password, which by default is set to cisco)
- The Telnet password (applies to Telnet and SSH access)

To configure a master passphrase and encrypt all passwords, choose **Configuration > Device Management > Advanced > Master Passphrase** to open the Master Passphrase screen (see Figure 19-3).

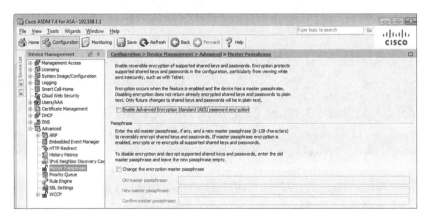

Figure 19-3 Master Passphrase Screen

To configure legal notification, click **Configuration > Device Management > Management Access > Command Line (CLI) > Banner** (see Figure 19-4).

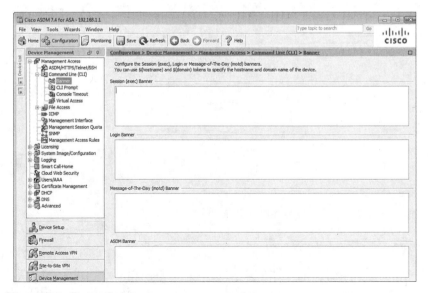

Figure 19-4 Banner Screen

Configuring Interfaces Using ASDM

To configure the Layer 3 interfaces, choose **Configuration > Device Setup > Interfaces** to open the Interfaces screen (see Figure 19-5).

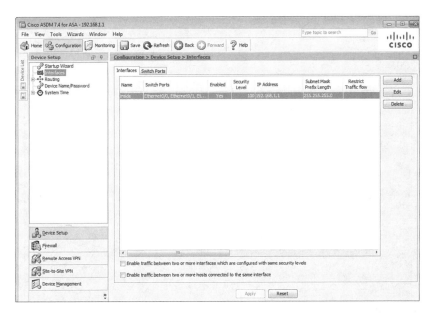

Figure 19-5   Interfaces Screen

In this window, you can create or edit the ASA inside, outside, and DMZ interfaces.

For example, to configure interface Ethernet 0/0 to be an outside interface in VLAN 2 with IP address 209.165.200.226/29, click the **Add** button to open the Add Interface window displayed in Figure 19-6.

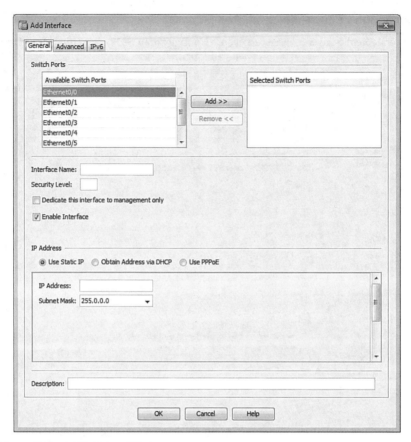

Figure 19-6 Add Interface Window

Ethernet 0/0 is highlighted by default. Add it to the Selected Switch Ports area by clicking **Add >>**. ASDM displays a Change Switch Port window, as shown in Figure 19-7.

Figure 19-7 Change Switch Port Window

Click **OK** to continue.

Assign the interface name **outside** with security level **0** and IP address **209.165.200.226** and subnet mask **255.255.255.248**, as shown in Figure 19-8.

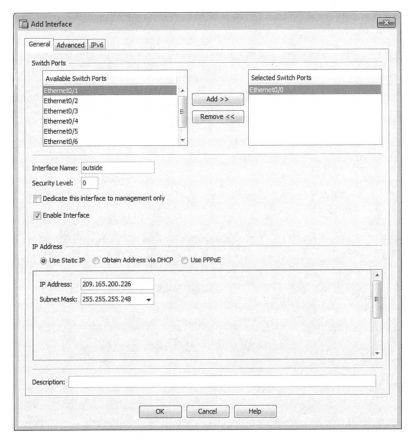

Figure 19-8   Add Interface Window with Change

The interface needs to be assigned to VLAN 2; therefore, click the **Advanced** tab. By default, ASDM wants to add the interface to VLAN 1. Change this setting to VLAN 2, as shown in Figure 19-9; then click **OK**.

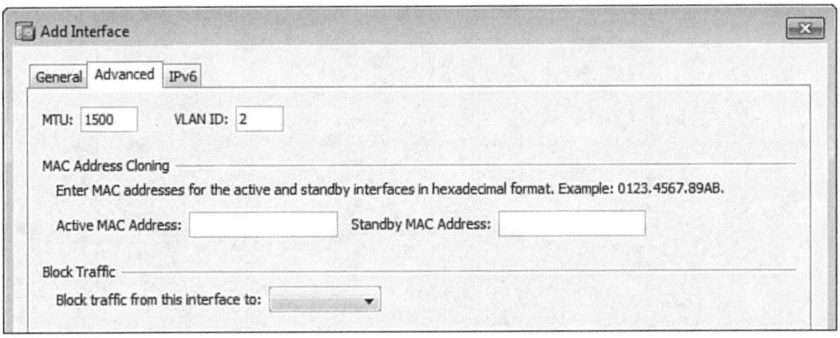

Figure 19-9   Change VLANs

ASDM now displays an updated Interface page highlighting the newly added outside interface, as shown in Figure 19-10.

Name	Switch Ports	Enabled	Security Level	IP Address	Subnet Mask Prefix Length	Restrict Traffic flow	
inside	Ethernet0/0, Ethernet0/1, Et...	Yes	100	192.168.1.1	255.255.255.0		Add
outside	Ethernet0/0	Yes	0	209.165.200.226	255.255.255.248		Edit
							Delete

Configuration > Device Setup > Interfaces

Interfaces | Switch Ports

Figure 19-10 Outside Interface Added

Next select the **Switch Ports** tab and the page displays the various port settings, as shown in Figure 19-11.

Configuration > Device Setup > Interfaces

Interfaces | Switch Ports

Switch Port	Enabled	Associated VLANs	Associated Interface Names	Mode	Protected	Duplex	Speed	
Ethernet0/0	No	2	outside	Access	No	auto	auto	Edit
Ethernet0/1	Yes	1	inside	Access	No	auto	auto	
Ethernet0/2	No	1	inside	Access	No	auto	auto	
Ethernet0/3	No	1	inside	Access	No	auto	auto	
Ethernet0/4	No	1	inside	Access	No	auto	auto	
Ethernet0/5	No	1	inside	Access	No	auto	auto	
Ethernet0/6	No	1	inside	Access	No	auto	auto	
Ethernet0/7	No	1	inside	Access	No	auto	auto	

Figure 19-11 Switch Port Screen

Notice how Ethernet 0/0 is not enabled yet. Click **Edit** to open the Edit Switch Port window, shown in Figure 19-12.

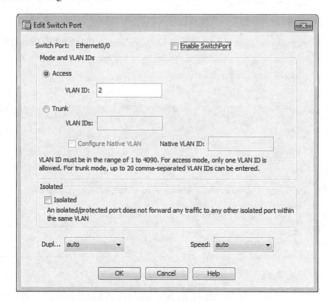

Figure 19-12 Edit Switch Port Screen

Then click **Enable SwitchPort** check box and click **OK**.

Finally, **Apply** the configuration and ASDM displays the updated Interface page, as shown in Figure 19-13.

Figure 19-13 Configured Outside Interface

Configuring the System Time Using ASDM

To change the system time, choose **Configuration > Device Setup > System Time > Clock** to open the Clock screen (see Figure 19-14).

Figure 19-14 System Time Clock Screen

From this screen, you can manually configure the time zone, date, and time. The time is displayed in the status bar in the bottom-right corner.

To configure NTP, choose **Configuration > Device Setup > System Time > NTP** to open the NTP screen (see Figure 19-15).

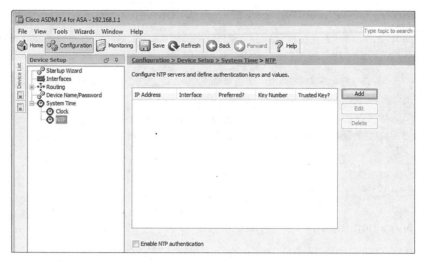

Figure 19-15 System Time NTP Screen

In this window, you can add, edit, or delete an NTP server. When adding a server, you can configure the IP address and authentication parameters. Time derived from an NTP server overrides any time set manually.

Clicking **Add** opens the Add NTP Server Configuration window, as shown in Figure 19-16.

Figure 19-16 Adding an NTP Server

From here the IP address and authentication parameters can be configured, as shown in the example in Figure 19-17.

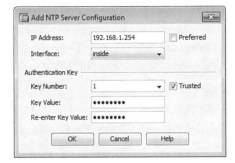

Figure 19-17 Adding an NTP Server Example

Click **OK** and the NTP page displays the newly added parameters, as shown in Figure 19-18.

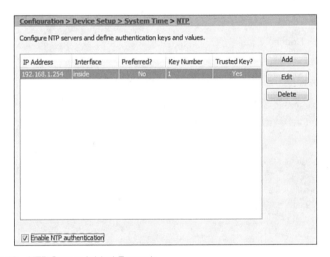

Figure 19-18 NTP Server Added Example

Finally, click the **Enable NTP authentication** check box and **Apply** the configuration.

Configuring Static Routing Using ASDM

Routing can be implemented by choosing **Configuration > Device Setup > Routing** as shown in Figure 19-19.

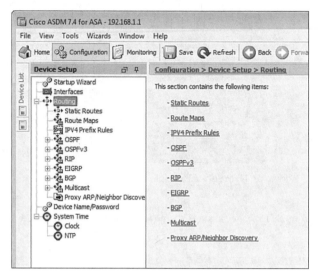

Figure 19-19   Routing Screen

From here, an administrator can enable IPv4 and IPv6 static and dynamic routing.

For example, to create a default static route to R1 located at 209.165.200.225, click **Configuration > Device Setup > Routing > Static Routes**, as shown in Figure 19-20.

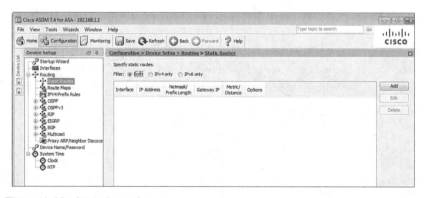

Figure 19-20   Static Route Screen

From here, static and default static routes can be entered or edited.

Click **Add** to open the Add Static Route window, as shown in Figure 19-21.

Figure 19-21   Add Static Route Window

Select outside from the Interface drop-down list and complete the details, as shown in Figure 19-22.

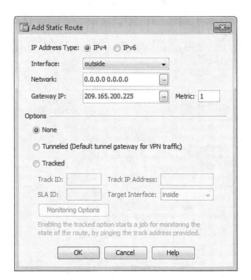

Figure 19-22   Add Static Route Window Example

Click **OK** to return to the Static Routes page, as shown in Figure 19-23.

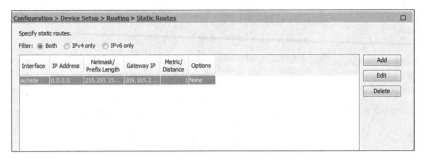

Figure 19-23   Static Route Added Example

Finally, click **Apply** to commit the changes.

Configuring Device Management Access Using ASDM

To configure management access for Telnet and SSH services, choose **Configuration > Device Management > Management Access > ASDM/HTTPS/Telnet/SSH**, as shown in Figure 19-24.

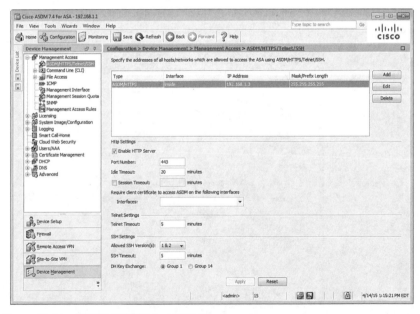

Figure 19-24   ASDM/HTTPS/Telnet/SSH Screen

In this window, an administrator can identify which host or networks can have access to the ASA via ASDM/HTTPS, Telnet, or SSH.

For example, to enable the 192.168.1.3 host SSH access, click **Add** and complete the information, as shown in Figure 19-25.

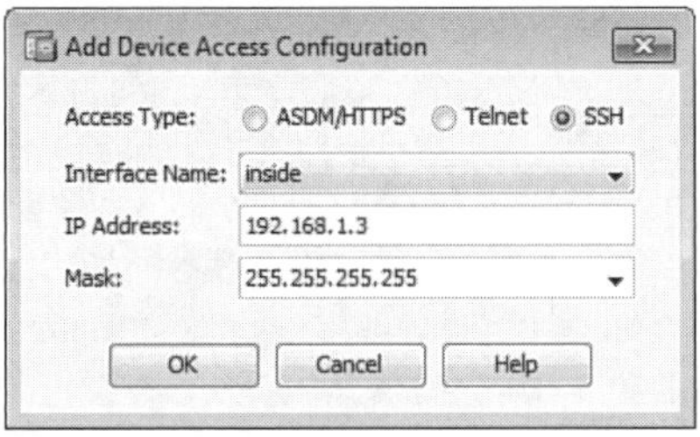

Figure 19-25   Add Device Access Configuration Window

Click **OK** to return to the main page and configure the SSH specifics, as shown in Figure 19-26.

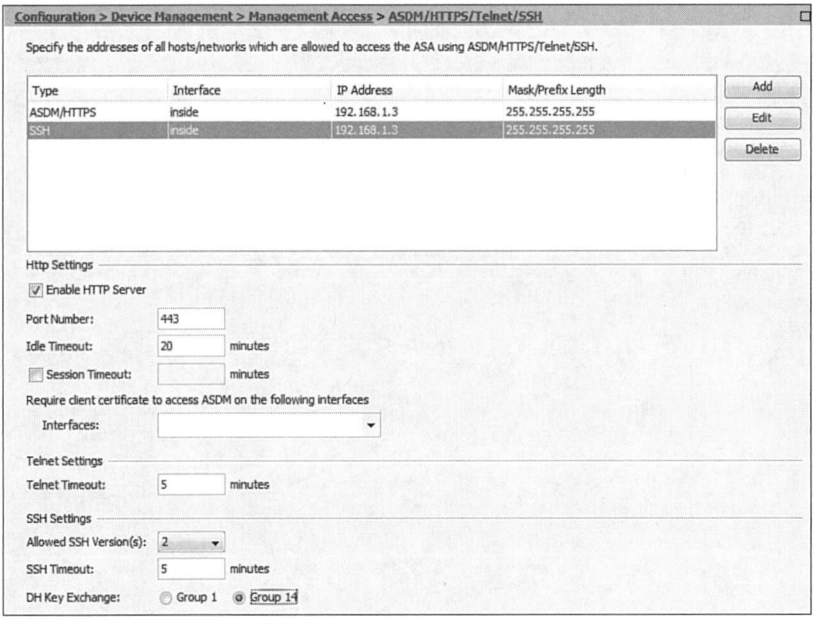

Figure 19-26   Add Device Access Configuration Window

Finally, click **Apply** to commit the changes.

CHAPTER 20

Configuring Cisco ASA Advanced Settings

This chapter covers the following topics:

ASA DHCP Services

- DHCP Client
- DHCP Server Services
- Configuring DHCP Server Example Using the CLI
- Configuring DHCP Server Example Using ASDM

ASA Objects and Object Groups

- Network and Service Objects
- Network, Protocol, ICMP, and Service Object Groups
- Configuring Objects and Object Groups Example Using ASDM

ASA ACLs

- ACL Syntax
- Configuring ACLs Example Using the CLI
- Configuring ACLs with Object Groups Example Using the CLI
- Configuring ACLs with Object Groups Example Using ASDM

ASA NAT Services

- Auto-NAT
- Dynamic NAT, Dynamic PAT, and Static NAT
- Configuring Dynamic and Static NAT Example Using the CLI
- Configuring Dynamic NAT Example Using ASDM
- Configuring Dynamic PAT Example Using ASDM
- Configuring Static NAT Example Using ASDM

AAA Access Control

- Local AAA Authentication
- Server-Based AAA Authentication

- Configuring AAA Server-Based Authentication Example Using the CLI
- Configuring AAA Server-Based Authentication Example Using ASDM

Modular Policy Framework Service Policies

- Class Maps, Policy Maps, and Service Policies
- Default Global Policies
- Configuring a Service Policy Example Using ASDM

ASA DHCP Services

You can configure the ASA as follows:

DHCP client	An interface is configured to receive its IP address and Dynamic Host Configuration Protocol (DHCP)-related information from an upstream device.
DHCP server	The Adaptive Security Appliance (ASA) provides IP addresses and DHCP-related information to inside hosts.

DHCP Client

Instead of manually configuring an IP address on a switch virtual interface (SVI), you can configure the ASA as a DHCP client:

ciscoasa(config-if)# ip address dhcp [setroute]	Requests an IP address from the upstream device.
	The setroute keyword automatically installs a default route to the upstream device.

NOTE: Alternatively, you can configure the ASA as a PPP over Ethernet (PPPoE) client connecting to an upstream digital subscriber line (DSL) device by using the ip address pppoe [setroute] command.

DHCP Server Services

Use the following commands to configure an ASA as a DHCP server:

ciscoasa(config)# dhcpd address[start-of-pool]-[end-of-pool] inside	Define the pool of IP addresses and assign the pool to inside users. NOTE: The start-of-pool and end-of-pool IP addresses are separated by a required hyphen (-).
ciscoasa(config)# dhcpd enable interface-name	Enable the DHCP server service (daemon) on the specified interface of the ASA. NOTE: The inside interface is usually configured to provide DHCP services by using the dhcpd enable inside command.

NOTE: For the ASA 5505, the maximum number of DHCP client addresses varies depending on the license. If the limit is 10 hosts, the maximum available DHCP pool is 32 addresses. If the limit is 50 hosts, the maximum available DHCP pool is 128 addresses. If the number of hosts is unlimited, the maximum available DHCP pool is 256 addresses.

Use the following commands to manually configure DHCP options:

ciscoasa(config)# **dhcpd domain** *domain-name*	Configure the DNS domain name.
ciscoasa(config)# **dhcpd dns** *dns-ip-address*	Configure the DNS domain name.
ciscoasa(config)# **dhcpd wins** *wins-ip-address*	Configure a WINS server address (if applicable).
ciscoasa(config)# **dhcpd lease** *seconds*	Configure the lease time in seconds. The default is 3600 seconds (1 hour).
ciscoasa(config)# **dhcpd option** *value*	Configure the DHCP option code. Option code is in the range 0–255.

NOTE: If the ASA outside interface is configured as a DHCP client, you can use the **dhcpd auto_config outside** global configuration command to redistribute DHCP options learned from the upstream device to the DHCP clients on the inside interface.

Configuring DHCP Server Example Using the CLI

Figure 20-1 shows the network topology for the DHCP server example.

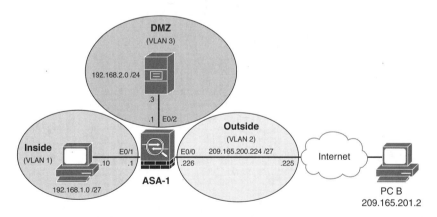

Figure 20-1 DHCP Server Topology Example

ASA-1(config)# **dhcpd address 192.168.1.11-192.168.1.30 inside**	Define the pool of IP addresses and assign the pool to inside users.
ASA-1(config)# **dhcpd enable inside**	Enable the DHCP server service (daemon) on the inside interface of the ASA.

`ASA-1(config)# dhcpd domain ccnas.com`	Define the domain name for DHCP clients.
`ASA-1(config)# dhcpd dns 209.165.200.225`	Define a Domain Name Service (DNS) server to DHCP clients.
`ASA-1(config)# dhcpd lease 7200`	Configure the lease time in seconds. The default is 3600 seconds (1 hour).

NOTE: To verify DHCP settings, use the `show dhcpd state` to display the current DHCP state for inside and outside interfaces, the `show dhcpd binding` command to display the current DHCP bindings of inside users, and the `show dhcpd statistics` command to display the current DHCP statistics.

NOTE: To clear the DHCP bindings or statistics, use the `clear dhcpd binding` or `clear dhcpd statistics` command.

Configuring DHCP Server Example Using ASDM

To enable DHCP server services, choose **Configuration > Device Management > DHCP > DHCP Server**. ASDM opens the DHCP Server screen (see Figure 20-2).

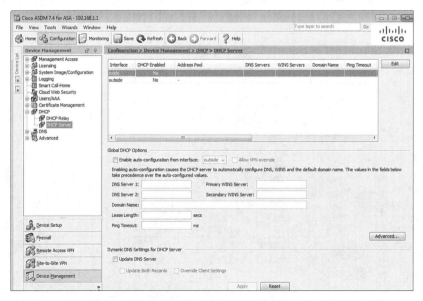

Figure 20-2   DHCP Server Screen

In this window, you can modify the general DHCP settings.

To enable DHCP services to inside users, click the inside interface and click the **Edit** button. ASDM then opens the Edit DHCP Server dialog, shown in Figure 20-3.

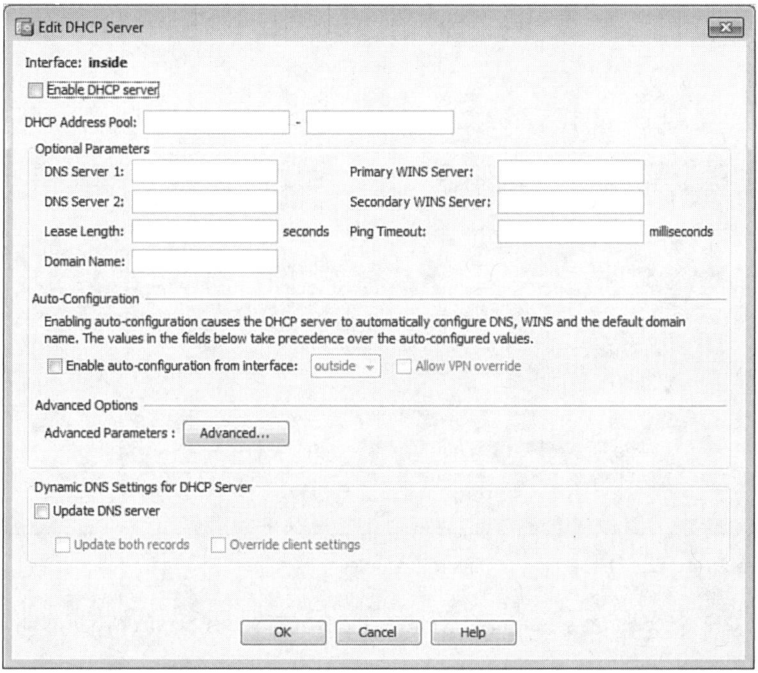

Figure 20-3   Edit DHCP Server Dialog

Figure 20-4 displays a sample DHCP configuration to provide DHCP server services to the inside using the 192.168.1.10 - 41 pool with a leased length of 12 hours.

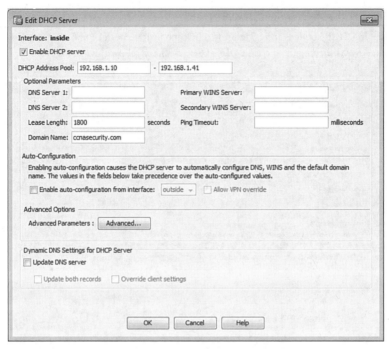

Figure 20-4 Edit DHCP Server Dialog Example

Click **OK** to accept the settings and return to the DHCP Server Services page as shown in Figure 20-5.

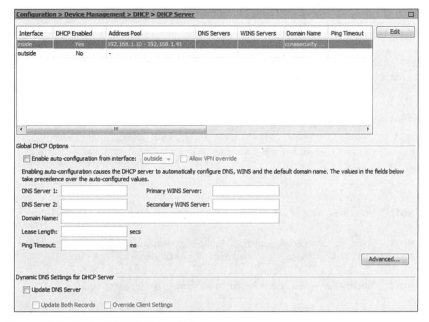

Figure 20-5   Revised DHCP Server Screen

Finally, click **Apply** to commit the changes.

ASA Objects and Object Groups

Objects make it easier to maintain configurations. When an object is modified, the change automatically applies to all rules that use the specified object. Objects are used in Network Address Translation (NAT), access lists, and nested into other object groups.

The ASA supports the following:

Objects	■ An object identifies an IP address/mask or a protocol (and a port).
	■ An object can be reused in several configurations.
	■ The ASA supports network objects and service objects.
	■ Objects are created using the `object` {`network` | `service`} `object-name` command.
Object groups	■ Object groups are used to group objects.
	■ Objects can be attached or detached from multiple object groups.
	■ You can create network, protocol, and Internet Control Message Protocol (ICMP)-type object groups created using the `object-group` {`network` | `protocol` | `icmp-type`} `group-name` command.
	■ You can also create service object groups by using `object-group` `service` `group-name` [`tcp` | `udp` | `tcp-udp`].

Network and Service Objects

A network object contains a single IP address/mask pair that can be identified using a host, subnet, or range of addresses.

Use the following commands to create or edit a network object:

ciscoasa(config)# **object network** *object-name*	Create or edit a network object and enter network object configuration mode.
ciscoasa(config-network-object)# {**host** *ip_addr* | **subnet** *net_addr net mask* | **range** *ip_addr_1 ip_addr_2*}	Assign the IP address to the named object. You can configure a host address, a subnet, or a range of addresses.

NOTE: Use the no form of any of these three commands to remove a network object.

NOTE: There can only be one statement in the network object. Entering a second IP address/mask pair will replace the existing configured statement.

NOTE: The description command could be used to document the object.

NOTE: The clear config object network command erases all network objects.

NOTE: To verify, use the show running-config object command.

A service object contains a protocol and optional source and/or destination port.

Use the following commands to create or edit a service object:

ciscoasa(config)# **object service** *object-name*	Create or edit a service object and enter service object configuration mode.

Use the following command to identify specific services:

ciscoasa(config-service-object)# **service** {*protocol* | **icmp** *icmp-type* | **icmp6** *icmp6-type* | {**tcp** | **udp**} [**source** *operator port*] [**destination** *operator port*]}	Specify an IP protocol name or number. You can optionally configure specific source or destination ports.

NOTE: The *protocol* argument specifies an IP protocol name or number.

NOTE: The tcp and udp keywords specify the protocol.

NOTE: The icmp keyword is used to identify a specific ICMP type.

NOTE: The *source* keyword specifies the source port, while the *destination* keyword specifies the destination port.

NOTE: The *operator port* argument specifies a single TCP/UDP port number. Valid keyword operators include eq, neq, lt, gt, and range. The default operator is eq when none is specified.

NOTE: There can be multiple `service` statements in the service object. Additional `service` commands are appended to the configuration.

NOTE: The `clear config object service` command erases all service objects.

To verify, use the `show running-config object` command.

NOTE: You cannot remove an object group or make an object group empty if it is used in a command.

Network, Protocol, ICMP, and Service Object Groups

Use the following commands to create a network object group:

`ciscoasa(config)# object-group network group-name`	Create or edit a network object group and enter network object group configuration mode.

Use the following commands to identify specific hosts or network object groups:

`ciscoasa(config-network-object-group)# network-object host ip-addr`	Assign an IP address to the named object.
`ciscoasa(config-network-object-group)# group-object group-name`	Assign an object group to the named object. **NOTE:** This allows for logical grouping of the same type of objects and construction of hierarchical object groups for structured configuration.

NOTE: Multiple hosts, networks, and objects can be added to a network object group.

NOTE: A network object group cannot be used to implement NAT. A network object is required to implement NAT.

A protocol-based object group combines IP protocols into one object.

Use the following commands to create a protocol object group:

`ciscoasa(config)# object-group protocol group-name`	Create or edit a protocol object group and enter protocol object group configuration mode.

Use one of the following commands to identify a protocol or other protocol object groups:

ciscoasa(config-protocol-object-group)# **protocol-object** *protocol*	Define the protocols in the group. **NOTE:** The *protocol* parameter is the IP protocol numeric identifier (1–254) or a keyword identifier (for example, **icmp, tcp, udp,** or **ip** to include all IP protocols).
ciscoasa(config-protocol-object-group)# **group-object** *group-name*	Assign an object group to the named object.

Use the following commands to create an ICMP object group:

ciscoasa(config)# **object-group icmp-type** *group-name*	Create or edit an ICMP object group and enter ICMP group object configuration mode.

Use one of the following commands to identify a protocol or other protocol object groups:

ciscoasa(config-icmp-object-group)# **icmp-object** *icmp-type*	Define the ICMP types in the group. Enter the command for each type.
ciscoasa(config-icmp-object-group)# **group-object** *group-name*	Assign an object group to the named object.

A service-based object group is used to group TCP, UDP, or TCP and UDP ports into an object. The ASA enables the creation of a service object group that can contain a mix of TCP services; UDP services; ICMP-type services; and any protocol such as Encapsulation Security Protocol (ESP), generic routing encryption (GRE), and TCP.

Use the following commands to create a service object group:

ciscoasa(config)# **object-group service** *group-name*	Create or edit a service group object and enter service object group configuration mode.

Use one of the following commands to identify a protocol or other protocol object groups:

ciscoasa(config-service-object-group)# **port-object eq** *service*	Add a port object to a service object group. Specify the decimal number or name of a TCP or UDP port for a service object.
ciscoasa(config-service-object-group)# **group-object** *group-name*	Assign an object group to the named object.

Configuring Objects and Object Groups Example Using ASDM

To configure a network object or a network object group in ASDM, choose
Configuration > Firewall > Objects > Network Objects/Groups. ASDM shows the
Network Object/Groups screen shown in Figure 20-6.

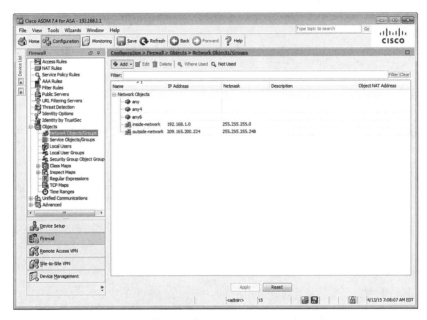

Figure 20-6   Network Objects/Groups Screen

From this window, the administrator can add, edit, or delete a network object or a
network object group, as shown in Figure 20-7.

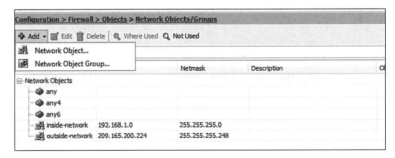

Figure 20-7   Adding a Network Object or Network Object Group

Figure 20-8 displays the Add Network Object window.

Figure 20-8   Add Network Object Window

Figure 20-9 displays the Add Network Object Group window.

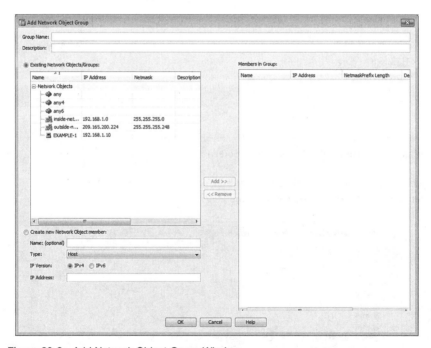

Figure 20-9   Add Network Object Group Window

To configure service objects, service object groups, ICMP object groups, or protocol object groups, choose **Configuration > Firewall > Objects > Service Objects/Groups**. ASDM opens the Service Objects/Groups screen, as shown in Figure 20-10.

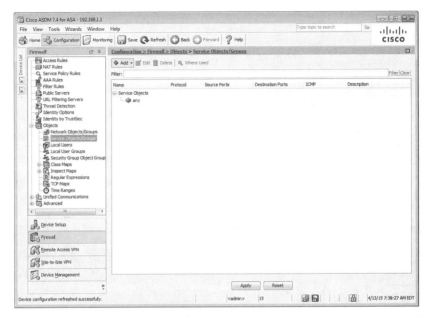

Figure 20-10   Service Objects/Groups Screen

From this window, the administrator can add, edit, or delete service objects or service object groups, ICMP object groups, and protocol object groups, as shown in Figure 20-11.

Figure 20-11   Adding a Service Object/Group

Figure 20-12 displays the Add Service Object window.

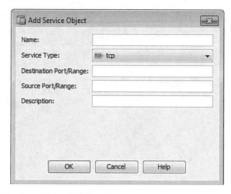

Figure 20-12   Add Service Object Dialog Box

Figure 20-13 displays the Add Service Group window.

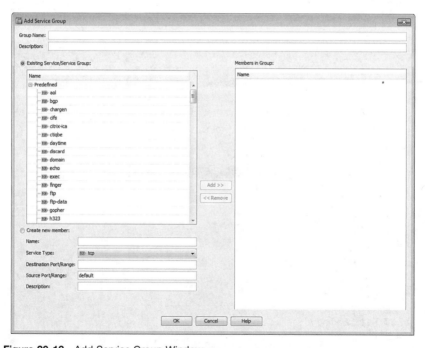

Figure 20-13   Add Service Group Window

ASA ACLs

Many similarities exist between ASA access control lists (ACLs) and IOS ACLs. For example, both

- Are made up of access control entries (ACEs)
- Are processed sequentially from top down
- Have an implicit deny any at the end
- Follow the rule of only one ACL per interface, per protocol, per direction

ASA ACLs differ from IOS ACLs as follows:

- ASA ACLs use a network mask rather than a wildcard mask (for example, 0.0.0.255).
- ASA ACLs are named rather than numbered. There are no numbered standard and extended ACLs, although you could name one with a number.
- By default, interface security levels apply access control without an ACL configured.

NOTE: Traffic from a more-secure interface (such as security level 100) is allowed to access less-secure interfaces (such as level 0). Traffic from a less-secure interface is blocked from accessing more-secure interfaces and requires an ACL to permit traffic to a higher security level.

The ASA supports five types of access lists:

Extended	■ Most common type of ASA ACL ■ Filters on source/destination port and protocol
Standard	■ Used for routing protocols, not firewall rules ■ Cannot be applied to interfaces to control traffic
IPv6	■ Used to support IPv6 addressing
Webtype	■ Used for clientless Secure Sockets Layer (SSL) virtual private networks (VPNs)
Ethertype	■ Specifies network layer protocol and only used with transparent firewall mode

NOTE: Use the `help access-list` privileged EXEC command to display the syntax for all the ACLs supported on an ASA platform.

NOTE: This section focuses on extended ACLs.

ACLs on a security appliance can be used for the following:

Through-traffic packet filtering	■ Traffic is passing through the appliance from one interface to another interface. ■ The configuration requires an ACL to be defined and then applied to an interface.
To-the-box traffic packet filtering	■ Traffic (for example, Telnet, or SSH, Simple Network Management Protocol [SNMP]) is destined for the appliance. ■ It filters traffic destined to the ASA management plane. ■ It is completed in one step but requires an additional set of rules to implement access control. ■ Also known as a management access rule.

ACL Syntax

You can use many options with ACLs. However, for most needs, a more useful and condensed version of the syntax is as follows:

```ciscoasa(config)# access-list id extended {deny | permit} protocol {source addr source mask} | any | host src host | interface src if name[operator port [port] {dest addr dest mask} | any | host dst host | interface dst if name [operator port [port]]}```	Create an extended ACL. **NOTE:** The `interface` keyword is used for to-the-box filtering. **NOTE:** Explanation of all ACL syntax is beyond the scope of this chapter.

NOTE: Use the `help access-list` command to view complete syntax information.

NOTE: To verify ACLs, use the `show access-list` and `show running-config access-list` commands.

NOTE: To erase a configured ACL, use the `clear configure access-list id` command.

After you configure an ACL to identify traffic allowed or denied by the ASA, the next step is to apply the ACL to an interface in either the inbound or the outbound direction.

Apply the ACL as follows:

```ciscoasa(config-if)# access-group acl-id {in | out} interface interface-name [per-user-override | control-plane]```	Applies the ACL to the interface. **NOTE:** The `control-plane` keyword is used for to-the-box filtering.

NOTE: To allow connectivity between interfaces with the same security levels, the `same-security-traffic permit inter-interface` global configuration command is required.

NOTE: To enable traffic to enter and exit the same interface, such as when encrypted traffic enters an interface and is then routed out the same interface unencrypted, use the `same-security-traffic permit intra-interface global` configuration command.

Configuring ACLs Example Using the CLI

PC-A and PC-B are external hosts that require access to the two internal servers. Each server provides web and email services.

Figure 20-14 shows the network topology for the ACL example.

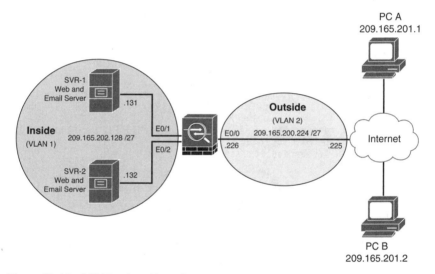

Figure 20-14 ACL Topology Example

`ASA-1(config)# access-list ACL-IN`
`remark Permit PC-A -> Server A for`
`HTTP / SMTP`
	Enter a remark.

`ASA-1(config)# access-list`
`ACL-IN extended permit tcp host`
`209.165.201.1 host 209.165.202.131`
`eq http`
	Permit PC-A HTTP access to SVR-1.

`ASA-1(config)# access-list`
`ACL-IN extended permit tcp host`
`209.165.201.1 host 209.165.202.131`
`eq smtp`
	Permit PC-A email access to SVR-1.

`ASA-1(config)# access-list ACL-IN`
`remark Permit PC-A -> Server B for`
`HTTP / SMTP`
	Enter a remark.

`ASA-1(config)# access-list`
`ACL-IN extended permit tcp host`
`209.165.201.1 host 209.165.202.132`
`eq http`
	Permit PC-A HTTP access to SVR-2.

`ASA-1(config)# access-list`
`ACL-IN extended permit tcp host`
`209.165.201.1 host209.165.202.132`
`eq smtp`
	Permit PC-A email access to SVR-2.

`ASA-1(config)# access-list ACL-IN`
`remark Permit PC-B -> Server A for`
`HTTP / SMTP`
	Enter a remark.

`ASA-1(config)# access-list`
`ACL-IN extended permit tcp host`
`209.165.201.2 host 209.165.202.131`
`eq http`
	Permit PC-B HTTP access to SVR-1.

`ASA-1(config)# access-list`
`ACL-IN extended permit tcp host`
`209.165.201.2 host 209.165.202.131`
`eq smtp`
	Permit PC-B email access to SVR-1.

`ASA-1(config)# access-list ACL-IN`
`remark Permit PC-B -> Server B for`
`HTTP / SMTP`
	Enter a remark.

`ASA-1(config)# access-list`
`ACL-IN extended permit tcp host`
`209.165.201.2 host 209.165.202.132`
`eq http`
	Permit PC-B HTTP access to SVR-2.

`ASA-1(config)# access-list`
`ACL-IN extended permit tcp host`
`209.165.201.2 host 209.165.202.132`
`eq smtp`
	Permit PC-B email access to SVR-2.

`ASA-1(config)# access-list ACL-IN` `extended deny ip any any log`	Configure the implicit **deny** statement to log all failures.
`ASA-1(config)# access-group ACL-IN` `in interface outside`	Apply the ACL to all incoming traffic on the outside interface.

Configuring ACLs with Object Groups Example Using the CLI

`ASA-1(config)# object-group` `protocol TCP`	Create a protocol object group called **TCP**.
`ASA-1(config-protocol)#` `protocol-object tcp`	Match all TCP traffic.
`ASA-1(config-protocol)# exit`	Return to global configuration.
`ASA-1(config)# object-group` `network Internet-Hosts`	Create a network object group called **Internet-Hosts**.
`ASA-1(config-network)#` `network-object host 209.165.201.1`	Identify a network host (PC-A).
`ASA-1(config-network)#` `network-object host 209.165.201.2`	Identify a network host (PC-B).

`ASA-1(config-network)# exit`	Return to global configuration.
`ASA-1(config)# object-group` `network Internal-Servers`	Create a network object group called **Internal-Servers**.

`ASA-1(config-network)#`
`network-object host`
`209.165.202.131`
	Identify a server host (SVR-1).

`ASA-1(config-network)#`
`network-object host`
`209.165.202.132`
	Identify a server host (SVR-2).

`ASA-1(config-network)# exit`	Return to global configuration.
`ASA-1(config)# object-group` `service HTTP-SMTP tcp`	Create a service object group called **HTTP-SMTP**.
`ASA-1(config-service)# port-object` `eq smtp`	Identify Layer 4 services (SMTP).
`ASA-1(config-service)# port-object` `eq www`	Identify Layer 4 services (HTTP).
`ASA-1(config-service)# exit`	Return to global configuration.

`ASA-1(config)# access-list ACL-IN`
`remark Only permit PC-A / PC-B ->`
`servers`
	Enter an ACL remark.

`ASA-1(config)# access-list ACL-IN`
`extended permit object-group`
`TCP object-group Internet-Hosts`
`object-group Internal-Servers`
`object-group HTTP-SMTP`
	Permit the Internet-Hosts object services identified in TCP when going to the Internal-Servers object for services identified in HTTP-SMTP.

`ASA-1(config)# access-list ACL-IN` `extended deny ip any any log`	Configure the implicit **deny** statement to log all failures.
`ASA-1(config)# access-group ACL-IN` `in interface outside`	Apply the ACL to all incoming traffic on the outside interface.

Configuring ACLs with Object Groups Example Using ASDM

To open the Access Rules screen, choose **Configuration > Firewall > Access Rules**. ASDM then opens the Access Rules screen, as shown in Figure 20-15.

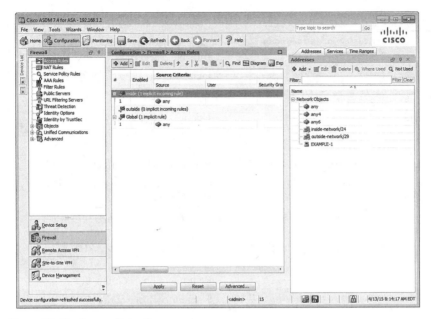

Figure 20-15   Access Rules Screen

From this screen, all ACL rules are displayed. You can add, edit, and delete rules.

To add a rule, highlight the interface you want to add a rule to and click **Add** to open the Add Access Rule dialog shown in Figure 20-16.

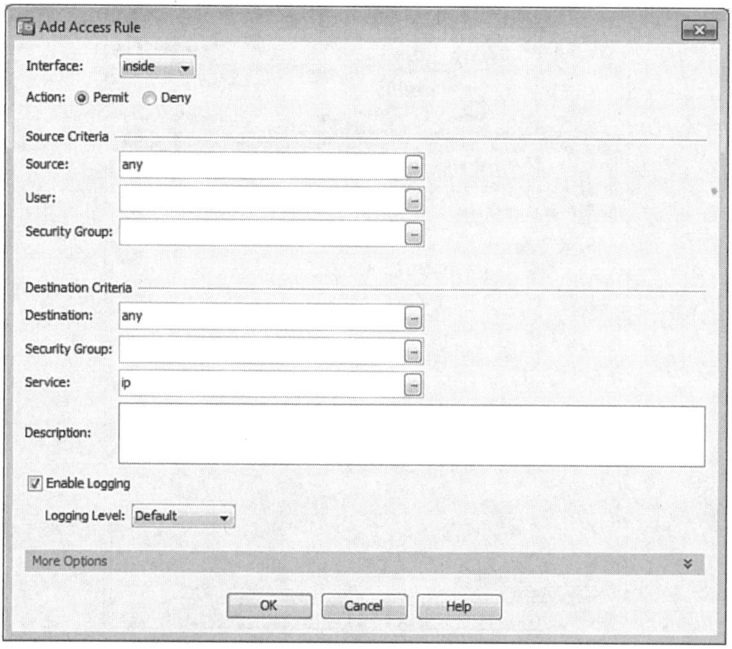

Figure 20-16 Add Access Rule Dialog

A useful feature in the Access Rules screen is the Diagram option. Selecting an access rule and then clicking **Diagram** in the Access Rules screen opens a graphical representation of the highlighted policy, as shown in the bottom section of Figure 20-17.

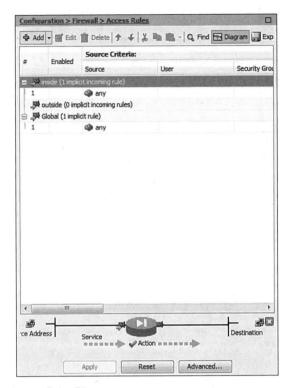

Figure 20-17   Access Rules Diagram

ASA NAT Services

Like IOS routers, the ASA supports the following Network Address Translation (NAT) and Port Address Translation (PAT) deployment methods:

Inside NAT	▪ Typical NAT deployment method where the ASA translates the internal host address to a global address. ▪ The ASA restores return traffic to the original inside IP address.
Outside NAT	▪ Deployment method used where traffic from a lower-security interface is destined for a higher-security interface. ▪ This method may be useful to make a host on the outside appear as one from a known internal IP address.
Bidirectional NAT	▪ Both inside NAT and outside NAT are used together.

Auto-NAT

The Auto-NAT feature has simplified the NAT configuration as follows:

1. Create a network object.

2. Identify hosts networks to be translated.

3. Define the **nat** command parameters.

The following are the three steps in a simple PAT configuration:

```
ASA-1(config)# object network NAT-CFG
ASA-1(config-network-object)# subnet 192.168.1.0 255.255.255.224
ASA-1(config-network-object)# nat (inside,outside) dynamic interface
```

> **NOTE:** Before ASA Version 8.3, NAT was configured using the **nat, global,** and **static** commands.

> **NOTE:** The **global** and **static** commands are no longer recognized.

Dynamic NAT, Dynamic PAT, and Static NAT

Cisco ASA supports the following common types of NAT:

Dynamic NAT	<ul><li>Many-to-many translation.</li><li>Typically deployed using inside NAT.</li></ul>
Dynamic PAT	<ul><li>Many-to-one translation.</li><li>Usually an inside pool of addresses to overload an outside interface or outside address deployed using inside NAT.</li></ul>
Static NAT	<ul><li>A one-to-one translation.</li><li>Usually an outside address mapping to an internal server deployed using outside NAT.</li></ul>
Twice-NAT	<ul><li>ASA Version 8.3 NAT feature that identifies both the source and destination address in a single rule (**nat** command).</li><li>Used when configuring remote-access IPsec and SSL VPNs.</li><li>Twice-NAT is beyond the scope of the chapter.</li></ul>

Dynamic NAT requires two network objects to be configured:

- The first network object identifies the pool of public IP addresses to translate to.

- The second network object binds inside addresses to the first network object.

Create a network object to identify the pool of public IP addresses.

ciscoasa(config)# **object network** public-pool-obj	Create a network object and enter network object configuration mode.
ciscoasa(config-network-object)# {**host** ip_addr | **subnet** net_addr net_mask | **range** ip_addr_1 ip_addr_2}	Identify the public IP pool of IP addresses using a host address, a subnet, or a range of addresses.

Create the network object that identifies the inside hosts and enable Dynamic NAT:

ciscoasa(config)# **object network** nat-object-name	Create a network object and enter network object configuration mode.
ciscoasa(config-network-object)# {**subnet** net_addr net_mask | **range** ip_addr_1 ip_addr_2}	Identify the inside IP pool of IP addresses using a subnet or a range of addresses.
ciscoasa(config)# **nat** (real-ifc, mapped-ifc) **dynamic** public-pool-object	Enable NAT to dynamically translate traffic from real-ifc to mapped-ifc using the public-pool network object. **NOTE:** The parentheses and comma (,) are required.

Dynamic PAT only requires one network object to be configured.

Create a network object that identifies the inside hosts and enable Dynamic NAT:

ciscoasa(config)# **object network** pat-obj-name	Create a network object and enter network object configuration mode.
ciscoasa(config-network-object)# {**subnet** net_addr net_mask | **range** ip_addr_1 ip_addr_2}	Identify the inside IP pool of IP addresses using a subnet or a range of addresses.
ciscoasa(config)# **nat** (real-ifc,mapped-ifc) **dynamic** [**interface** | ip-address]	Enable NAT to dynamically overload the outside interface IP address or overload a specified IP address. **NOTE:** The parentheses and comma (,) are required. **NOTE:** PAT could also be configured to overload a public pool of addresses if configured with the pat-pool mapped-obj parameter.

Static NAT maps an inside IP address to an outside public address to provide access to web servers by outside hosts. Static NAT requires one network object and an ACL to permit outside hosts access to the internal IP address.

Create a static NAT network object:

ciscoasa(config)# **object network** *static-nat-obj-name*	Create a network object and enter network object configuration mode.
ciscoasa(config-network-object)# **host** *ip_addr*	Identify the inside host IP address.
ciscoasa(config)# **nat** *(real-ifc,mapped-ifc)* **static** *mapped-ip-addr*	Enable NAT to statically map an inside address to an outside address. **NOTE:** The parentheses and comma (,) are required.
ciscoasa(config)# **access-list** *acl-id* **extended permit ip any host** *inside_host*	Create an extended ACL to permit outside users access to the internal IP address.
ciscoasa(config-if)# **access-group** *acl-id* **interface outside**	Apply the ACL to allow incoming static NAT traffic.

NOTE: Use the **show run object** command to display the network object, and use the **show run nat** command to display the NAT running configuration.

Configuring Dynamic and Static NAT Example Using the CLI

Translate inside users to a public pool and permit outside users access to SVR-1. Figure 20-18 shows the network topology for the NAT example.

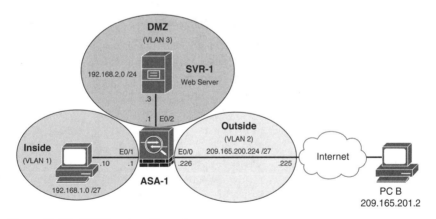

Figure 20-18   NAT Topology Example

ASA-1(config)# **object network** **NAT-POOL**	Create the public pool network object.
ASA-1(config-network-object)# **range 209.165.200.240 209.165.200.246**	Assign the outside public pool IP addresses.
ASA-1(config-network-object)# **exit**	Return to global configuration mode.
ASA-1(config)# **object network NAT**	Create the Dynamic NAT object.

`ASA-1(config-network-object)#` `subnet 192.168.1.0 255.255.255.224`	Identify the inside hosts to translate from.
`ASA-1(config-network-object)# nat` `(inside,outside) dynamic NAT-POOL`	Dynamically translate traffic inside users to the NAT-POOL network object.
`ASA-1(config)# object network` `DMZ-NAT`	Create the static NAT network object.
`ASA-1(config-network-object)#` `host 192.168.2.3`	Identify the inside SVR-1 IP address.

`ASA-1(config-network-object)#`
`nat (dmz,outside) static`
`209.200.165.227`
	Statically map the public IP address to the identified SVR-1 address.

`ASA-1(config-network-object)# exit`	Return to global configuration mode.

`ASA-1(config)# access-list`
`PCB->SVR1 permit ip any host`
`192.168.2.3`
	Create an ACL permitting outside users to access the inside SVR-1 server.

`ASA-1(config)# access-group` `PCB->SVR1 in interface outside`	Apply the ACL to the outside interface.

NOTE: Unlike IOS ACLs, the ASA ACL `permit` statement must permit access to the internal private demilitarized zone (DMZ) address. External hosts access the server using its public static NAT address, and the ASA translates it to the internal host IP address and applies the ACL.

Configuring Dynamic NAT Example Using ASDM

To configure Dynamic NAT in ASDM, first configure the public pool network object. Choose **Configurations > Firewall > Objects > Network Objects/Groups** to open the Network Objects/Groups screen, as shown in Figure 20-19.

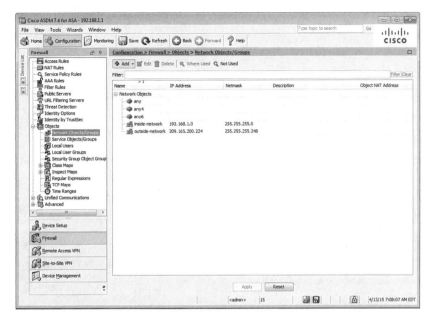

Figure 20-19 Network Objects/Groups Screen

Click **Add** > **Network Object** to display the Add Network Object dialog shown in Figure 20-20.

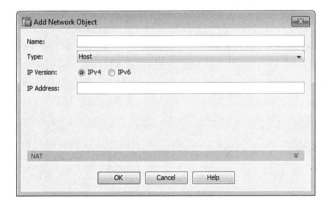

Figure 20-20 Add Network Object Dialog

Figure 20-21 displays an example of creating the first network object identifying the range of useable public IP addresses.

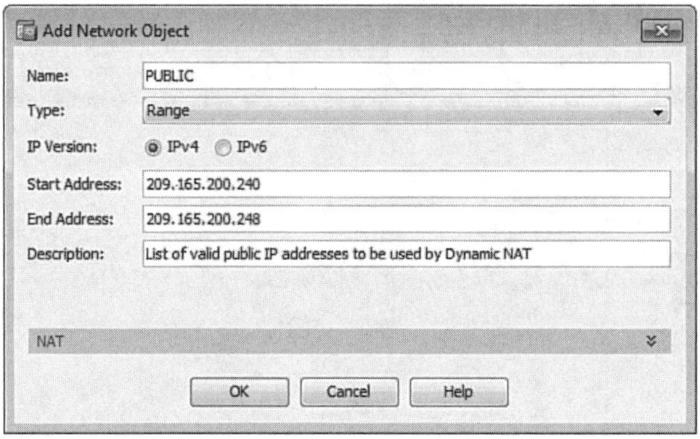

Figure 20-21   Add Network Object Dialog Example

Next, create the Dynamic NAT network object.

Click **Add > Network Object** a second time, and click the drop-down NAT arrows to display the configurable NAT parameters.

Then do the following:

- Enter the NAT network object name.
- Identify the inside network address and subnet mask.
- Check the **Add Automatic Address Translation Rules** box.
- Identify the type of NAT as Dynamic (other options include Dynamic PAT and Static).
- Click the **Translated Addr** ellipsis (**...**) to open the Browse Translated Addr window.
- Select the public pool network object name and click **OK**.

Figure 20-22 shows the revised Add Network Object window.

Figure 20-22   Creating a Dynamic NAT Network Object

Review the settings and click **OK** to complete the NAT configuration.

To view the NAT configuration, choose **Configuration > Firewall > NAT Rules**.

Configuring Dynamic PAT Example Using ASDM

Dynamic PAT is configured in ASDM by creating a network object that binds inside addresses to the outside interface. To configure Dynamic PAT, click **Configurations > Firewall > Objects > Network Objects/Groups** and then click **Add > Network Object** to display the Add Network Object window. Initially, the NAT section is hidden when creating the network object. Click **NAT** to expand the section and continue.

Figure 20-23 displays a sample dynamic PAT network object.

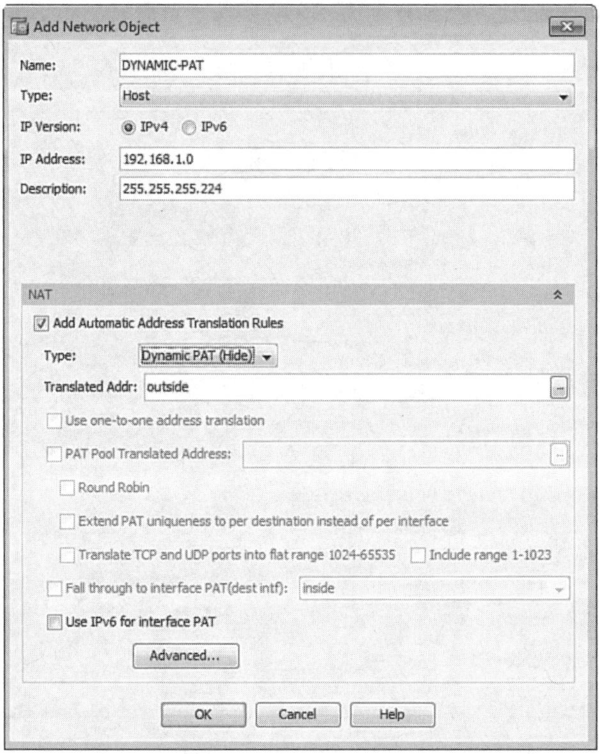

Figure 20-23   Creating a Dynamic PAT Network Object

Click **OK** and **Apply** the changes.

Configuring Static NAT Example Using ASDM

Static NAT is often used to enable an inside server to be accessed by outside hosts.
It is configured in ASDM by creating a network object binding an inside address to an outside address.

To configure Static NAT in ASDM, click **Configurations** > **Firewall** > **Objects** > **Network Objects/Groups** and then click **Add** > **Network Object**. This opens the Add Network Object page.

Figure 20-24 displays an example of configuring a static NAT network object.

Figure 20-24 Creating a Static NAT Network Object

Click **Advanced** to identify the source and destination interfaces as shown in Figure 20-25.

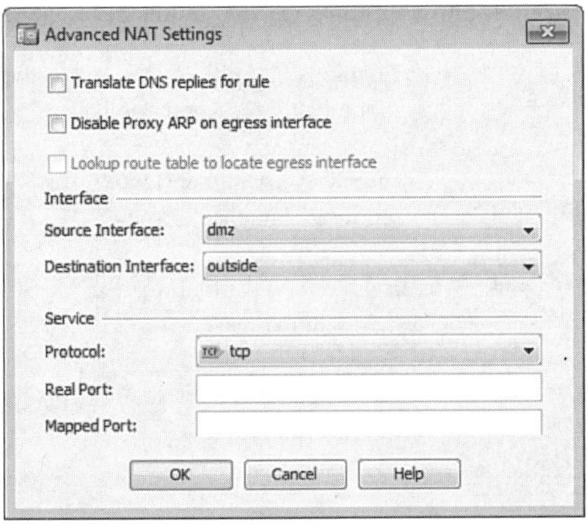

Figure 20-25 Identifying Source and Destination Interface

Click **OK** and **Apply** the changes.

AAA Access Control

You can configure Cisco ASA to authenticate using the following:

Local user database	▪ Local authentication, authorization, and accounting (AAA) stores usernames and passwords locally on the ASA, and users authenticate against the local database. ▪ Ideal for small networks that do not need a dedicated AAA server.
Server-based authentication	▪ Server-based AAA authentication is a much more scalable method than local AAA authentication. ▪ It uses an external database server resource leveraging RADIUS or TACACS+ protocols.

NOTE: Both methods are commonly used to provide a fallback mechanism.

Local AAA Authentication

ciscoasa(config)# **username** *name* **password** *password* [**privilege** *priv-level*]	Create a local user account.

NOTE: To erase a user from the local database, use the `clear config username` [*name*] command.

NOTE: To view all user accounts, use the `show running-conf username` command.

Enable AAA authentication for the privilege EXEC mode, HTTP, SSH, or Telnet access:

ciscoasa(config)# **aaa authentication enable console LOCAL**	Enable AAA authentication for the privileged EXEC mode using the local database.
ciscoasa(config)# **aaa authentication http console LOCAL**	Enable AAA authentication for HTTP access using the local database.
ciscoasa(config)# **aaa authentication ssh console LOCAL**	Enable AAA authentication for SSH access using the local database.
ciscoasa(config)# **aaa authentication telnet console LOCAL**	Enable AAA authentication for Telnet access using the local database.

Server-Based AAA Authentication

Server-based AAA authentication is a much more scalable solution that uses an external database server resource leveraging RADIUS or TACACS+ protocols.

Server-based AAA authentication lets you do the following:

- Create a TACACS+ or RADIUS AAA server group.
- Add a AAA server and parameters to the AAA server group.
- Configure server-based AAA authentication.

`ciscoasa(config)# aaa-server`
`server-tag protocol [tacacs+ |`
`radius}`
	Create a TACACS+ or RADIUS AAA server group.
	
	NOTE: Other protocols include `http-form`, `kerberos`, `ldap`, `nt`, and `sdi`. All are beyond the scope of this chapter.

`ciscoasa(config-aaa-server-group)#`
`aaa-server server-tag [(interface-`
`name)] host {server-ip | name}`
`[key]`
	Identify a AAA server and parameters to be part of the AAA server group.

`ciscoasa(config)# aaa`
`authentication {enable | http |`
`ssh | telnet} console server-tag`
`[LOCAL]`
	Enable server-based AAA authentication.

NOTE: To erase all AAA server configurations, use the `clear config aaa-server` command.

NOTE: To view all user accounts, use the `show running-config aaa-server` command.

Configuring AAA Server-Based Authentication Example Using the CLI

Figure 20-26 shows the network topology for the server-based AAA authentication example.

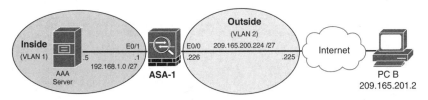

Figure 20-26   Server-Based AAA Authentication Topology

`ASA-1(config)# username admin password cisco123 privilege 15`	Create a local user account for fallback purposes.
`ASA-1(config)# aaa-server TACACS-SVR protocol tacacs+`	Create a AAA server group using the TACACS+ protocol.
`ASA-1(config-aaa-server-group)# aaa-server TACACS-SVR (inside) host 192.168.1.5 cisco123`	Identify a server and password key.
`ASA-1(config-aaa-server-host)# exit`	Return to global configuration mode.
`ASA-1(config)# aaa authentication enable console TACACS-SVR LOCAL`	Enable privilege EXEC to use server-based AAA authentication with the local database for fallback.
`ASA-1(config)# aaa authentication http console TACACS-SVR LOCAL`	Enable HTTP to use server-based AAA authentication with the local database for fallback.
`ASA-1(config)# aaa authentication ssh console TACACS-SVR LOCAL`	Enable SSH to use server-based AAA authentication with the local database for fallback.
`ASA-1(config)# aaa authentication telnet console TACACS-SVR LOCAL`	Enable Telnet to use server-based AAA authentication with the local database for fallback.

Configuring AAA Server-Based Authentication Example Using ASDM

For fallback reasons, create a local user account. Open the User Accounts screen by selecting **Configuration > Device Management > Users/AAA > User Accounts** as shown in Figure 20-27.

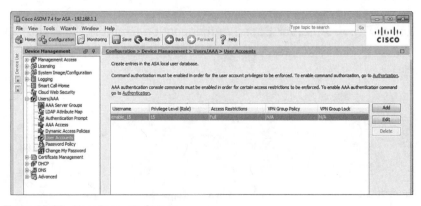

Figure 20-27   User Accounts Screen

To add a user, click **Add** and complete the Add User Account window as shown in the example in Figure 20-28.

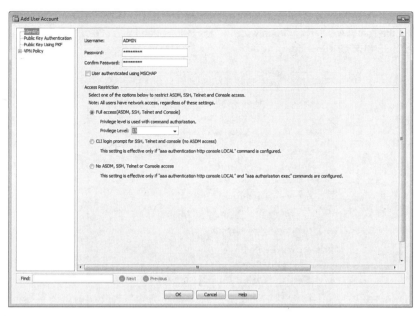

Figure 20-28 Add User Account Window

Once the specifics have been configured, click **OK** to continue.

To create the AAA server groups, click **Configuration** > **Device Management** > **Users/AAA** > **AAA Server Groups** to open the AAA Server Groups screen shown in Figure 20-29.

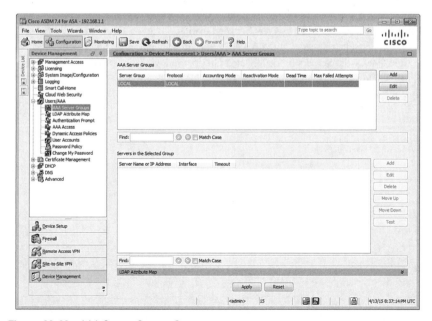

Figure 20-29 AAA Server Groups Screen

To add a server group, click **Add** on the right side of the AAA Server Groups page to open the Add AAA Server Group window. The example in Figure 20-30 is adding a RADIUS-SERVERS group.

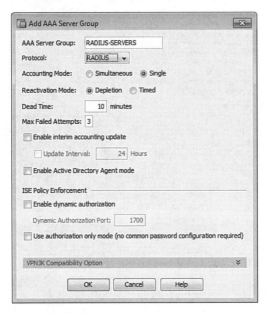

Figure 20-30 Add AAA Server Group

Once the specifics have been configured, click **OK** to continue.

To add the AAA servers to the server groups, click **Configuration** > **Device Management** > **Users/AAA** > **AAA Server Groups**. To add a server to a specific Server Group, select a server in the AAA Server Group window and then click **Add** on the right side of the Servers in the Selected Group window. This opens the **Add AAA Server** window. The example in Figure 20-31 adds a server to the RADIUS-SERVERS group.

Figure 20-31 Add AAA Server Example

Figure 20-32 displays the AAA Server Groups page with the configured changes.

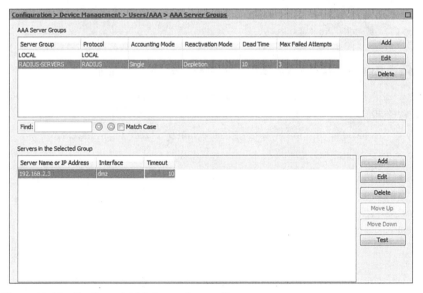

Figure 20-32 Configured AAA Server Groups Screen

To bind the authentication with the AAA Server Groups and local database, click **Configuration > Device Management > Users/AAA > AAA Access**, as shown in Figure 20-33.

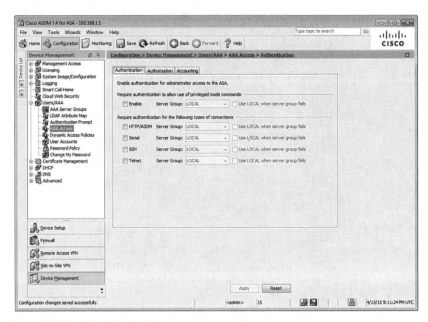

Figure 20-33   Authentication Screen

From this page, an administrator can choose to configure AAA for the enable, HTTP, Serial, SSH, and Telnet access.

Modular Policy Framework Service Policies

Modular Policy Framework (MPF) configuration defines a set of rules for applying firewall features to the traffic that traverses the ASA. You can use MPF for the following:

- Advanced application layer traffic inspection by classifying at Layers 5–7
- Rate-limiting
- Traffic inspection and quality of service (QoS)

Cisco MPF uses these three configuration objects to define modular, object-oriented, hierarchical policies, as illustrated in Figure 20-34.

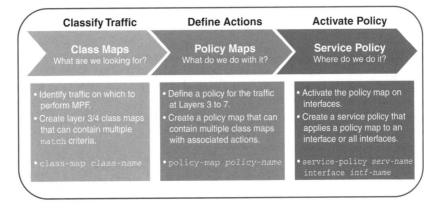

Figure 20-34   Modular Policy Framework

NOTE: Although the MPF syntax is similar to the IOS Cisco Modular QoS CLI (MQC) syntax and Cisco Common Classification Policy Language (C3PL) syntax, the configurable parameters differ. For instance, the ASA provides more configurable actions and support for Layer 5–7 inspections.

To configure MPF on an ASA, you must complete four steps:

1. Optionally configure extended ACLs to identify specific granular traffic.

2. Configure the class map to identify traffic.

3. Configure a policy map to apply actions to those class maps.

4. Configure a service policy to attach the policy map to an interface.

Class Maps, Policy Maps, and Service Policies

Create a class map to identify specific Layer 3/4 traffic:

`ciscoasa(config)# `**`class-map`** `class-map-name`	Create a Layer 3 or 4 class map and enter class-map configuration mode.
`ciscoasa(config)# `**`class-map type`** **`management`** `class-map-name`	Create a Layer 3 or 4 class map for to-the-box traffic and enter class-map configuration mode. **NOTE:** Two other variations of the command include the **`class-map type inspect`** command, which is used to define special actions for application inspection traffic, and the **`class-map type regex`** command to use with regular expressions (for example, to match specific URLs). Both are beyond the scope of this chapter.

NOTE: The names `class-default` and any name that begins with `_internal` or `_default` are reserved.

Define the traffic to include in the class by matching one of the following characteristics:

`ciscoasa(config-cmap)# match any`	Match all traffic to which you want to apply actions.
`ciscoasa(config-cmap)# match access-list` `acl-id`	Match packets specified by an extended ACL. **NOTE:** Other match keywords include `dscp`, `flow`, `port`, `precedence`, `rtp`, and `tunnel-group`. All are beyond the scope of this chapter.

NOTE: The `description` keyword could be used to document the class map.

NOTE: Unless otherwise specified, include only one `match` command in the class map.

NOTE: To display information about the class map configuration, use the `show running-config class-map` command.

NOTE: To remove all class maps, use the `clear configure class-map` command.

Create a policy map to assign actions to traffic configured in Layer 3/4 class maps:

`ciscoasa(config)# policy-map` `p-map-name`	Specify a name for this policy map (up to 40 characters in length). **NOTE:** Another variation of the command is `policy-map type inspect` `p-map-name` command. The command is beyond the scope of this chapter.

Identify the class map:

`ciscoasa(config-pmap)# class` `class-map-name`	Assign a class map to a policy map where you can assign actions to the class map traffic and enter config policy map class mode. **NOTE:** The class name `class-default` is a reserved name.

NOTE: The `description` keyword could be used to document the policy map.

Assign one of the following actions:

ciscoasa(config-pmap-c)# **set connection**	Configure connection parameters.
ciscoasa(config-pmap-c)# **police** {**input** | **output**} *rate-bps*	Rate-limit traffic for this class.
ciscoasa(config-pmap-c)# **inspect** *protocol*	Configure protocol inspection services. **NOTE:** There are many different *protocol* keywords, including **dns**, **ftp**, **http**, **icmp**, **ipv6**, and more. All are beyond the scope of this chapter.

NOTE: Other configurable policy map actions that are beyond the scope of this chapter include **priority**, **service-policy**, **shape**, **ips**, **flow-export**, and more.

The service policy enables the policy map globally on all interfaces or on a specific interface:

ciscoasa(config)# **service-policy** *p-map-name* [**global** | **interface** *intf*]	Enable a set of policies globally or apply them on an interface.

Default Global Policies

By default, the ASA configuration includes a policy that matches all default application inspection traffic and applies inspection to the traffic on all interfaces (a global policy).

The global policy consists of the following MPF framework:

- A default class map called **inspection_default** that matches a special keyword **default-inspection-traffic** that includes all common protocols
- A global policy map called **global_policy** that assigns protocol inspection action to the **inspection_default** class map
- A global service policy that enables the policy map **global_policy** globally

The default class map matches common TCP/UDP traffic:

ciscoasa(config)# **class-map inspection_default**	Edit the default class map and enter class-map configuration mode.
ciscoasa(config-cmap)# **match default-inspection-traffic**	Special keyword to match the default ports for all inspections. **NOTE:** Matches specific common traffic including DNS (UDP 53), FTP(TCP 21), HTTP (TCP 80), ICMP, SMTP(TCP 25), TFTP (UDP 69), and more.

NOTE: There is also a global class map called `class-default` that matches all remaining traffic. This is a special class map that is applied implicitly at the end of all Layer 3 and 4 policy maps and essentially tells the ASA to not perform any actions on all other traffic.

The global policy map is called `global_policy`:

`ciscoasa(config)# policy-map global_policy`	Enter global policy map.
`ciscoasa(config-pmap)# class inspection_default`	Specify the action for the default class map.

The service policy applies it globally to all interfaces:

`ciscoasa(config)# service-policy global_policy global`	Enable a set of policies globally.

The default policy configuration includes the following commands:

```
class-map inspection_default
 match default-inspection-traffic
!
policy-map type inspect dns preset_dns_map
 parameters
   message-length maximum client auto
   message-length maximum 512
policy-map global_policy
 class inspection_default
   inspect dns preset_dns_map
   inspect ftp
   inspect h323 h225
   inspect h323 ras
   inspect ip-options
   inspect netbios
   inspect rsh
   inspect rtsp
   inspect skinny
   inspect esmtp
   inspect sqlnet
   inspect sunrpc
   inspect tftp
   inspect sip
   inspect xdmcp
!
service-policy global_policy global
```

Configure Service Policy Example Using ASDM

To configure a service policy using ASDM, choose **Configuration** > **Firewall** > **Service Policy Rules** and click **Add**. ASDM then opens the Service Policy Rules screen shown in Figure 20-35.

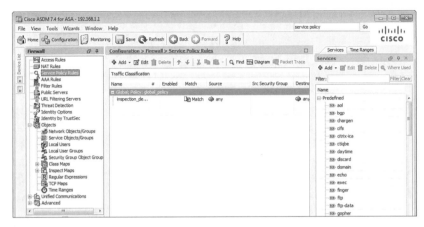

Figure 20-35   Service Policy Rules Screen

CHAPTER 21

Configuring Cisco ASA VPNs

This chapter covers the following topics:

Remote-Access VPNs

- Types of Remote-Access VPNs

ASA SSL VPNs

- Client-Based SSL VPN Example Using ASDM
- Clientless SSL VPN Example Using ASDM

ASA Site-to-Site IPsec VPN

- ISR IPsec VPN Configuration
- ASA Initial Configuration
- ASA VPN Configuration Using ASDM

Remote-Access VPNs

Enterprise users are requesting support for their mobile devices, including smartphones, tablets, notebooks, and a broader range of laptop manufacturers and operating systems.

This shift has created a challenge for IT security. The solution is the use of Secure Sockets Layer (SSL) virtual private networks (VPNs) to secure access for all users, regardless of the endpoint from which they establish a connection.

Both Cisco Integrated Services Routers (ISR) and Adaptive Security Appliances (ASA) provide IPsec and SSL VPN capabilities. However, an ISR supports up to 200 concurrent sessions per device while an ASA can support up to 10,000 concurrent sessions per device. The ASA is usually the choice when supporting a large remote networking deployment.

Types of Remote-Access VPNs

The ASA supports three types of remote-access VPNs:

Clientless SSL VPN	<ul><li>Clientless SSL VPN remote access (using a web browser).</li><li>Browser-based VPN, which lets users establish a secure, remote-access VPN tunnel to the ASA.</li><li>After authentication, users access a portal page and can access specific supported internal resources.</li></ul>

Client-based SSL or IPsec VPN	▪ SSL or IPsec (IKEv2) VPN remote access (using Cisco AnyConnect Client). ▪ Provides full-tunnel SSL VPN connection but requires a VPN client, such as the Cisco AnyConnect VPN client to be installed on the host. ▪ The AnyConnect client can be manually preinstalled on the host or downloaded on demand to a host via a browser. ▪ After authentication, the user's PC is assigned an internal IP address and can access network resources as though they were on the local network.
IPsec (IKEvl) VPN	▪ IPsec (IKEvl) VPN remote access (using Cisco VPN client).

NOTE: Clientless VPNs do not require administrative privileges on the host. However, client-based VPNs initially require administrative access to install Cisco AnyConnect.

ASA SSL VPN

ASA SSL VPNs can be configured manually or by using the ASDM VPN Wizard. To start the VPN Wizard using the menu bar: choose **Wizards > VPN Wizards >** (see Figure 21-1).

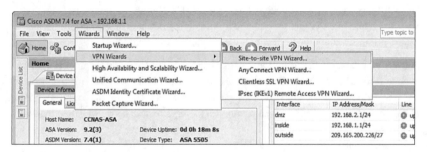

Figure 21-1   Choosing a VPN Wizard

Client-Based SSL VPN Example Using ASDM

In this example, the ASA is configured to support client-based SSL VPN. Remote users can establish an SSL connection using the Cisco AnyConnect client.

Figure 21-2 shows the network topology for the client-based SSL VPN example.

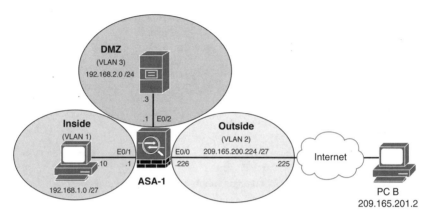

Figure 21-2 Client-Based SSL VPN Topology Example

To configure a client-based SSL VPN using the Cisco AnyConnect Mobility Client, use the VPN Wizard by choosing **Wizards > VPN Wizards > AnyConnect VPN Wizard** as shown in Figure 21-3.

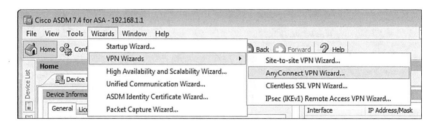

Figure 21-3 AnyConnect VPN Wizard

The VPN Wizard Introduction window then opens, as shown in Figure 21-4. Click **Next** to continue.

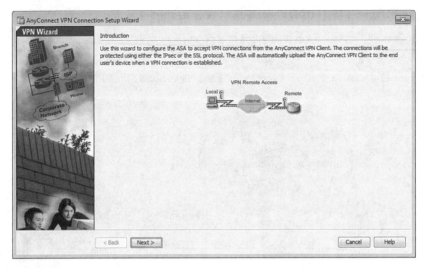

Figure 21-4 AnyConnect VPN Connection Setup Wizard's Introduction Window

Next, the wizard shows the Connection Profile Identification window, as shown in Figure 21-5.

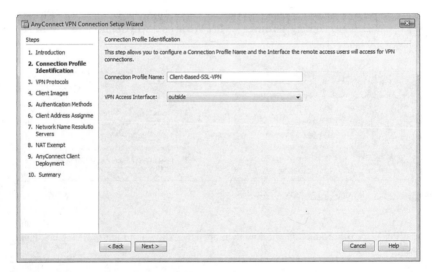

Figure 21-5 Connection Profile Identification Window

Configure a connection profile name for the connection and identify the interface to which remote users will connect.

Click **Next** to continue to display the VPN Protocol window shown in Figure 21-6.

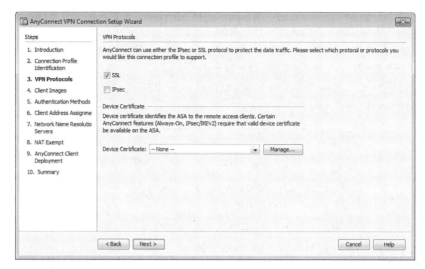

Figure 21-6 VPN Protocols Window

The choices are SSL and/or IPsec. A third-party certificate can also be configured.

NOTE: By default, the ASA uses a self-signed certificate to send to the client for authentication. Optionally, the ASA may be configured to use a third-party certificate purchased from a well-known certificate authority, such as VeriSign. In the event that a certificate is purchased, it may be selected in the Device Certificate drop-down menu.

By default, SSL and IPsec are selected; however, in this example only SSL will be used so IPsec is unchecked. Click **Next** to continue. The Client Images window opens as shown in Figure 21-7.

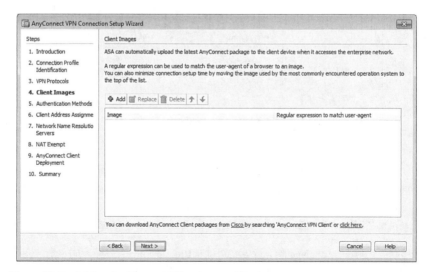

Figure 21-7 Adding AnyConnect Client Images Window

This window allows you to identify client images that a connecting host can download. If a host does not have the AnyConnect VPN client preinstalled, the ASA can be configured to provide the AnyConnect software to the host. The Client Images window is where you specify the client file's location.

To identify the location and AnyConnect Client version, click **Add** to open the Add AnyConnect Client Image window, as shown in Figure 21-8.

Figure 21-8   Add AnyConnect Client Image Window

Click **Browse Flash** to open the Browse Flash window, as shown in Figure 21-9, and navigate to the desired AnyConnect Client version.

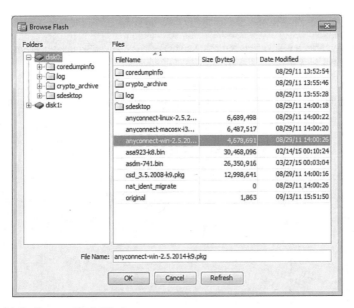

Figure 21-9   Browse Flash Window

Three AnyConnect versions are available (Linux, MAC OS, and Windows).

NOTE: If there is no image file on the ASA, click **Upload** in the Add AnyConnect Client Image window to upload a copy from the local machine.

Select the client version and click **OK** to display a revised Add AnyConnect Client Image window, as shown in Figure 21-10.

Figure 21-10   Revised Add AnyConnect Client Image Window

Click **OK** to return to the Client Images window, as shown in Figure 21-11.

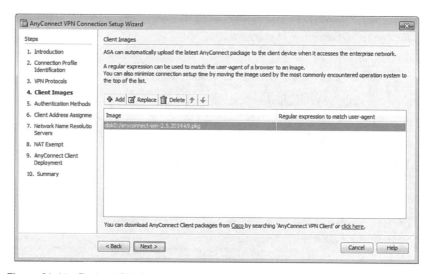

Figure 21-11   Revised Client Images Window

The window now displays the client image that will be available for clients to download.

NOTE: Repeat the process to add other client images.

Click **Next** to continue.

The Authentication Methods window opens, as shown in Figure 21-12.

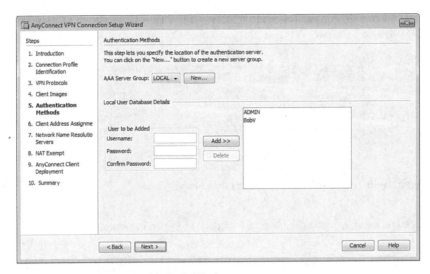

Figure 21-12 Authentication Methods Window

You can add the location of the AAA authentication server.

In this window, the authentication method can be defined. Click **New** to enter the location of the AAA server. If a server is not identified, the local database is used.

To add a new user, enter the username and password and then click **Add**.

Click **Next** to continue.

The Client Address Assignment window opens, as shown in Figure 21-13.

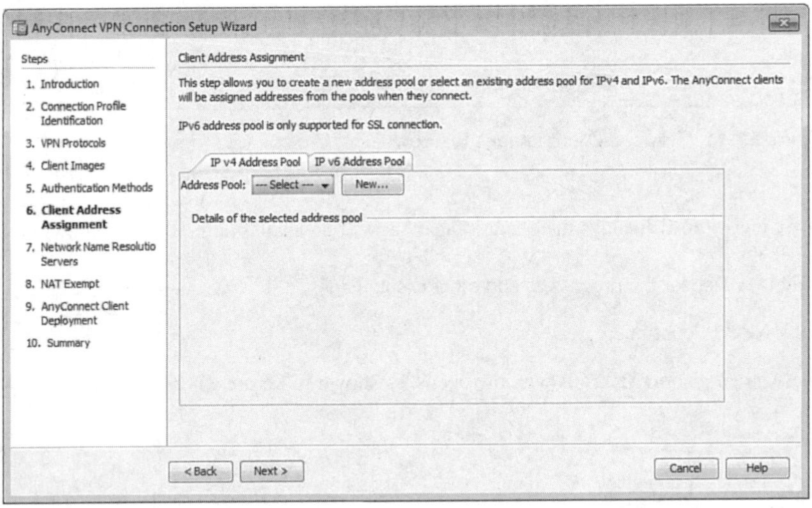

Figure 21-13 Client Address Assignment Window

Create a new pool of private inside addresses that the remote users will be assigned once authenticated.

You can choose a preconfigured IP address pool from the Address Pool drop-down menu. Otherwise, to create a new pool, click **New** to open the Add IPv4 Pool window as shown in Figure 21-14.

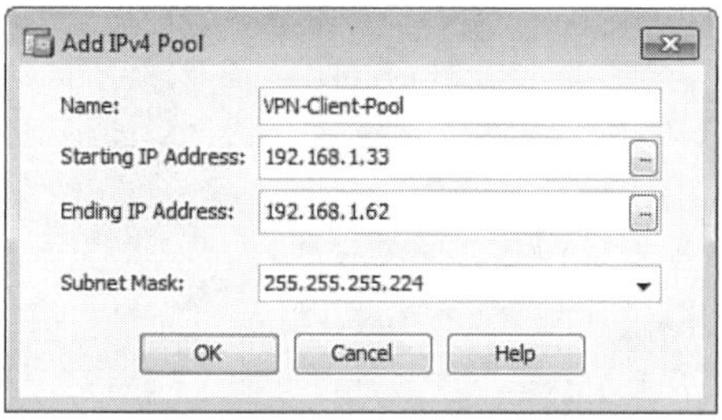

Figure 21-14   Add IPv4 Pool Window

In this window, identify the pool name, the starting and ending IP addresses, and associated subnet mask. In the figure, a client pool named VPN-Client-Pool is created that will hand out IPv4 addresses from the 192.168.1.33 to 192.168.1.62 with a /27 mask to connecting clients.

Click **OK** to return to the Client Address Assignment window displayed in Figure 21-15.

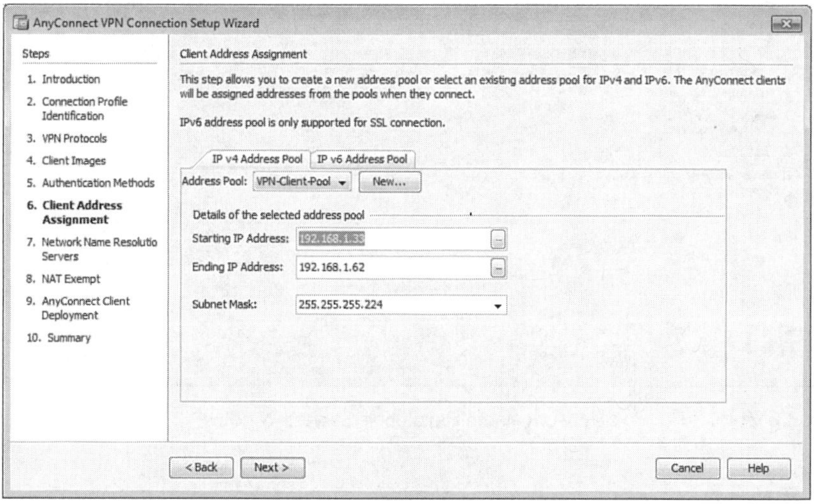

Figure 21-15   Revised Client Address Assignment Window

Click **Next** to continue and display the Network Name Resolution Servers window, as shown in Figure 21-16.

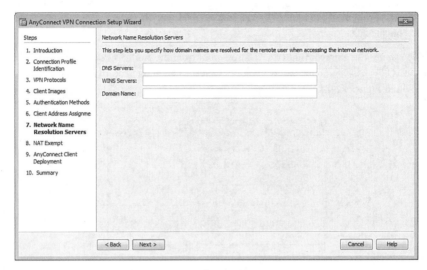

Figure 21-16 Network Name Resolution Servers Window

Enter the Domain Name System (DNS)-related information as shown in Figure 21-17.

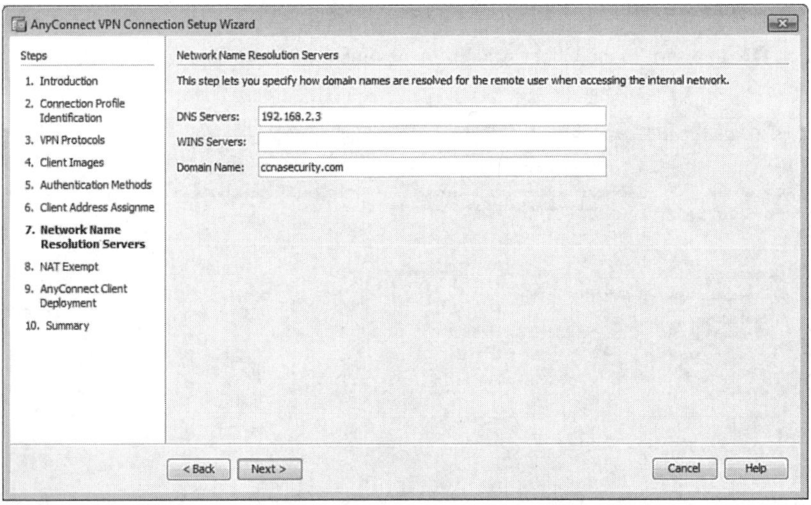

Figure 21-17 Revised Network Name Resolution Servers Window

Click **Next** to continue.

The NAT Exempt window opens, as shown in Figure 21-18.

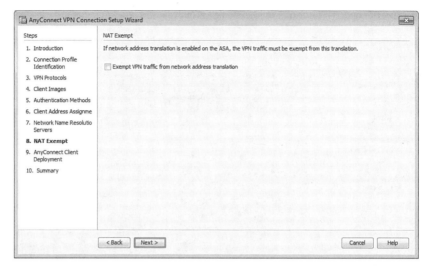

Figure 21-18   NAT Exempt Window

If Network Address Translation (NAT) is configured on the ASA, a NAT exemption rule must be created for the configured IP address pool. Like IPsec, SSL client address pools must be exempt from the NAT process because NAT translation occurs before encryption functions.

Check the **Exempt VPN traffic from network address translation** check box to reveal the details of the exemption, as shown in Figure 21-19.

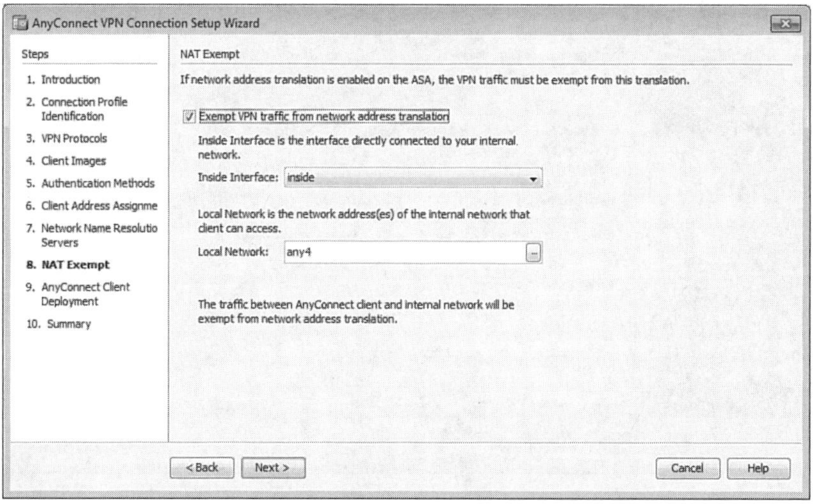

Figure 21-19   NAT Exempt Details Window

Click **Next** to open an information screen shown in Figure 21-20.

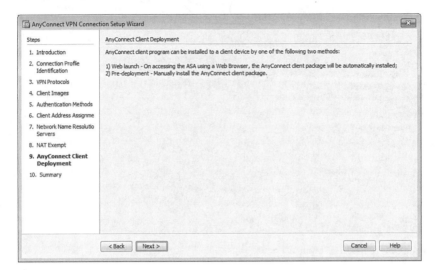

Figure 21-20   AnyConnect Client Deployment Informational Window

This is simply an informational page explaining that the AnyConnect client can be deployed using a web launch or pre-deployed on the host.

Click **Next** again and the VPN Wizard displays a summary of the configured selection, as shown in Figure 21-21.

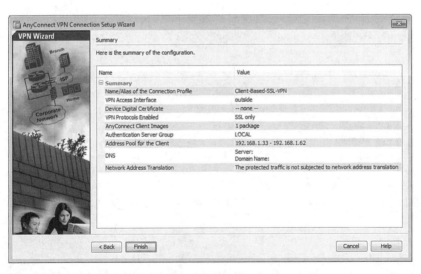

Figure 21-21   Summary of the Client Images

Review the information displayed. If correct, click **Finish**. Otherwise, click **Back** and correct the misconfiguration.

The configuration is then committed to the ASA, and the AnyConnect Connection Profiles screen opens, as shown in Figure 21-22.

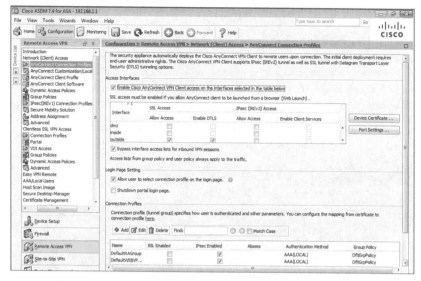

Figure 21-22   AnyConnect Connection Profiles Screen

From this screen, you can specify VPN client access on the interfaces you select, and you can select, add, edit, and delete connections. You can also specify whether you want to allow a user to select a particular connection at login.

Scrolling down to the bottom of the page displays the Connection Profiles on the ASA. Figure 21-23 displays the details in the Connection Profiles section of the window.

Name	SSL Enabled	IPsec Enabled	Aliases	Authentication Method	Group Policy
DefaultRAGroup		✓		AAA(LOCAL)	DfltGrpPolicy
DefaultWEBVP...		✓		AAA(LOCAL)	DfltGrpPolicy
Clientless-SSL-...				AAA(LOCAL)	Clientless-SSL-Policy
Client-Based-S...	✓		Client-Based-SS...	AAA(LOCAL)	GroupPolicy_Client-Ba...

Let group URL take precedence if group URL and certificate map match different connection profiles. Otherwise, the connection profile that matches the certificate map will be used.

Figure 21-23   Connection Profiles Section

The profile can be edited or deleted. A new connection profile can also be added.

To verify the configuration, you must do the following from a remote host:

1. Open a web browser and enter the login URL for the SSL VPN into the Address field.

2. If the AnyConnect client requests confirmation that this is a trusted site, accept and proceed. The ASA performs a series of compliance checks, platform detection, and finally selects/downloads the software package. A security warning displays if AnyConnect must be installed. It is important that the security appliance is added

as a trusted network site. After the client completes the autodownload, the web session automatically launches the Cisco AnyConnect SSL VPN Client.

Clientless SSL VPN Example Using ASDM

In this example, the ASA is configured to support clientless SSL VPN. Clientless VPNs are typically used when remote users are either using a noncorporate computer, and therefore don't have administrative privileges to install software, or because we want to limit their access to specific applications/bookmarks. For this reason, the remote host uses a secure web browser connection to access select network resources.

Use the VPN Wizard by choosing **Wizards > VPN Wizards > Clientless SSL VPN Wizard** as shown in Figure 21-24.

Figure 21-24   AnyConnect VPN Wizard

The Clientless SSL VPN Connection window opens, as shown in Figure 21-25.

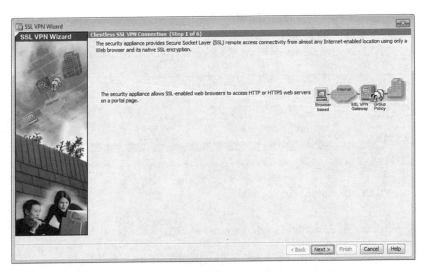

Figure 21-25   Clientless SSL VPN Connection Introduction Window

Click **Next** to continue.

The SSL VPN Interface window appears, as shown in Figure 21-26.

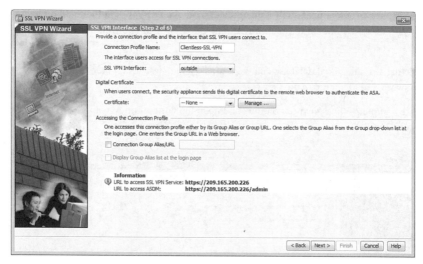

Figure 21-26   SSL VPN Interface Window

Configure a connection profile name for the connection and identify the interface to which remote users will connect.

> **NOTE:**   The SSL VPN Interface screen provides links in the Information section. These links identify the URLs that need to be used for the SSL VPN service access (login) and for Cisco ASDM access (to access the Cisco ASDM software download).

Click **Next** to continue and display the User Authentication window, as shown in Figure 21-27.

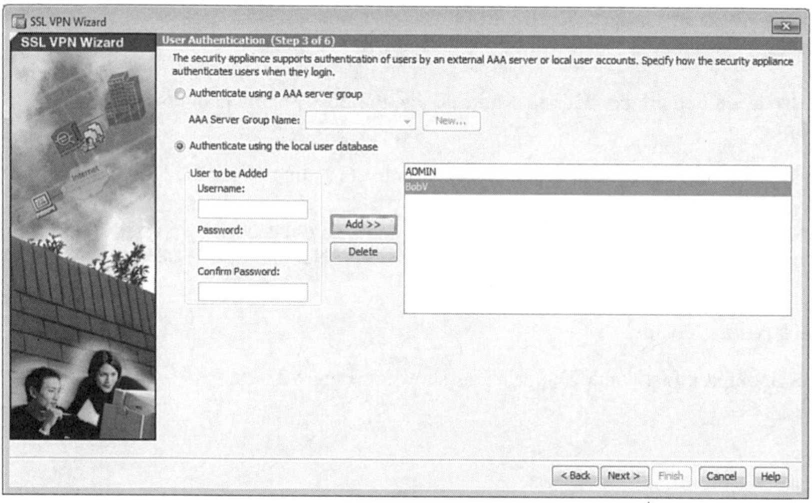

Figure 21-27   User Authentication Window

Identify how remote users will authenticate. You can configure authentication using a AAA server by checking the radio button. Click **New** to enter the location of the AAA server.

Alternatively, the local database can be used. To add a new user, enter the username and password and then click **Add**.

Once complete, click **Next** to continue and open the Group Policy window, as shown in Figure 21-28.

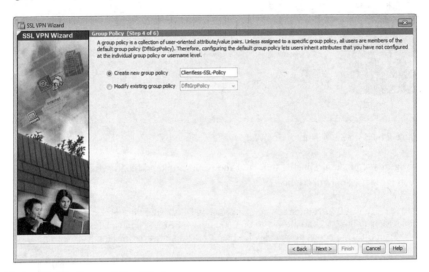

Figure 21-28   Group Policy Window

Identify a group policy that will be associated with the authenticated remote user.

> **NOTE:**   If you are configuring a new policy, the policy name cannot contain any spaces.

By default, the created user group policy inherits its settings from the DfltGrpPolicy.

> **NOTE:**   You may modify these settings after the wizard has been completed by navigating to **Configuration > Remote Access VPN > Clientless SSL VPN Access > Group Policies**.

Click **Next** to continue.

The Bookmark List window appears, as shown in Figure 21-29.

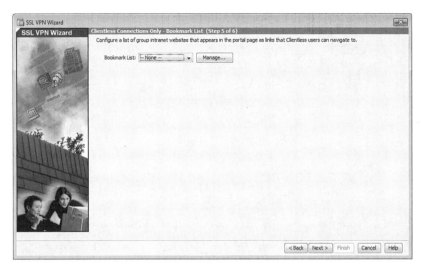

Figure 21-29   Bookmark List Window

A bookmark list is a set of URLs configured to be used in the clientless SSL VPN web portal. If bookmarks are already listed, use the Bookmark List drop-down menu, choose the bookmark you want, and click **Next** to continue with the SSL VPN Wizard.

To add bookmarks, click **Manage** to open the Configure GUI Customization Objects window shown in Figure 21-30.

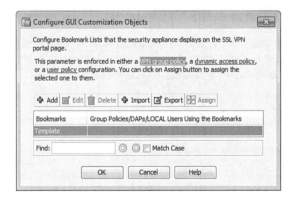

Figure 21-30   Configure GUI Customization Objects Window

Click **Add** to open the Add Bookmark List window shown in Figure 21-31.

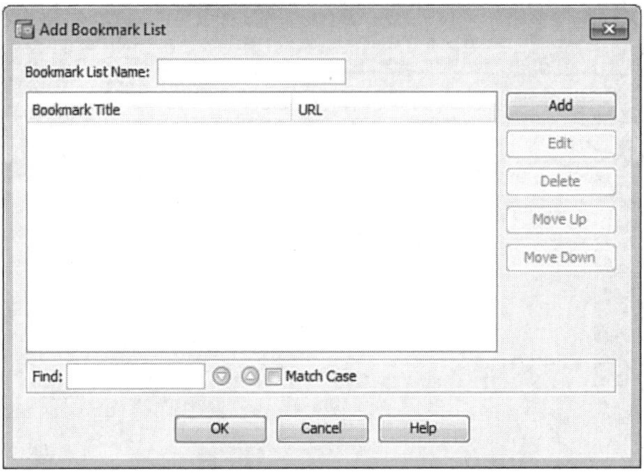

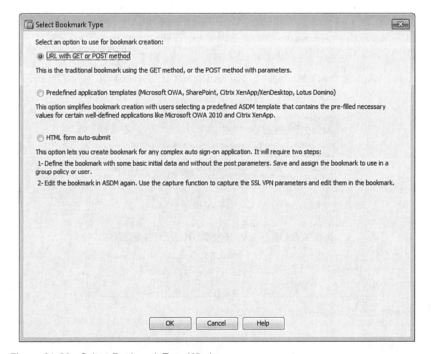

Figure 21-31   Add Bookmark List Window

Enter a bookmark list name and click **Add** again to open the Select Bookmark Type window shown in Figure 21-32.

Figure 21-32   Select Bookmark Type Window

There are three types of bookmarks that can be created, as identified in the window. To add a traditional bookmark, select the URL with the GET or POST method and click **OK** to open the Add Bookmark window shown in Figure 21-33.

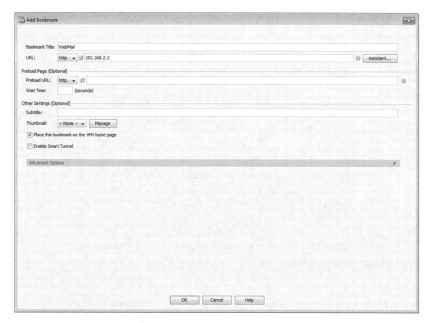

Figure 21-33 Add Bookmark Window

Enter a name for the bookmark in the Bookmark Title field. The name cannot contain spaces. Next enter the URL value, which could be HTTP, HTTPS, FTP, or Common Internet File System (CIFS), and the server destination IP address or hostname to be used with the bookmark entry. In our example, we are creating a bookmark named WebMail located at IP address 192.168.2.3.

When the specifics are configured, click **OK** in the Add Bookmark window to return to the Add Bookmark List window. The newly created bookmark and specifics are displayed as shown in Figure 21-34.

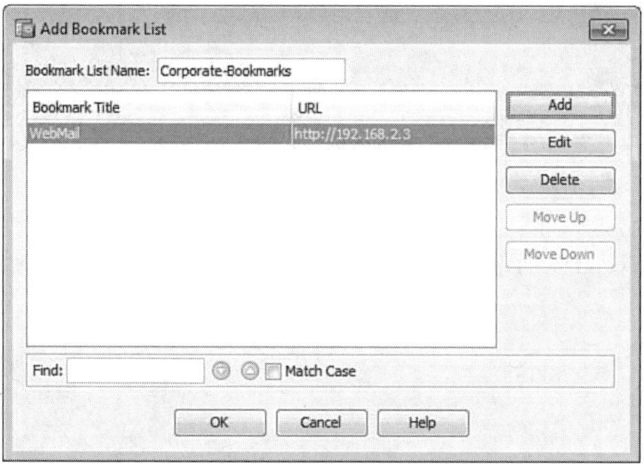

Figure 21-34 Revised Add Bookmark List Window

Click **OK** to return to the Configure GUI Customization Objects window as shown in Figure 21-35.

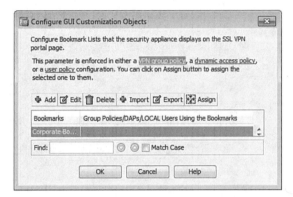

Figure 21-35 Revised Configure GUI Customization Objects Window

Click **OK** to return to the Bookmark List window shown in Figure 21-36.

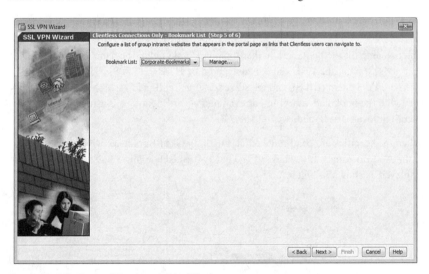

Figure 21-36 Revised Bookmark List Window

Click **Next** to continue. The Summary screen will open as shown in Figure 21-37.

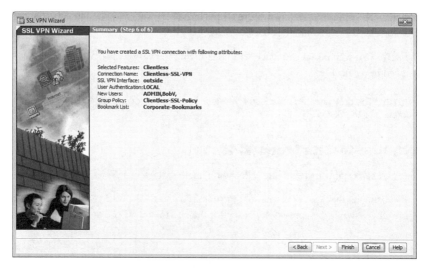

Figure 21-37   SSL VPN Wizard Summary Screen

Review the information displayed. If correct, click **Finish**. Otherwise, click **Back** and correct the misconfiguration.

The configuration is then committed to the ASA, and the AnyConnect Connection Profiles screen opens as shown in Figure 21-38.

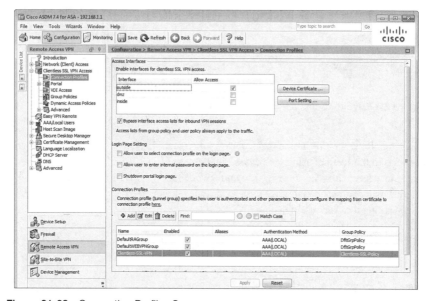

Figure 21-38   Connection Profiles Screen

To verify the configuration, open (from a remote host) a web browser and enter the login URL for the SSL VPN into the Address field.

The ASA SSL web portal web page will open listing the various bookmarks previously assigned to the profile.

NOTE: The browser URL must use Hypertext Transfer Protocol Secure (HTTPS) to connect to the SSL VPN.

ASA Site-to-Site IPsec VPN

The ASA can establish site-to-site VPNs with another ASA or ISR router.

In this example, the ASA is configured to support a site-to-site VPN with an ISR router. Figure 21-39 shows the network topology for the site-to-site VPN example.

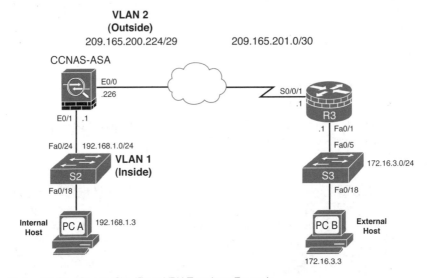

Figure 21-39 Site-to-Site IPsec VPN Topology Example

In the topology, the ISR has an inside network on the 172.16.3.0/24 network and connects to the Internet using the network address 209.165.201.0/30. The ASA has an inside interface with security level 100 on network 192.168.1.0/24 and connects to the Internet using an outside interface with security level 0 on network 209.165.200.224/29. Users exiting the ASA use dynamic PAT.

ISR IPsec VPN Configuration

The ISR router VPN configuration consists of five tasks:

Step 1. Configure the interfaces and static route:

```
R3(config)# interface GigabitEthernet0/1
R3(config-if)# description R3 LAN
```

```
R3(config-if)# ip address 172.16.3.1 255.255.255.0
R3(config-if)# exit
R3(config)#
R3(config)# interface Serial0/0/1
R3(config-if)# description WAN Connected to the Internet
R3(config-if)# ip address 209.165.201.1 255.255.255.252
R3(config-if)# exit
R3(config)#
R3(config)# ip route 0.0.0.0 0.0.0.0 S0/0/1
R3(config)#
```

Step 2. Configure the IPsec Policy for IKE Phase 1:

```
R3(config)# crypto isakmp policy 10
R3(config-isakmp)# encryption 3des
R3(config-isakmp)# hash sha
R3(config-isakmp)# group 2
R3(config-isakmp)# authentication pre-share
R3(config-isakmp)#
R3(config-isakmp)# crypto isakmp key SECRET-KEY address 209.165.200.226
R3(config)#
```

Step 3. Configure the IPsec Policy for IKE Phase 2 and an ACL to define interesting
       traffic:

```
R3(config)# crypto ipsec transform-set ESP-TUNNEL esp-3des esp-sha-hmac
R3(cfg-crypto-trans)# mode tunnel
R3(cfg-crypto-trans)# exit
R3(config)#
R3(config)# ip access-list extended VPN-ACL
R3(config-ext-nacl)# remark VPN ACL defining interesting traffic
R3(config-ext-nacl)# permit ip 172.16.3.0 0.0.0.255 192.168.1.0
0.0.0.255
R3(config-ext-nacl)# exit
R3(config)#
```

Step 4. Configure a crypto map for the IPsec policy:

```
R3(config)# crypto map S2S-MAP 10 ipsec-isakmp
% NOTE: This new crypto map will remain disabled until a peer and a
valid access list have been configured.
R3(config-crypto-map)# set peer 209.165.200.226
R3(config-crypto-map)# set transform-set ESP-TUNNEL
R3(config-crypto-map)# match address VPN-ACL
R3(config-crypto-map)# exit
R3(config)#
```

Step 5. Apply the crypto map to the outgoing interface:

```
R3(config)# interface Serial0/0/1
R3(config-if)# crypto map S2S-MAP
R3(config-if)#
```

ASA Initial Configuration

The ASA must be configured with complementary information. The following is the initial ASA 5505 configuration:

```
CCNAS-ASA(config)# enable password class
CCNAS-ASA(config)#
CCNAS-ASA(config)# interface vlan 1
CCNAS-ASA(config-if)# nameif inside
INFO: Security level for "inside" set to 100 by default.
CCNAS-ASA(config-if)# ip address 192.168.1.1 255.255.255.0
CCNAS-ASA(config-if)#
CCNAS-ASA(config-if)# interface e0/1
CCNAS-ASA(config-if)# switchport access vlan 1
CCNAS-ASA(config-if)# no shut
CCNAS-ASA(config-if)# exit
CCNAS-ASA(config)#
CCNAS-ASA(config)# interface vlan 2
CCNAS-ASA(config-if)# nameif outside
INFO: Security level for "outside" set to 0 by default.
CCNAS-ASA(config-if)# ip address 209.165.200.226 255.255.255.224
CCNAS-ASA(config-if)#
CCNAS-ASA(config-if)# interface e0/0
CCNAS-ASA(config-if)# switchport access vlan 2
CCNAS-ASA(config-if)# no shut
CCNAS-ASA(config-if)# exit
CCNAS-ASA(config)#
CCNAS-ASA(config)# route outside 0.0.0.0 0.0.0.0 209.165.200.225
CCNAS-ASA(config)#
CCNAS-ASA(config)# object network INSIDE-NET
CCNAS-ASA(config-network-object)# subnet 192.168.1.0 255.255.255.0
CCNAS-ASA(config-network-object)# nat (inside,outside) dynamic interface
CCNAS-ASA(config-network-object)#
CCNAS-ASA(config-network-object)# policy-map global_policy
CCNAS-ASA(config-pmap)# class inspection_default
CCNAS-ASA(config-pmap-c)# inspect icmp
CCNAS-ASA(config-pmap-c)# exit
CCNAS-ASA(config-pmap)# exit
CCNAS-ASA(config)#
```

```
CCNAS-ASA(config)# http server enable
CCNAS-ASA(config)# http 192.168.1.0 255.255.255.0 inside
CCNAS-ASA(config)#
```

ASA VPN Configuration Using ASDM

The site-to-site configuration is easier to do using the ASDM Site-to-Site VPN Wizard. The following steps provide an example of how to use the wizard to complete the site-to-site VPN implementation.

To configure a site-to-site IPsec VPN use the VPN Wizard by choosing **Wizards > VPN Wizards > Site-to-Site VPN Wizard** as shown in Figure 21-40.

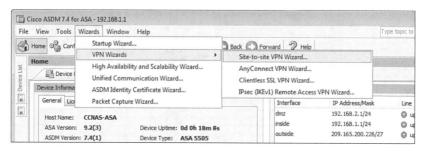

Figure 21-40   Site-to-Site VPN Wizard

The VPN Wizard Introduction window then opens, as shown in Figure 21-41.

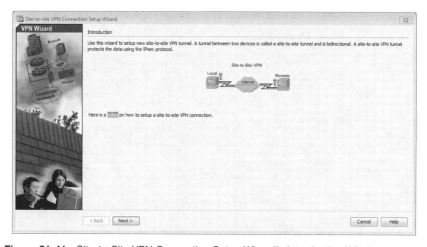

Figure 21-41   Site-to-Site VPN Connection Setup Wizard's Introduction Window

Click **Next** to continue and open the Peer Device Identification window, as shown in Figure 21-42.

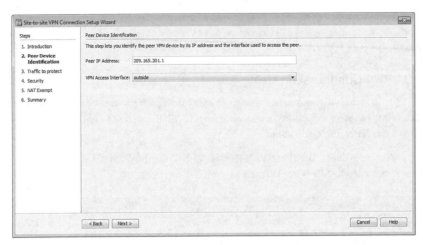

Figure 21-42   Peer Device Identification Window

Enter the reachable IP address of the peer. In this example, this is 209.165.201.1.

This window allows you to identify the interface the ASA will use to connect to the peer. In this example, the crypto map is applied to the outside interface.

Click **Next** to continue and open the Traffic to Protect window, as shown in Figure 21-43.

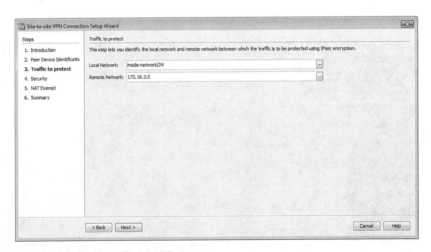

Figure 21-43   Traffic to Protect Window

This window allows you to identify interesting traffic by identifying the local network and the remote network. These networks protect the traffic using IPsec encryption. In this example, traffic from the 192.168.1.0 network going to the 172.16.3.0 network will initiate the VPN connection to be established.

Click **Next** to continue and open the Security window, as shown in Figure 21-44.

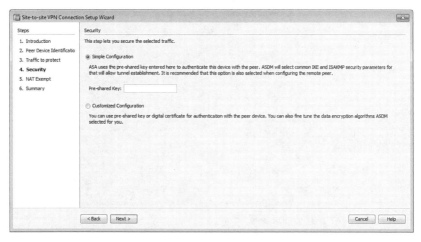

Figure 21-44   Security Window

This window provides two security options:

Simple Configuration	Uses a pre-shared keyword to use when authenticating with the identified peer.
	It selects common IKE and ISAKMP security parameters to establish the tunnel.
Customized Configuration	Uses either a pre-shared key or a digital certificate to authenticate with the identified peer.
	The IKE and ISAKMP security parameters can also be specifically selected.

In this example, the Simple Configuration option is used.

Enter the pre-shared key **SECRET-KEY** and click **Next** to continue and open the NAT Exempt window, as shown in Figure 21-45.

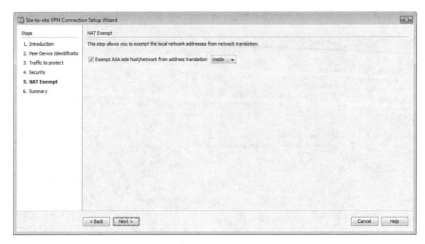

Figure 21-45   NAT Exempt Window

Outgoing traffic from inside hosts to the remote VPN network should not have their IP addresses translated by NAT. Select the **Exempt ASA side host/network from address translation** check box.

Click **Next** to continue and open the Summary window, as shown in Figure 21-46.

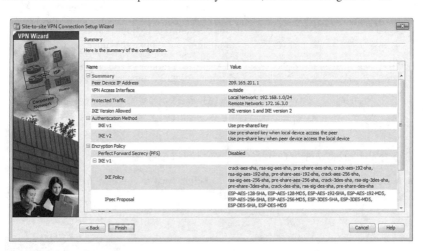

Figure 21-46   Summary Window

Verify that the information configured in the Site-to-Site VPN Wizard is correct. Use Back to alter any of the configuration parameters.

Click **Finish** to deliver the commands to the ASA.

The configuration is then committed to the ASA and the Site-to-Site Connection Profiles screen opens as shown in Figure 21-47.

Figure 21-47   Site-to-Site VPN Connection Profiles Screen

From this window, the VPN configuration can be verified and edited. To test the tunnel, internal traffic must attempt to reach the remote network.

The VPN can be monitored by clicking **Monitoring > VPN.**

Index

Numerics

3DES (Triple Data Encryption Standard), 155

802.1X authentication, 65-68
  configuring, 66-68

A

AAA (authentication, authorization, and accounting), 58
  accounting, 65
  authentication, configuring server-based authentication, 61-64
  authorization, 64
  local authentication, 260
  local authentication, configuring, 58-60
  server-based authentication, 261-266
aaa command, 59-60
access attacks, 10-11
access rules, 127-128
access-class command, 45
access-list command, 116
accountability, 14
accounting, 65
ACLs (access control lists), 40
  antispoofing, 112-117
  ASA ACLs, 243-249
    configuring, 245-249
    syntax, 244-245
  configuring, 110-112
  design guidelines, 108
  in IPv6, 121-124

IPv6
  configuring, 123-124
  filtering, 122-123
  implicit entries, 122
mitigating ICMP abuse, 115-116
mitigating threats with, 108
named extended ACLs, 111-112
numbered extended ACLs, 110-111
object groups
  configuring, 119-121
  in extended ACLs, 119
  network object groups, 117-118
  service object groups, 118-119
permitting traffic, 114
statements, 108-109
address spoofing attacks, 83-84
administrative threats, 3
advanced wizards (ASDM), 204
adware, 6
AES (Advanced Encryption Standard), 155
alarms, 136
ALE (annualized loss expectancy), 17
alert-severity command, 145
amplification attacks, 12
anomaly-based IPS, 137
anti-evasion techniques, 138-139
antispoofing, 40, 112-117
AnyConnect, 31
ARO (annualized rate of occurrence), 17
ARP attacks, 71, 80-82
asymmetric encryption algorithms, 156, 161-162
  PKI, 162-165
    characteristics, 165
    standards, 163-164
    topologies, 164

W

X-Y-Z

REGISTER YOUR PRODUCT at CiscoPress.com/register

Access Additional Benefits and SAVE 35% on Your Next Purchase

- Download available product updates.
- Access bonus material when applicable.
- Receive exclusive offers on new editions and related products.
  (Just check the box to hear from us when setting up your account.)
- Get a coupon for 35% for your next purchase, valid for 30 days.
  Your code will be available in your Cisco Press cart. (You will also find
  it in the Manage Codes section of your account page.)

Registration benefits vary by product. Benefits will be listed on your account
page under Registered Products.

CiscoPress.com – Learning Solutions for Self-Paced Study, Enterprise, and the Classroom
Cisco Press is the Cisco Systems authorized book publisher of Cisco networking technology,
Cisco certification self-study, and Cisco Networking Academy Program materials.

At CiscoPress.com you can

- Shop our books, eBooks, software, and video training.
- Take advantage of our special offers and promotions (ciscopress.com/promotions).
- Sign up for special offers and content newsletters (ciscopress.com/newsletters).
- Read free articles, exam profiles, and blogs by information technology experts.
- Access thousands of free chapters and video lessons.

Connect with Cisco Press – Visit CiscoPress.com/community
Learn about Cisco Press community events and programs.

Cisco Press